**CRITICAL PUBLISHING**

# Children Forsaken

Child Abuse from Ancient to Modern Times

**Other books you may be interested in:**

*Active Social Work with Children with Disabilities*
Julie Adams and Diana Leshone				ISBN 9781910391969

*Observing Children and Families: Beyond the Surface*
Gill Butler						ISBN 9781910391624

*Supporting Troubled Young People*
Steven Walker						ISBN 9781912508730

*The W Word; Witchcraft labelling and child safeguarding in social work practice*
Prospera Tedam and Awura Adjoa				ISBN 9781912096008

www.criticalpublishing.com or contact our distributor Ingram Publisher Services, telephone 01752 202301 or email NBNi.Cservs@ingramcontent.com

**CRITICAL PUBLISHING**

# Children Forsaken

## Child Abuse from Ancient to Modern Times

Steven Walker

First published in 2021 by Critical Publishing Ltd

All rights reserved. No part of this publication may be reproduced, stored in a retrieval system, or transmitted in any form or by any means, electronic, mechanical, photocopying, recording or otherwise, without prior permission in writing from the publisher.

Copyright © 2021 Steven Walker

British Library Cataloguing in Publication Data

A CIP record for this book is available from the British Library

ISBN: 9781913453817

This book is also available in the following e-book formats:
EPUB ISBN: 9781913453831
Adobe e-book 9781913453848

The rights of Steven Walker to be identified as the Author of this work have been asserted by him in accordance with the Copyright, Design and Patents Act 1988.

Cover design by Out of House
Text design by Out of House
Project Management by Deanta Global Publishing Services, Dublin, Ireland
Printed and bound in Great Britain by 4edge, Essex

Critical Publishing
3 Connaught Road
St Albans AL3 5RX

www.criticalpublishing.com

# Disclaimer

*This book contains numerous references to other works and authors who have published their research and ideas about the history of child abuse. The author is grateful to them all. He has examined considerable amounts of data and findings in books, official reports, academic research, public inquiries, grey literature and online sources. They have all to the best of his knowledge been cited or referenced but please let us know if there are any omissions or errors and we will make the appropriate corrections as soon as possible.*

To my parents, Mary and James Walker, and all their children, grandchildren and great-grandchildren

# Praise for this book:

'The various historical constructions of childhood, child abuse and children's rights present us with evidence of the terrible ubiquity of child mistreatment, its changing forms and the necessity of child safeguarding and protection. This ambitious book paints an important and erudite picture of child abuse and social responses to it, bringing us up-to-date with a call for continued vigilance, compassion, and action.'

Professor Dr Jonathan Parker PhD, FAcSS, FHEA, FRSA
Professor of Society & Social Welfare
Bournemouth University, UK

'Steven has done a vast amount of research covering a massive range of topics and international perspectives. I admire him for embarking on this massive adventure. He has brought into focus child abuse previously raised in disparate ways not brought together before in one place.'

Dr Liz Davies
Emeritus Professor of Social Work
London Metropolitan University

'Steven Walker's book is an erudite and articulate antidote to the dominant Anglo-American narrative that child abuse was "discovered" in the 1960s. It presents an analysis with a global sweep, starting in Jericho in 7,000BC and finishing with the latest debates about the relationship between child abuse and poverty. Challenging popular notions that child abuse is perpetrated by evil or irrational individuals, it examines how child abuse has been woven into the fabric of our societies. A fascinating and thought-provoking read for anyone who wants to understand our current responses to child abuse.'

Dr Andrew Whittaker, Associate Professor in Social Work and Head of the Serious Violence Research Group, London South Bank University.

# Contents

|  | Meet the Author | x |
|---|---|---|
|  | Introduction | 1 |
| Chapter 1 | Child abuse in ancient times | 5 |
| Chapter 2 | Fairy tales, folklore and religion | 21 |
| Chapter 3 | Defining child abuse | 37 |
| Chapter 4 | Revealing child abuse | 57 |
| Chapter 5 | Children as labour | 75 |
| Chapter 6 | Child sexual abuse becomes public | 93 |
| Chapter 7 | The contemporary picture | 109 |
| Chapter 8 | Changing perceptions of children | 127 |
| Chapter 9 | Children's rights and parent support | 145 |
|  | *Bibliography* | 163 |
|  | *Index* | 177 |

# Meet the Author

*Steven is an alumnus of the London School of Economics and Political Science (MSc) he has written 15 books and contributed chapters to several others. He has presented his research at 12 international conferences and has a total of 35 years' experience in child protection and CAMHS. He is campaigning to save his local library from closure and is raising money for his local foodbank.*

# Introduction

*There can be no keener revelation of a society's soul than the way in which it treats its children.*

Nelson Mandela

Recent media revelations about historic child sexual abuse by men in powerful positions of authority and responsibility such as sports coaches and priests, plus stories of cruel physical abuse and cover-ups by powerful institutions, have created a modern narrative that has shocked many people. Yet these stories only go back in time 50 or 60 years with brave survivors finding their voices as older women and men. However, there is ample evidence dating back to the earliest times of human history that clearly shows child abuse is not a new phenomenon. It has existed since the beginning of recorded history.

Our current concept about what constitutes child abuse is a result of redefining, relabelling and the way modern society reflects on previous generations of education, social care and child-rearing practices. Alongside attempts at consciousness-raising there have been major legal changes to the safeguarding and protection of children from harm often prompted by children's charities and campaigners to try to enshrine children's rights into every aspect of social and economic policies. But these only began in earnest towards the turn of the twentieth century.

In 1895 the National Society for the Prevention of Cruelty to Children summarised its findings about the way children were mistreated:

*by battering, with shovels, pots, straps, ropes, boots, pokers, boiling water and fire. It described neglected children as miserable, vermin-infested, filthy, cold, ragged, pale, malnourished and feeble. Children were put out to beg, abducted by drunkards and vagrants, little girls were sexually abused, some with abnormalities or disfigurements were sold to circuses to be exhibited as freaks of nature.*

Further back in time there is ample evidence of similar cruelty against children. According to De Mause (1998), the further back in history one goes the more massive the neglect and cruelty one finds and the more likely children are to have been killed, rejected, beaten, terrorised and sexually abused by their caretakers. The history of humanity is founded upon the abuse of children. Most historical families once practised infanticide, erotic beating and incest. Most states have sacrificed and mutilated their children in rituals designed to appease ancient deities to end droughts and help guarantee good harvests. Even today, humans continue to arrange the daily killing, maiming, molestation and starvation of children through our social, military and economic activities in postcolonial wars or proxy conflicts between superpowers.

This book illustrates how child abuse is pernicious and endures persistently despite attempts to stop it or minimize its occurrence. In the ultramodern cyber world, child abuse is arguably easier and spreading, with paedophiles particularly adept at hiding beyond the reach of law enforcement. Economic crises and climate change are also prompting conditions to arise where child abuse happens in the context of poverty, poor housing conditions, lack of access to physical and mental health services, and in the form of sex trafficking, forced marriages, honour killings, or military conflicts where children are used as soldiers or flee as refugees and asylum seekers in perilous journeys. Most child abuse happens within families. The recent pandemic has, according to the latest research, unleashed a tidal wave of abuse within families (Romanou & Belton, 2020).

Country reports in a UN study (2006) show that children under ten years of age are at significantly greater risk than older children of severe violence perpetrated by family members and people closely associated with the family. Public information messages about stranger danger are a dangerous, misleading focus of attempts at child protection when every evidence base available shows conclusively that child abuse is likely to happen in the family home involving a parent, sibling or close relative. The WHO study also reported estimates that in children less than 18 years of age the worldwide prevalence of sexual violence involving forced intercourse and touch is 73 million for boys and 150 million for girls.

The Crime Survey for England and Wales (ONS, 2020) estimated that one in five adults aged 18 to 74 years experienced at least one form of child abuse, whether emotional abuse, physical abuse, sexual abuse, or witnessing domestic violence or abuse, before the age of 16 years (8.5 million people). In addition, an estimated 1 in 100 adults aged 18 to 74 years experienced physical neglect before the age of 16 years (481,000 people); this includes not being taken care of or not having enough food, shelter or clothing, but it does not cover all types of neglect.

An estimated 3.1 million adults aged 18 to 74 years were victims of sexual abuse before the age of 16 years; this includes abuse by both adult and child perpetrators. Prevalence was higher for females than males for each type of abuse, with the exception of physical abuse where there was no difference. Many cases of child abuse remain hidden; around one in seven adults who called the National Association for

People Abused in Childhood's (NAPAC) helpline had not told anyone about their abuse before. It is possible to identify 227,530 child abuse offences recorded by the police in the year ending March 2019.

The UK child protection charity, Childline, delivered 19,847 counselling sessions to children in the UK where abuse was the primary concern in the year ending March 2019; sexual abuse accounted for nearly half (45%) of these and has become the most common type of abuse counselled by Childline in recent years. At 31 March 2019, 52,260 children in England were the subject of a child protection plan (CPP) and 2820 children in Wales were listed in the child protection register (CPR) because of experience or risk of abuse or neglect; neglect was the most common category of abuse in England and emotional abuse was the most common in Wales. As of 31 March 2019, 49,570 children in England and 4810 children in Wales were looked after by their local authority because of experience or risk of abuse or neglect. Around half of adults (52%) who experienced abuse before the age of 16 years also experienced domestic abuse later in life, compared with 13% of those who did not experience abuse before the age of 16 years.

In their US study, Eckenrode et al (2014) used county-level data to examine the relationship between income inequality and child maltreatment, using a widely used and validated measure of inequality. County-level data extracted for all 3142 US counties between 2005 and 2009 and child maltreatment data obtained from the US Children's Bureau's National Child Abuse and Neglect Data System found significant associations between levels of income inequality across US counties and higher county-level rates of child maltreatment. These findings resonate with other studies that indicate an association between inequality and child abuse and neglect. For example, Gilbert et al (2011) investigated child maltreatment variation in trends and policies across England, Sweden, Western Australia, Manitoba and New Zealand. Their study identified lower levels of maltreatment incidence in Sweden than in the USA, which were consistent with lower rates of child poverty and parent risk factors and policies providing higher levels of universal support for parenting in Sweden. These studies suggest that, compared to countries with higher levels of inequality, countries with lower levels of inequality are likely to enjoy lower rates of child abuse (Bywater et al, 2016).

Stopping child abuse and neglect on a global scale requires different solutions for each country to reassess the way children are perceived and how the laws in each nation help or hinder children's safety. One of the major risk factors in child abuse is poverty, so by supporting developing economies by reducing debt and providing other international aid is a small but significant step forwards that rich nations can afford to take. Developed countries have more resources to tackle child abuse but the political will needs to be there to move the needs of vulnerable children up politicians' agenda. A commonly heard aphorism is: *there are no votes in children*. Legal, technocratic and bureaucratic changes have made little impact on the prevalence of child abuse. Instead they have created defensive practice among social workers, families feeling persecuted and under unfair surveillance, and created a legal industry that is wasting public money indulging in blame games.

Children's rights and those influencers who support them need to be front and centre of any policy changes and responses to rising numbers of abused children, especially in the age of the internet where much harm can take place. This will require a shift in parents' and other adults' perceptions of childhood and the place of children in society. School settings are ideal places where models and methods of parenting can be taught, giving the parents of the future some education and resources to draw upon in later life. Schools can nurture and foster respectful relationships alongside teaching children their legal rights. Increased resources for parents to access support services when they feel they are unsafe or a risk to their children are needed at scale in every locality, especially among disadvantaged families. The combination of improved children's rights and better parent support is a powerful one; the evidence is there to justify investment, whether on a cost benefit basis or simply on moral and humanitarian grounds. Children are the future; they deserve our collective support, and the sooner the better.

*Steven Walker, MPhil, MSc, BA (Hons), PG. Dip, FHEA.*
*January 2021*

## Chapter 1 | Child abuse in ancient times

# Introduction

Child abuse has always been with us; it cuts across country borders, continents, and cultures. Infanticide is the ultimate form of child abuse. Many people may think that killing children was a part of ancient cultures, consigned to primitive barbaric sacrifices or dreadful economic necessity in times when food was scarce and no social or advanced healthcare systems existed. Yet, according to the children's organisation UNICEF, approximately 95,000 children are murdered each year globally (UNICEF, 2011).

Being murdered in childhood is strongly associated with age, gender and geography with the majority of cases involving death at the hands of a parent. Drawing on data collected as part of the UNODC Crime Trends Survey, UNODC estimates that a total of 205,153 children aged 0 to 14 years lost their lives worldwide as a result of homicide during the ten-year period 2008–2017. Of these, roughly six in ten were male (59 per cent) and four in ten were female (41 per cent). Over the same period, a total of 1,691,869 adolescents and young adults between the ages of 15 and 29 were intentionally killed. Around 86 per cent of these were male and 14 per cent were female (UNDOC, 2019).

Researchers have examined evidence from ancient texts, drawings, pottery and archaeological digs to show that even very small children have been deliberately killed throughout history. These acts took place in the context of ritual sacrifice by ancient cultures worldwide as offerings to deities, or children were killed because they were female or born disabled. In China, India, Mexico and Peru, for example, children were cast into rivers in the belief this would bring fine harvests and good fortune. In other early cultures, the blood and flesh of infants was thought to confer vigour and health, and as a result, it was fed to expectant mothers or favoured siblings. Kings were worshipped as gods in some ancient societies, and were expected to guarantee bountiful harvest and prevent catastrophes such as earthquakes or torrential rains. If the King failed in his godly duties his subjects expected him to give himself in sacrifice. Kings would therefore offer a son as a sacrificial substitute (Lynch, 1985).

Girls had a particularly bad time as gendered thinking regarded them as less useful than male children. According to Castleden (2002), *'Girls were given in sacred marriage to the goddess Inanna in Uruk as early as 3000 BC. The temple was at liberty to either keep the girls to be trained as priestesses, pass them off as concubines, or just put them on the street as prostitutes'.*

An ancient form of infanticide was the burial alive of children in foundations of buildings and other structures. The earliest evidence consists of the remains of infants interred in the walls of the city of Jericho in 7000 BC. Infanticide was practised in early Scandinavian cultures and in European countries nearly into the twentieth century. Children's remains have been found in the foundations or walls of buildings across the world.

*Pottery furnaces were consecrated in China with the shedding of children's blood. Children were probably immured in the dykes of the German city of Oldenburg until the seventeenth century. The practice of putting children in the foundations of buildings was also common in ancient India.*

(Mason, 1972)

Infanticide during antiquity has usually been played down despite hundreds of clear references by ancient writers that it was an accepted, everyday occurrence. Children were thrown into rivers, flung into dung-heaps and cess pits, potted in jars to starve to death, and exposed on hills and roadsides, a prey for birds, food for wild beasts to rend (Euripides, *Ion*, 504). To begin with, any child that was not perfect in shape and size, or cried too little or too much, or was otherwise than was expected in the gynaecological writings was generally killed.

Beyond this, the firstborn was usually allowed to live especially if it was a boy. Girls were, in a patriarchal hierarchy, valued little. The result was a large imbalance of males over females, which was typical of the West until well into the Middle Ages, when the killing of legitimate children was probably much reduced. The killing of illegitimate children does not affect the sex ratio, since both sexes are generally killed. Available statistics for antiquity show large surpluses of boys over girls. Until the fourth century AD, neither law nor public opinion found infanticide wrong in either Greece or Rome (De Mause, 1974). Those few passages which modern classicists consider as a condemnation of infanticide seem to indicate just the opposite, such as Aristotle's:

*As to exposing or rearing the children born, let there be a law that no deformed child shall be reared; but on the ground of number of children, if the regular customs hinder any of those born being exposed, there must be a limit filed to the procreation of offspring.*

(Viljoen, 1959)

Musonius Rufus, sometimes called The Roman Socrates, is often quoted as opposing infanticide, but his piece *'Should Every Child That Is Born Be Raised?'* quite clearly only says that since brothers are very useful they should not be killed. But more ancient writers openly approved of infanticide, saying, like Aristippus, that a man could do what he wants with his children, for '*do we not cast away from us our spittle, lice and such like, as things unprofitable, which nevertheless are en-gendered and bred even out of our own selves*'. Or, like Seneca, they pretend only sickly infants are involved:

*Mad dogs we knock on the head; the fierce and savage ox we slay; sickly sheep we put to the knife to keep them from infecting the flock; unnatural progeny we destroy; we drown even children who at birth are weakly and abnormal. Yet it is not anger, but reason that separates the harmful from the sound.*

(Brett, 1991)

The theme of exposure loomed large in myth, tragedy, and the New Comedy, which is often built around the subject of how funny infanticide is. In Menander's *Girl from Samos*, much fun is made of a man trying to chop up and roast a baby. In his comedy The *Arbitrants*, a shepherd picks up an exposed infant, considers raising it, then changes his mind, saying, '*What have I to do with the rearing of children and the trouble*'. He gives it to another man, but has a fight over who got the baby's necklace (De Mause, 1974).

# The archaeological and cultural evidence

According to Sandra Wheeler, a bio-archaeologist at the University of Central Florida, and her colleagues (Wheeler et al, 2013), much can be learned about cultural attitudes of violence towards children from the analyses of their skeletal remains and mortuary patterns of the communities in which they lived and died. She used a bio-archaeological approach integrating biological, sociocultural and physical environments, in 2013, to analyse the 2000-year-old remains of a 2–3-year-old child from Kellis 2, a Romano-Christian period cemetery in the Dakhleh Oasis, Egypt:

*The skeletal remains showed an unusual pattern of trauma and healing events, possibly indicating multiple episodes of non-accidental trauma. Macroscopic, radiographic, and histologic analyses showed the extent of the skeletal trauma and healing, while stable carbon and nitrogen analyses of bone and hair revealed metabolic disturbances and changes in diet correlated with these traumatic events.*

Results from the differential diagnosis demonstrated that skeletal fracture and healing patterns were consistent with repeated non-accidental trauma, which may or may not have resulted in death. In addition, this may also represent the earliest documented case of violence against children from an archaeological context.

In Greek mythology, Medea was the granddaughter of the sun god Helios, and ran away from her father's house to marry the hero Jason. In Euripides's play she is portrayed as a sinful mother who killed her children to avenge Jason's marital infidelity. This early rendition of maternal infanticide endures even today, in modern times, when women who kill their children are portrayed as the worst kind of human. Compared to men who more often kill children, mothers are demonised and subjected to the worst kind of misogyny. Despite the evidence from multiple cases of such women found to be suffering from postnatal depression accompanied by untreated psychosis, or being failed by health and social care agencies, they receive longer prison sentences than men. Tabloid reporting is notoriously harsher towards women who murder than towards men. Euripides makes Medea breach a fundamental taboo, echoing modern attitudes and media stereotypes about the mystical bond between mother and child, and the assumption of unconditional maternal love.

A research study from 2005 (Friedman et al) examined more than 250 news reports on maternal infanticide in the US to see how journalists present these cases. It concluded that women tend to be presented in oversimplistic terms, either as being driven to insanity due to caring so much, or as fundamentally heartless. Jason and the Chorus try to present Medea as inhuman to make sense of her actions. The implication is that a proper human being would be incapable of acting as Medea does and, so perhaps, that normal people are safe from such things. Modern reporters similarly present mothers who kill as mad or bad to help provide distance from other women who might at times feel like killing their children but refrain from doing so.

*Euripides points to the broader societal pressures that lie behind what she does. She argues that her situation is an inevitable hazard of the patriarchal rules governing marriage in the Greek world: women are dependent on their husbands, vulnerable, and easily driven to desperation. The chorus of Corinthian wives accepts this argument and promise to help Medea achieve vengeance, swayed by the idea that they too could have been in her place.*

(Swift, 2014)

## Ancient Greece and the Mediterranean

Philo of Alexandria was a Hellenistic Jewish philosopher who lived in Alexandria, in the Roman province of Egypt. Philo used philosophical allegory to harmonise Jewish scripture, mainly the Torah, with Greek philosophy. His method followed the practices of both Jewish exegesis and Stoic philosophy. His allegorical exegesis was important for some Christian Church Fathers, but he had very little credence within Rabbinic Judaism. He adopted allegorical instead of literal interpretations of the Hebrew Bible. He spoke out clearly against the horrors of infanticide:

*Some of them do the deed with their own hands; with monstrous cruelty and barbarity they stifle and throttle the first breath which the infants draw or throw them into a river or into the depths of the sea, after attaching some heavy substance to make them sink more quickly under its weight. Others take them to be exposed in some desert place, hoping, they themselves say, that they may be saved, but leaving them in actual truth to suffer the most distressing fate.*

(Colson, 1962)

Some attempts were made to pay parents to keep children alive in order to replenish the dwindling Roman population, but it was not until the fourth century AD that real change was apparent. The law began to consider killing an infant as murder only in 374 AD. Yet even the opposition to infanticide by the Catholic Church often seemed to be based more on their concern for the parent's soul than with the child's life. After the Council of Vaison (442 AD), however, some progress emerged when the care of abandoned children was formally acknowledged as a Christian duty, and by 787 AD Bishop Dateo of Milan founded the first asylum solely for abandoned infants.

Other countries followed much the same pattern of evolution. According to Kosloski (2020), the Catholic Church created laws to try to eradicate infanticide and provide options for struggling families. Villages were advised to create shelters for poor families in order to protect children from being killed due to the burden of feeding them. Mothers with no other parent were encouraged to leave their newborns in the entrances to churches. This concept continued well into the twentieth century, and today newborns are still left in church entrances or near hospitals.

# Pederasty across cultures

Evidence of pederasty alongside infanticide has emerged in recent years by researchers studying ancient remains and written sources. These reveal that it was common among Minoans, for example, for a father to make a financial transaction with an older man, or *philetor* (befriender), to abduct his son and take him out to the woods for sexual purposes. This relationship was called *harpagmos*; it was public, a common occurrence and considered a normal part of a young man's development (Bloch, 1988).

References in ancient Greek literature to sexual relationships between men and boys typically portray this as a normal part of human development or as a ritual period of life in preparation for military or religious service. In the seventh century BC, clear evidence emerges of mythical stories illustrating the sexual abuse of mortals by gods such as Zeus, Poseidon, Apollo and Dionysus, to name a few. Some scholars have tended to accept the concept that the ancient pederasts' activities were beneficial to boys, that they were *'educating boys in the habits and ways of manhood and of citizenship'*. However, Bloch (1988) explores the subject of sex between men and boys from the point of view of the child rather than the adult, drawing evidence both from ancient literature and from modern medicine to reveal how deeply troubling and damaging the pederastic experience must have been for many Greek boys.

It is without doubt that the child in antiquity lived their earliest years in a society which tolerated and even approved of sexual abuse. Growing up in Greece and Rome often included being abused sexually by older men. The exact form and frequency of the abuse varied according to area and date. In Crete and Boeotia, pederastic marriages and honeymoons were common (De Mause, 1974). Abuse was less frequent among aristocratic boys in Rome, but sexual use of children was everywhere evident in some form. Boy brothels flourished in every city, and men could even contract for the use of a rent-a-boy service in Athens for a certain period of time. A writer at the time, Musonius Rufus wondered whether such a boy would be justified in resisting being abused:

*I knew a father so depraved that, having a son conspicuous for youthful beauty, he sold him into a life of shame. If, now, that lad who was sold and sent into such a life by his father had refused and would not go, should we say that he was disobedient.*

(Brett, 1991)

The ancient philosophers began to engage in debate and earnest discussion about the sexual abuse of children. Aristotle's main objection to Plato's idea that children should be held in common was that when men had sex with boys they wouldn't know if they were their own sons, which Aristotle says would be *'most unseemly'*.

Plutarch said the reason why freeborn Roman boys wore a gold ball around their necks when they were very young was so men could tell which boys it was not proper to use sexually when they found a group in the nude (Babbit, 1928). Plutarch's statement was only one among many which indicate that the sexual abuse of boys was not limited to those over 11 or 12 years of age, as most scholars assume. Sexual abuse by pedagogues and teachers of smaller children may have been common throughout antiquity (De Mause, 1974).

# Child sacrifice

Modern researchers have discovered considerable evidence that child sacrifice was practised by the Irish Celts, the Gauls, the Scandinavians, the Egyptians, the

Phoenicians, the Moabites, the Ammonites and, in certain periods, the Israelites. Thousands of bones of sacrificed children have been dug up by archaeologists, often with inscriptions identifying the victims as firstborn sons of noble families, reaching in time all the way back to the Jericho of 7000 BC. Sealing children in walls, foundations of buildings and bridges to strengthen the structure was also common from the building of the wall of Jericho to as late as 1843 in Germany (e Mause, 1998).

The Minoan civilization in ancient Crete, dating from 3000 BC, is considered to be the first civilisation in Europe. However, an expedition to Knossos by the British School of Athens excavated a mass grave of child sacrifices which revealed clear evidence of cannibalism (Alexiou and Warren, 2004). There was abundant evidence that their flesh had been carefully cut away, as with butchered animals. The children appear to have been in good health, discounting the idea that they had died prematurely and were eaten to supplement the adults' diet. The evidence shows that the children were slaughtered and their flesh cooked and possibly eaten in a sacrificial ritual made in the service of a deity to assure an annual renewal of fertility and a good harvest.

Another dig near Knossos revealed the remains of a 17-year-old found to have been sacrificed circa 1800 BC. He had been trussed up before being ritually murdered with a bronze dagger engraved with a boar's head that lay beside him. The practice of infanticide continued when barbarian tribes took over Europe attempting to ensure future generations would not repopulate and seek vengeance.

To this day, when children play *London Bridge Is Falling Down*, they are apparently acting out a sacrifice to a river goddess when they catch the child at the end of the game. The hypothesis that the song refers to the burying, or immurement, perhaps alive, of children in the foundations of the bridge was first advanced by Alice Bertha Gomme (later Lady Gomme) in *The Traditional Games of England, Scotland and Ireland* (1894–98). This was based around the idea that a bridge would collapse unless the body of a sacrificed human was buried in its foundations and that the watchman is actually a child sacrifice, who will then watch over the bridge as it ages.

Colson (1962) argues:

*In Rome, sacrifice of children led an underground existence. The emperor Julianus killed many boys as a magic rite and because of a portent the Senate decreed that no male born that year should be reared. While Pliny the Elder spoke of men who sought to secure the leg-marrow and the brain of infants. More frequent was the practice of killing your enemy's children, often in great numbers, so that noble children not only witnessed infanticide in the streets but were themselves under continual threat of death depending on the political fortunes of their fathers.*

# Ancient Middle East

There are references in the Tanakh (Hebrew Bible) 500 BC pointing to an awareness of human sacrifice practice in the history of the ancient Near East. The king of Moab reportedly gives his firstborn son and heir as a whole burnt offering in a temple sacrifice (De Mause, 1974). The Tanakh suggests that the Ammonites offered child sacrifices to the deity *Moloch* while the Torah contains a number of imprecations against and laws forbidding child sacrifice, and human sacrifice in general. The Tanakh denounces human sacrifice as a barbaric custom of Baal worshippers. James Kugel (1997) argues that the Torah's specifically forbidding child sacrifice indicates that it happened in Israel as well. The mention of Topeth in Isaiah 30:27–33 indicates an acceptance of child sacrifice in the early Jerusalem practices, to which the law in Leviticus 20:2–5 forbidding child sacrifice is a response. However, some scholars have stated that at least some Israelites and Judahites believed child sacrifice was a legitimate religious practice (Smith, 1990).

Genesis relates the binding of Isaac, by Abraham to present his son Isaac, as a sacrifice on Mount Moriah. It was apparently a test of faith which he agrees to. The story ends with an angel stopping Abraham at the last minute and making Isaac's sacrifice unnecessary by providing a ram, caught in some nearby bushes, to be sacrificed instead. It is possible that the story contains traces of a tradition in which Abraham does sacrifice Isaac and modern versions are the product of censorship and efforts to disguise such cruelty. The most extensive accounts of child sacrifice in the Hebrew Bible refer to those carried out in Gehenna by the two kings of Judah, Ahaz and Manasseh of Judah.

In the Book of Judges, the figure of Jephthah makes a vow to God promising that in return for granting him victory in a war with the Ammonite enemy he would sacrifice the first living person he met at his front door. This turned out to be his own daughter and he duly carried out the promise made to God. In the Book of Exodus, a further startling example of the way children were considered disposable is illustrated in the killing of tens of thousands of Egyptian children, which is celebrated today as the Jewish festival of Passover. The story relates how Israelites were enslaved in ancient Egypt. Yahweh, the god of the Israelites, appears to Moses in a burning bush and commands Moses to confront Pharaoh. To show his power, Yahweh inflicts a series of ten plagues on the Egyptians, culminating in the tenth plague the death of the firstborn. This is what is reported in Exodus:

*About midnight I will go throughout Egypt. Every firstborn son in Egypt will die, from the firstborn son of Pharaoh, who sits on the throne, to the firstborn of the slave girl, who is at her hand mill, and all the firstborn of the cattle as well. There will be loud wailing throughout Egypt – worse than there has ever been or ever will be again.*

(Exodus 11:4–6)

# Ancient Latin America

There are accounts, from around 1499, in the historical archive that the Aztecs performed child sacrifice to appease the angry gods who had flooded Tenochtitlan, an area now recognized as the capital of early Mexico (Sahagun, 1996). Archaeologists found remains of 42 children indicating that these children were sacrificed to the deity *Tlaloc* in the offerings of the Great Pyramid of Tenochtitlan by the Aztecs of pre-Columbian Mexico. Ample evidence has discovered that human sacrifice was an everyday activity in Tenochtitlan and children were not exempt.

*The Aztecs believed that, if sacrifices were not given to Tlaloc, the rain would not come and their crops would not grow. In every case, the 42 children, mostly males aged around six, were suffering from serious cavities, abscesses or bone infections that would have been painful enough to make them cry continually. Tlaloc required the tears of the young so their tears would wet the earth. As a result, if children did not cry, the priests would sometimes tear off the children's nails before the ritual sacrifice.*

(Sahagun, 1996)

The Inca culture frequently sacrificed children in a ritual called '*qhapaq hucha*'. Their frozen corpses have been discovered in the South American mountaintops. The first of these corpses, a female child who had died from a blow to the skull, was discovered in 1995. Other methods of sacrifice included strangulation and simply leaving the children, who had been given an intoxicating drink, to lose consciousness in the extreme cold and low-oxygen conditions of the mountaintop, and to die of hypothermia (Reinhard, 2010).

In Maya culture, people believed that supernatural beings had power over their lives and this is one reason that child sacrifice occurred. The sacrifices were essentially to satisfy the supernatural beings. This was done through *k'ex*, which is an exchange or substitution of something. Through *k'ex* infants would substitute more powerful humans.

*It was thought that supernatural beings would consume the souls of more powerful humans and infants were substituted in order to prevent that. Infants were believed to be good offerings because they had a close connection to the spirit world through liminality, which allowed parents to believe that their children would continue to live albeit in some altered form. Child sacrifice was preferred when there was a time of crisis and transitional times such as famine and drought.*

(Scherer, 2012)

There is archaeological evidence of infant sacrifice in tombs where the infant has been buried in urns or ceramic vessels. There have also been depictions of child sacrifice in art. Some art includes pottery and steles as well as references to infant sacrifice in mythology and art depictions of the mythology. According to De Castellanos, the Moche of northern Peru practised mass sacrifices of boys. The Timoto-Cuicas offered human sacrifices. Until colonial times, child sacrifice persisted secretly in Laguna de Urao (Mérida). Feasts and human sacrifices were done in honour of *Icaque*, an Andean pre-Hispanic goddess (De Castellanos, 2014).

The BBC reported that archaeologists in northern Peru found evidence of what could be the world's largest single case of child sacrifice in 2018. The pre-Columbian burial site, known as Las Llamas, contains the skeletons of 140 children who were between the ages of 5 and 14 when they were ritually sacrificed during a ceremony about 550 years ago. The site is located near the modern-day city of Trujillo. The burial site was apparently built by the ancient Chimú empire. It is thought the children were sacrificed as floods caused by the El Nino weather pattern ravaged the Peruvian coastline.

Researchers did not find just bones at the site but also footprints that have survived rain and erosion. The small footprints indicate the children were marched to their deaths from Chan Chan, an ancient city a mile away from Las Llamas. The children's skeletons contained lesions on their breastbones, which were probably made by a ceremonial knife. Dislocated ribcages suggest that whoever was performing the sacrifices may have been trying to extract the children's hearts (BBC, 2018).

## Ancient North Africa

Carthage (modern-day Tunisia) was notorious for its child sacrifice practices. Plutarch (ca. 46–120 AD), Tertullian, Orosius and Diodorus Siculus mention this practice. The ancestors of Carthage, Canaanites, were also mentioned performing child sacrifices in the Hebrew Bible, and by some Israelites at a place called the Tophet (roasting place). Some of these sources suggest that children were roasted to death on a heated bronze statue. According to Diodorus Siculus:

*There was in their city a bronze image of Cronus extending its hands, palms up and sloping toward the ground so that each of the children when placed thereon rolled down and fell into a sort of gaping pit filled with fire.*

(Picard, 1935)

Sites within Carthage and other Phoenician centres have revealed the remains of young children in large numbers. Some historians interpret this as evidence for frequent and prominent child sacrifice to the god Baal-hamon. These all mention the burning of children as offerings to Cronus or Saturn, the chief god of Carthage. There is a consensus among scholars that Carthaginian children were sacrificed by their parents, who would make a vow to kill the next child if the gods would grant them a favour, for instance, that their shipment of goods was to arrive safely in a foreign port (Stager and Wolff, 1984). They placed their children alive in the arms of a bronze statue of the lady *Tanit*.

The hands of the statue extended over a brazier into which the child fell once the flames had caused its limbs to contract and its mouth to open. The child was thus alive and conscious when burned. Claims concerning Moloch and child sacrifice may have been made for negative-propaganda effect. The Romans and Israelites describe child sacrifice as a practice of their evil enemies. Some scholars think that after the Romans finally defeated Carthage and totally destroyed the city, they engaged in post-war propaganda to make their arch-enemies seem cruel and less civilised.

## Ancient Arabia

The Qur'an documents pagan Arabians sacrificing their children to idols. Pagan Arabs, it states, engaged in female infanticide, exploitation of the poor, usury, murder, false contracts, fornication, adultery and theft. Esposito (1988) states that Muhammad's insistence that each person was personally accountable not to tribal customary law but to an overriding divine law shook the very foundations of ancient Arabian society. Muhammad proclaimed a sweeping programme of religious and social reform that affected religious beliefs and practices, business contracts and practices, male–female and family relations. Esposito (1988) holds that the Qur'an's reforms consisted of wholesale changes and reforms that swept away time-honoured traditions in pre-Islamic Arabia. According to some scholars, Muhammad's condemnation of infanticide was the key aspect of his attempts to raise the status of women. A much-cited verse of the Qur'an that addresses this practice is:

*When the sun shall be darkened when the stars shall be thrown down when the mountains shall be set moving when the pregnant camels shall be neglected when the savage beasts shall be mustered when the seas shall be set boiling, when the souls shall be coupled, when the buried infant (mawudatu) shall be asked for what sin she was slain when the scrolls shall be unrolled.*

(Gallagher, 2009)

The true prevalence of gendercide in this time period is hard to determine. Donna Lee Bowen (2002) suggests that it was quite common but declining up to the establishment of Islam. The rationale was that by killing girls a form of birth control was legitimized among destitute families unable to feed large numbers of children. Boys also had status as future workers and heads of households.

Though the belief that pre-Islamic Arabs regularly practised female infanticide has become common among both Muslims and Western writers, few surviving sources reference the practice before Islam. An inscription in Yemen, dating to approximately 400 BC, forbidding the practice is the sole mention of it in pre-Islamic records.

## Medieval evidence

Written English began to spread in the fifteenth century in Britain and offers some valuable evidence and insight into the treatment of children and the wider family and social context of their lives. What emerges is a picture of extreme and formal deference that children were made to show their parents, the harshness of home and school discipline, and the constant physical abuse of boys, girls and young servants. The choice of partners for the daughters of well-off parents was based ruthlessly on power, prestige and money, and very young girls were basically sold off to the highest bidder. One account (Trevelyan, 1977) refers to a young daughter who hesitated to agree to marry an ugly widower of 50 years' age, and was beaten regularly for three months constantly two or three times every week.

In the eleventh century, according to Kissane (2017), for example, the surviving ordinances of Canterbury Cathedral indicate that Archbishop Lanfranc ordered boy recruits to be governed by a monk of mature age and discretion, who was to supervise them going to bed and to be present should any other monk wish to speak to them. This process clearly sought to minimise opportunities for monks guilty of past sexual abuse. The bulk of surviving records into abuses in the medieval era have avoided destruction or editing of the truth, and provide testimony of sexual abuse despite efforts of the Church of England and Catholic Church to conceal or deny the truth in order to avoid tainting their reputations. They remain remarkably similar to the cases currently being heard by the UK Independent Inquiry into Child Sexual Abuse (IICSA). This very modern investigation has revealed countless examples of church collusion with paedophile priests, cover-ups, denial and a lack of care for traumatized children (Kissane, 2017).

Kissane (2017) provides an example of the medieval culture from the case of an eight-year-old girl raped by a much older man. The case dragged on and was eventually heard at Lincoln in 1355, having taken almost a decade to come to court and with no clear resolution after the trial. According to the Latin record, a prominent local man, Hugh de Outhorp, raped the eight-year-old then enlisted his brother, a local court official, in a cover-up. He also used threats against the mother and child to try to cover up his crime. The case was eventually heard but with no satisfactory outcome.

Such incidents bear many of the hallmarks of cases currently under investigation by the Independent Inquiry into Child Sexual Abuse (IICSA), with power and influence being used to suppress due legal process. While no outcome is recorded in the case of Agnes, she remains representative of many other girls who experienced sexual abuse. Some even died from violent sexual assaults, including Alice, daughter of William Ambroys, whose back was broken after being thrown on to the bed of her attacker in 1309. For men found guilty of *rape*, a term sometimes inclusive of violent sexual assault, the punishment was clear, at least in principle.

Following the introduction of new legislative measures in 1285, perpetrators were ordered be hanged, though in the vast majority of cases this did not happen (Kissane, 2017). Attitudes towards child sexual abuse were conditioned by rural societies' custom of intermarriage in family groups, incest between siblings, or by fathers. The canonical age of consent for intercourse, set by the medieval church at 12 years of age, set the parameters for what was considered normal and permissible.

Around the year 1500, an assistant to the Venetian ambassador to England was struck by the strange attitude to parenting that he had encountered on his travels (BBC, 2014a). He was struck at the different childcare practices he witnessed or heard about compared to those of the Continent.

It was for the children's own good, he was told, but he suspected the English preferred having other people's children in the household because they could feed them less, sexually abuse them and work them harder. His remarks shine a light on a system of child-rearing that operated across Northern Europe in the medieval and early modern period. Many parents of the poor classes sent their children away from home to work as servants or apprentices, while only a small minority went into the church or to university.

Model letters and diaries in medieval schoolbooks indicate that leaving home was traumatic. *'For all that was to me a pleasure when I was a child, from three years old to 10… while I was under my father and mother's keeping, be turned now to torments and pain'*, complains one boy in a letter given to pupils to translate into Latin. Illiterate servants had no means of communicating with their parents, and the difficulties of travel meant that even if children were only sent 20 miles (32 km) away they could feel completely isolated (Kremer, 2014).

Peter Damian (1007–72), later canonised and declared a doctor of the church, learned about the destructive power of evil early in his life. As a child in Ravenna, Italy, Damian lost both of his parents and spent time with an abusive older brother before another brother, who was archpriest of Ravenna, took him in and saw to his education. In the diocesan cathedral school he attended, Damian became increasingly scandalised by the behaviour of both students and professors (Anderson, 2005).

Complaints from Damian about the church's unwillingness to confront the sexual behaviour of the clergy, however, met with inaction. In 1049, Damian wrote to Pope Leo IX (1048–54) about the cancer of sexual abuse that was spreading through the church: boys and adolescents were being forced and seduced into performing acts of sodomy by priests and bishops; there were problems with sexual harassment among higher clergy; and many members of the clergy were keeping boy concubines. Damian warned the Pope that bishops were contributing to the growth of the problem by their failure to enforce church discipline. Members of the clergy who sexually abused others demonstrated by their actions that they had no fear of God, Damian argued:

*Such men were afraid only of being despised by the people and of losing their positions; they would do anything to avoid being stripped of their clerical status and identity. Knowing that their bishop would not remove them from their office and ministry gave such men license to continue in their wickedness. Thus in failing to discipline abusive members of the clergy, the bishops stood as guilty as the men who committed the crimes.*
(Anderson, 2005)

This is again reminiscent of the revelations from the IICSA into sexual abuse of children within many UK churches. Priests and bishops convinced their victims that they were wicked and responsible for the degrading and painful acts, threatened them with grotesque punishments or suggested their parents would be imprisoned. These clergymen then sought confession and the sanctity and secrecy it guaranteed in order to cover their tracks. Despite hearing of criminal activities against the most vulnerable children, church leaders colluded with cover-ups and themselves committed criminal offences by not reporting such crimes.

# The European Reformation and Enlightenment

In the early sixteenth century, the Protestant Reformation challenged the principles and authority of the Roman Catholic Church throughout Europe. It marked the beginning of intellectual challenges to the concept of Biblical truth and the emergence of scientific, rationale explanations for disease, weather events, celestial phenomena and much else. But before Newton's *Principia* sparked the intellectual sea change known as the Enlightenment when scientific principles began to challenge religious orthodoxy, the first flickers of the Enlightenment had begun with the Renaissance and Reformation. The Enlightenment was an intellectual and cultural movement that occurred in eighteenth-century Europe. It heralded the first inkling of a change in the perception of children. With regard to healthcare for children, the first English language paediatric text, *The Boke of Children*, appeared in 1545 and was based on ancient Greek, Roman and Arab treatises which advocated the care and education of children.

But despite the changes that the Reformation and Enlightenment brought to the education of children and young people, most European children remained for a long time illiterate or barely literate. In addition, children's lives were bleak and short with infant mortality rates calculated at between 20 and 40 per cent until the late eighteenth century. By this time scientific advances had enabled the discovery of a vaccine for smallpox, a deadly, killer disease. There was also considerable resistance from the Establishment and wealthy classes to the concept of universal education perceiving it as a threat to their privileges and entitlement to lucrative occupations or positions of power.

The earliest known organised schools in England were connected to the church. Augustine established a church in Canterbury in 598, which included a school for the study of religious texts, and in 604 this was joined by another school at what is now Rochester Cathedral. Further schools were established throughout the British Isles in the seventh and eighth centuries, generally following one of two forms: grammar schools to teach Latin, and song schools to train singers for cathedral choirs. Corporal punishment was meted out on a regular basis by some teachers who derived sadistic pleasure in harming children. During the Middle Ages, schools were established to teach Latin grammar to the sons of the aristocracy destined for priesthood or monastic work with the ministry, or in government or the lucrative legal profession. Out of 4.3 million children of primary school age in England and Wales, 1 million were in purely voluntary schools and 1.3 million were in state-aided schools, but the remaining 2 million had no access to schools whatsoever (Gillard, 2018).

William Forster's Elementary Education Act 1870 required partially state-funded board schools to be set up to provide elementary (primary, in modern parlance) education in areas where existing provision was inadequate. Board schools were managed by elected school boards. The schools remained fee-charging, but poor parents could be exempted. Education in England remained closely linked to religious institutions until the nineteenth century, although charity schools and grammar schools, which were open to children of any religious beliefs, became more common in the early modern period. Nineteenth-century reforms expanded education provision and introduced widespread state-funded schools. By the 1880s, education was compulsory for children aged 5 to 10, with the school-leaving age progressively raised since then, most recently to 18 in 2015 (Middleton, 1970).

The rational approach to government in the Enlightenment, which led to the American and French revolutions, encouraged the idea that a wider suffrage required an educated electorate. By the early nineteenth century, some American states had established educational standards and teacher training institutions. The French government secularised and centralised its education system, forming elementary, secondary schools and special lycées intended as high schools with the aim of creating a class of government and military figures to perpetuate patriotism and national pride (Marten, 2018).

Widespread education in theory provided some protection for children because children who were abused could be noticed by teachers. However, school children were brutalised into submission by those in authority, scared to complain about abuse, and there was no effective child protection resources or training. Disturbed or disruptive behaviour as a result of abuse was considered naughty and punished, while schools then, as now, themselves attracted those with harmful intent towards children who learned how to exploit the vulnerable and stop them disclosing abuse. Instead of schools being sanctuaries of safety and learning for children, they remained for many decades places where children could be physically and sexually abused, bullied by teachers or other students, where rote learning squashed individuality and creativity, and children's voices and agency were completely ignored.

## Chapter 2 | Fairy tales, folklore and religion

*Discipline your children and they will give you peace of mind and will make your heart glad.*

Proverbs 29:17

# Introduction

Fairy tales and their origins in folklore and some religious texts are a very popular children's literary genre. But there is a dark side to what most parents feel is a normal childhood rite of passage.

The Brothers Grimm wrote many popular fairy tales in the early nineteenth century These tales have increasingly been subject to scholarly scrutiny due to the amount of violence, cruelty, cannibalism and other horrific elements in them. Maria Tatar, in particular, has researched the theme of child abuse in the tales (Tatar, 2018). Tatar translated 36 tales from German into English and analysed them for traces of child abuse. She defined and clarified what she meant by abuse and focused on neglect, emotional abuse, physical abuse and sexual abuse. In 20 of the 36 tales examined, she identified one or more types of abuse.

*Many tales are about children who suffer from neglect like Hansel and Gretel. Their parents abandon them in the woods because they couldn't afford to feed them anymore. Emotional abuse is another type of child abuse that prevails in the tales. Cinderella, for instance, goes through emotional abuse the moment her mother dies and a stepmother and stepsisters enslaved her. Most of the tales have a physical abuse theme like Snow White in which her stepmother attempts to kill her stepdaughter out of jealousy.*

(Tatar, 2018)

Kyhoon suggests that the tales, even disguised in fantastical ways and relying on a reader's vivid imagination, still portrayed the reality of children's abuse during the period of time they were written. The appeal of fairy stories may unconsciously enable adults reading to their children to provide warnings or moral aphorisms about good versus evil. Thus these perennial tales managed to live through many historical times and still capture the attention of the twenty–first-century reader for their realistic themes (Kyhoon, 2014).

# The impact on children

In the late seventeenth century, it was commonly believed that fairies could scare people to death or harbour evil intent.

*They were thought to be descended from fallen angels, thereby playing into a religious context of devilish forces intent on causing harm and to have the power to cause cataclysmic events. Despite their modern image as harmless playmates, the fairies feared by ordinary people caused them to flee their homes, to revere fairy trees and paths, and to abuse or even kill infants or adults held to be fairy changelings. Such beliefs lingered on in places well into the twentieth century.*

(Sugg, 2018)

Children subjected to such beliefs may have suffered from anxiety. Often associated with witchcraft and black magic, fairies were also closely involved with reports of ghosts and poltergeists. In literature and art, fairies often retain this edge of danger. Distraught over a sick or disabled child, parents would torture, or sometimes kill, what they believed to be a changeling, a malevolent stand-in for a stolen baby (Sugg, 2018).

The legend of the Pied Piper of Hamelin is an example of how folklore features children at risk. Enraged by non-payment for ridding the town of a plague of rats, the piper vows to take revenge. By playing his pipe, he attracts the town's children and 130 of them follow him out of town and are never seen again.

Fairies were associated with evil-doing; they were malevolent, powerful, mystical beings from another dimension. They could appear out of thin air or secret themselves in forests, caves or forbidden territory. They could charm small children, mesmerize them and change shape to trick and deceive. They had the power to cure sickness or conversely cause illness in livestock or people.

While ordinary people still believed in the limitless power of fairies until less than a century ago, the educated also believed it in the era of the witch persecutions. Witches were held responsible for every sort of natural negative event. Fairies or fairyland was quite often referenced in their trials. Although Joan of Arc was tried as a religious heretic, rather than a witch, the latter association was emphasised by her tormentors, and it is notable that in 1431 her interrogators used as evidence in her trial the fact that she used to play around a 'fairy tree' in her childhood village. It has been estimated that in the mid-eighteenth century up to 1000 women were killed during the peak of witch trials in the UK conducted by religious fanatics.

Fairies, vampires or witches could be grouped together as demonic characters with the potential to kill. The latter pair could suck out your blood, soul or breath, or extract the essence from food. In the twentieth century that iconic *other*, the alien abductor, updated this basic assault with reports of clinical probings or the removal of human eggs or sperm. In the pre-scientific cultures of the fairy or the witch, however, the most potent emblem of life was simply one's own baby or child. The result of this was that, for most of history children were taught to fear them or were frightened by tales of children being abducted at night by supernatural beings. Generations of small children still fear the monster under the bed or have nightmares possibly derived from seemingly innocuous fairy stories at bedtime readings (Sugg, 2018).

## Changelings

Some children were believed by their parents to be changelings, either false children or children possessed by an evil spirit that could be driven from the child through abuse and punishment. In her book *The Burning of Bridget Cleary* (1999) about a woman killed by her husband in an attempt to exorcise fairy spirits from her, folklorist Angela Bourke of the National University of Ireland notes that many accounts can be found in nineteenth-century newspapers and police reports of suspected child-changelings in Ireland being placed on red-hot shovels, drowned or otherwise mistreated or killed.

*Throughout Europe and in Celtic territories in particular, fairies were believed to steal babies and children especially boys, and especially those with blue eyes and fair hair leaving fairy substitutes in their place. Around the end of the nineteenth century beliefs that fairies had swapped their children were so strong that some parents would kill or torture their offspring in an exorcise attempt to rid them of the perceived evil and accompanying family curse.*

(Briggs, 1976)

When Martin Luther recommended drowning a changeling, it was because the child's appearance showed it to have no soul. In the seventeenth century, even the most rational Christians used changeling as a loose synonym for the mentally disabled, with dramatist Elkanah Settle echoing Luther when he talked, in 1694, of '*some coarse half-souled fairy changeling*' (Sugg, 2018).

The changeling often met with violence being advised or performed by the local fairy doctor. In some cases, such rituals were used on actual sick children thought to be fairy-struck seen as in danger of abduction. Carole Silver (1999) cites changelings killed by foxglove baths in Wales in 1857, and in Donegal in the 1870s and 1890s. Susan Eberly (2012) tells of a Scottish case, in Caerlaverock, where a ceaselessly crying baby was thrown onto hot coals. Eberly (2012) has argued convincingly that modern-day responses of parents to disabled children still sometimes mingle anger and guilt, and that such emotions could well have fed into the violence directed at changelings. In the twentieth century, it was not uncommon for new-born severely disabled children to be left to die by nursing staff and midwives. Silver has suggested that one benefit of the changeling belief was the way it shifted blame for the child's condition into a thoroughly separate, supernatural realm, beyond human control.

Silver suggests that changeling beliefs offered two important benefits. First, they allowed people to shift from being helpless victims to active combatants of the perceived problem. Second, they gave an otherwise frighteningly arbitrary condition a meaning, a known and accepted place within a shared framework of explanation. The craving for certainty at times when rational thought and scientific evidence were limited was powerful, and thus easy to understand superstitions gained credibility. It provided a justification for the horrific treatment of innocent children.

*Immersed in rivers or placed at the margin of coastal tides, stood on hot coals or hung over fires, exposed in freezing weather, bathed in poisonous foxglove essence, beaten, threatened and subjected to forms of exorcism, these babies and children sometimes survived, sometimes not.*

(Silver, 1999)

The Ancient Greek legend of Oedipus provided Freud with the ideal vehicle for articulating his theory of infantile sexuality and the son's death wish aimed at the father with a sexual desire for the mother. The legend tells of King Laius of Thebes and Queen Jocasta who are warned by a prophet that their expected child would grow up to murder his father and marry his mother. At birth the baby's feet are pierced and he is left to die in the mountains. The child is saved by peasants and eventually grows up as the son of a foreign king and queen.

Oedipus meets a stranger on the road and kills him after an argument not realising that this is in fact his real father King Laius. Oedipus eventually realises that he is indeed the murderer of his own father and in a violent torment blinds himself. Jocasta on learning of the news commits suicide thus completing the tragedy. The Oedipus legend, according to psychoanalysts, serves to illustrate the unconscious struggles taking place in a child's sexual development where a male child feels intense emotional desire to replace its father. But it also sows a seed of distrust between adults and children with children portrayed as harbouring murderous thoughts (Walker, 2005).

Childhood fairy stories and legends are often experienced as bedtime reading or narrated by a parental/carer figure. They are usually extraordinary tales involving fantastical characters and situations where magic is woven in a world outside the physical daily world inhabited during the waking day. Good and evil usually feature in a struggle during trials and tribulations, morality also features; so unwittingly parents are introducing, albeit in an imaginary way, the idea that death is a potential risk (Walker, 2010). Children's earliest and widely held fears are the death of one or both parents, so by reading these stories to their children parents were ironically implanting the message that the very person they were becoming fully dependent upon was at risk of dying. Before printed books these myths and legends were part of narrative communication; storytelling was a vital part of entertainment as well as education. For example, the tale of Little Red Riding Hood can be used as a way for parents to warn children not to talk to strangers. However, a benign intent could backfire by implanting in a child the concept that they are at risk from abduction and harm by a stranger.

## Towards deeper cultural meaning

Favat (1977) suggests that a child's interest in the fairy tale is at some level a natural search for a world more ordered than their current experience where they are striving for resolution to an internal crisis.

*It is a salutary utilisation of an implicit cultural device in order to invest the real world with the constructs of the tale. Thus the fairy tale reflects a process of struggle against experiences of suppression and authoritarian control. The more traditional fairy tales represent a regressive notion of family life where arbitrary authority in the form of Kings and Queens mete out justice.*

(Favat, 1977)

The third-person narrative voice in Hans Christian Anderson's 'The Tinderbox' (Anderson, 1913) speaks of the social tensions encountered by a young person born into a poor family but who aspires to a higher social station in life. He is recruited by a witch to retrieve a fortune but instead of returning it to her he keeps it, kills the witch and assumes enormous power and influence. The young man deposes the ruling monarchs and becomes the head of state. The tale implants the idea that children are susceptible to malignant influence, and can murder to achieve wealth and power.

Many characters in fairy tales are under a spell of some kind, often transformed into an animal shape. The task of the heroine or hero is to try to spot the genuine person underneath the disguise or spell. This theme occurs across cultures and time in verbal and written renditions. Although there is more often a happy ending to fairy stories, this is not universally the case. For example, in the Cinderella-like tale 'Why the Sea Moans' from Brazil, the spell must work itself out for bad or good, and in the amazing Inuit story 'A Whale's Soul and Its Burning Heart' the spell that is broken due to constant meddling is life itself (Walker, 2005).

Charles Lutwidge Dodgson better known by his pen name, Lewis Carroll, was an English writer of children's fiction, notably *Alice's Adventures in Wonderland* and its sequel *Through the Looking-Glass.* Dodgson was obsessed with small children and painted or photographed them naked. Some late twentieth-century biographers, including Morton N. Cohen in his *Lewis Carroll: A Biography* (1995), Donald Thomas in his Lewis Carroll: *A Portrait with Background* (1995) and Michael Bakewell in his *Lewis Carroll: A Biography* (1996), have suggested that Dodgson's interest in children had an erotic element and that he might have been a paedophile. Cohen, in particular, speculates that Dodgson's *'sexual energies sought unconventional outlets'*, and further writes:

*We cannot know to what extent sexual urges lay behind Charles's preference for drawing and photographing children in the nude. He contended the preference was entirely aesthetic. But given his emotional attachment to children as well as his aesthetic appreciation of their forms, his assertion that his interest was strictly artistic is naïve. He probably felt more than he dared acknowledge, even to himself.*

(Cohen, 1995)

Cohen goes on to note that Dodgson tried to convince many of his friends that his attachment to the nude female child form was free of any eroticism, but Cohen adds that later generations have been able to look beneath the surface and assess the content through the prism of what we now know to be a long history of child sexual abuse. He argues that Dodgson may even have wanted to marry the 11-year-old Alice Liddell, who was the template for the character in his most famous book, and that this was the cause of the unexplained break with the Liddell family in June 1863.

## Storytelling as therapeutic support

Parents, counsellors, social workers and psychotherapists will understand that storytelling is an important way of communicating with children at many levels, especially children traumatised by abuse. There is the physical sensation of hearing a trusted voice speaking in expressive ways to fire the imagination. There is the story itself which could be full of emotional and cognitive content. Then there is the imagination of the listening child as they interpret the story and then build a mental picture to paint the narrative. The story probably contains a message at an obvious moral level such as good versus bad, or at an allegorical level (Walker, 2010). Communication as we know is both ways, so a child can derive immense pleasure from telling an adult stories they have learnt and then watching their reactions. Or the story could conjure up fears and fantasies, increasing anxiety and worries (Sunderland, 2001).

However, the effect of the use of myths and legends with children cannot be predicted or assumed. The significance adults attach to a particular story and the assumption that it will have a benign impact on a troubled young person could provoke an unintended negative result. This could happen when attempting to link a depressive reaction to a family bereavement with stories involving death such as Jesus or Muhammad. In the case of Jesus and his literal resurrection, a child could become more anxious at the thought of a relative rising from the dead. The Jewish story of Jairus's daughter contains several potential layers of meaning (Walker, 2010). In it the father pleads with Jesus to help his dying daughter. Although the girl dies before Jesus reaches her, he carries on and says the girls is not dead but sleeping. He holds her hand and tells her to rise which she immediately does. Jesus orders food for her and she makes a quick recovery. Crompton (1996) suggests several layers of meaning:

- » Female children had little status then – yet her father and a male healer come to her aid providing a message that female children are equally important.

- » Jesus heals the girl showing diagnostic ability – children are often labelled as too disturbed, delinquent or beyond help yet in this story the child was helped.

- » The significance of food could represent an eating disorder – so the story illustrates how a young woman with this problem can be supported back to health.

- » The girl could have been commencing her period – Jewish men were not allowed to touch menstruating women; therefore, by holding her hand he demonstrates that no child is too unclean or unacceptable to receive care from an adult.

The story of Hansel and Gretel can be interpreted in several ways but it seems to fit well with the need for a child embarking on a significant milestone by going to full-time education at about five years of age. This is a time of great change and particularly an important separation from parental control. The story is one of stepping out into a potentially dangerous world where a threatening enemy is symbolised by the witch character (Walker, 2010). The children triumph of course and in so doing are representing the child reader who can derive reassurance and understanding of separation anxieties. For a female child reading the story it offers a role model of a younger child who becomes less dependent on her brother and eventually actually defeats the witch (Bettelheim, 1991). However, it also plants the seed of an idea that maybe the witch could succeed and harm the lost children.

Cinema cartoon films have been used as a vehicle for mass exposure of some of the more famous fairy tales yet because of the dominance of one producer the range of material offered is culturally narrow. Various critiques of the organisations that make these cartoons have focused on the ideological nature of the treatment of fairy tales in order to conform to a rigid formula promoting family values, the victory of good over evil and the reinforcement of idealised heterosexual marital relationships. The Hollywood animated cartoon was, it is argued, developed from, expressed and was frequently controlled by a number of shifting and often contradictory discourses about sexuality, race, gender, class, leisure and creativity (Smoodin, 1993).

Children and young people have the capacity to conjure feelings of faith and hope when experiencing emotional and psychological distress.

*Myths legends and fairy stories as part of their early child development offer a rich source of material to draw from and enlist in direct work. Fairies often act in a healing capacity in mythology, or they appear as agents between the world of human affairs and the invisible forces of nature. They also possess powers in advance of mortals achieving superhuman tasks, but they can also run into trouble and sometimes rely on assistance from humans to succeed .*

(Williams, 1997)

Fairy stories in particular can be used to engage children when conventional ordinary dialogue is inadequate or unsuccessful at promoting therapeutic engagement and process. If we accept that childhood tales form a building block in the construction of the child's fantasy world and therefore their personality development, then this offers an opportunity to understand the variety of meanings and influences contained therein at many levels (Walker, 2011). Myths are poetic tales explaining why the world is the way it is and why people behave the way they do. They usually involve gods and goddesses or spirits. Legends are stories about events that may or may not have taken place a long time ago.

The fairy realm is a central aspect of cultures all over the world, yet until very recently the mainstream school and young person's literature reflected a narrow spectrum of examples from a Eurocentric base. Classic tales read in classrooms or appearing in popular culture on television or in annual pantomimes, such as Jack and the Beanstalk, Cinderella or Puss in Boots, neglect the rich diversity of stories from around the world (Walker, 2005). Aladdin, for example, while incorporated into mainstream pantomime is actually one of *The Arabian Nights* stories told over 1001 nights by Sheherazade to King Shahryar as part of a lost collection of Persian tales circa AD 850.

# Religion and spirituality

The Western model of psychological illness linked to child abuse tends to ignore the religious or spiritual aspects of the culture in which it is based. However, Eastern, African and Native American cultures tend to integrate them (Fernando, 2002). Spirituality and religion as topics in general do not feature often in the child protection literature, yet they can be components of a child and young person's psychological well-being offering a source of strength and hope in trying circumstances. Children for whom family and faith backgrounds are inseparable may need encouragement to feel comfortable in multi-faith settings.

It is important to address this dimension as part of the constellation of factors affecting children and adolescents, bearing in mind the positive and sometimes negative impact spiritual or religious beliefs might have on their mental health. It is well understood that children communicate about feelings and experiences more easily through responses to stories. Direct work that allows them to use their imaginations and access their own spirituality through stories can be liberating (Walker, 2010).

*Multiple caregiving of young children in Australian aboriginal culture has attracted concerns based on Western notions of attachment theory and the need for secure attachment relationships with primary carers. However, research has demonstrated that Aboriginal children can sustain and thrive with multiple attachment figures that are wholly consistent with societal norms.*

(Yeo, 2003)

Indeed, there are sometimes lengthy absences from parents related to important sacred initiations or religious ceremonies considered necessary for the child or young person's spiritual development. However, each individual child has a unique personality and some may find separation like this traumatic and abusive.

In South American countries, the influence of the Catholic Church and family planning combined with poverty, a history of military dictatorships and a culture of machismo has produced a culture of extreme social inequality where children can easily drift into prostitution, child labour or become homeless. In these conditions, authoritarian family structures create a climate where domestic violence and child abuse thrives (Ravazzola, 1997). Here, however, liberation theology translates Christian concepts into activity that challenges the prevailing order offering hope of better circumstances and prospects through revolutionary struggle. Children and young people can thus link religion with empowerment and liberation from inequitable and socially unjust conditions.

# Established churches and child abuse

The latest UK Independent Inquiry into Child Sexual Abuse recent report (IICSA, 2020) about the Catholic Church and Birmingham Archdiocese has uncovered another layer of church secrecy and cover-up about child abuse going back nearly 100 years. The Inquiry found more than 130 allegations of child sexual abuse had been made against 78 individuals associated with the Archdiocese since the 1930s. The true scale of offending is likely to be far higher.

The IICSA report examined the Church's response to child sexual abuse by investigating the cases of four priests: James Robinson, Samuel Penney, John Tolkien and an anonymous priest ciphered as RC-F167. It also shows how the previous investigations by the Church – the Nolan and Cumberlege reports, produced in 2001 and 2007 respectively – were both whitewashes. Robinson, a serial child abuser, was simply moved to another parish after complaints were first made in the 1980s. The police were not informed and there was no internal investigation.

In 1985, he fled to the US after being confronted by a victim who recorded their conversation. However, he continued to receive financial support from the Archdiocese for seven years. In 2003, the BBC broadcast a documentary in which the programme makers tracked down Robinson to a caravan park in California and confronted him. The then Archbishop of Birmingham, Vincent Nichols, now a cardinal and the highest-ranking Catholic in the UK, issued a press release complaining about the programme and accusing the BBC of anti-Catholic bias. Similarly, when the Archdiocese was alerted to allegations against Penney, the Vicar General in charge of investigating them instead attempted to help him evade arrest and leave the UK (Daily Telegraph, 2019).

# Religious cults

Raine and Kent (2019) argue that the unique aspects of religion facilitate institutional and interpersonal grooming of children and young people in ways that often differ from forms of manipulation in secular settings. Drawing from Christianity (Catholicism, Protestantism and Seventh-day Adventism) and various sects (the Children of God, the Branch Davidians, the Fundamentalist Church of Jesus Christ of Latter-Day Saints, a Hindu ashram and the devadasis), their research shows how some religious institutions and leadership figures in them can slowly cultivate children and their caregivers into harmful and illegal sexual activity.

*A number of uniquely religious characteristics facilitate this cultivation, which includes: theodicies of legitimation; power, patriarchy, obedience, protection, and reverence towards authority figures; victims' fears about spiritual punishments; and scriptural uses to justify adult-child sex.*

(Raine and Kent, 2019)

In some religious sects, physical child abuse is widespread; the pain and suffering of children is horrendous, and sometimes results in the death of children at the hands of those who should be caring for and protecting them. Such abuse can have significant deleterious effects on people, both through their childhood and on into adulthood.

*There are an estimated one million children living in religious sects in the USA. Some of the information on child abuse in sects is highly disturbing, and it is clear that physical abuse does occur in some sects and sometimes at an extreme level to most children in that sect. In other sects, it is likely that little if any physical child abuse occurs. In still other sects, there may be differences between branches of the sects or between families in the sect.*

(Furnari, 2005)

The Children of God cult began in the United States in the late 1960s and built on the free love philosophy of counter-culture America. Its founder, David Berg, told members that God was love and love was sex, so there should be no limits, regardless of age or relationship. By the 1970s Berg's cult claimed to have 10,000 full-time members in 130 communities around the world. The religious sect, which was also known as The Family, has faced allegations of widespread sexual and physical abuse of children, including sexual violence, incest and brainwashing. Survivors told prosecutors of beatings, secrecy and brainwashing that belittled small children making them feel worthless and useless (BBC, 2019).

It operated at a number of sites in Scotland. The adults in the communes would have cult names, often Biblical, and frequently unrelated to their true identity which has presented issues in trying to gather evidence of their abuse. A sister was told that her brother had been excommunicated for incurable demon possession. However, he testified that he was ejected from the group after having a '*total mental breakdown*' at the age of 14. '*They tried to pray the demons out of me and it didn't work*', he says. '*Ultimately they had to excommunicate me but they had to force me out*' (BBC, 2019).

In 2018 a man linked to the Children of God religious cult in Scotland was convicted of four charges of sexually abusing his daughter and another child in Renfrewshire on the east coast of Scotland when they were part of the cult. Another member of the cult admitted in 2020 repeatedly raping two schoolgirls, aged 9 and 11, about 30 years ago (Daily Record, 2020).

# Covering up child abuse

Under cross examination at the Independent Inquiry into Historic Child Sexual Abuse, George Carey, the former Archbishop of Canterbury, admitted he offered uncritical support for a bishop accused of sexual abuse. Lord Carey said that with 25 years of hindsight, he realised he should not have been so generous in his views of Peter Ball, the former bishop of Lewes and then Gloucester, who was jailed in 2015 for sexually abusing vulnerable young men. He did not face a criminal trial for more than 20 years, by which time one of his victims had killed himself (Guardian, 2018).

Pope Francis in 2019 gathered 200 bishops and heads of religious orders from around the world for a global summit in Rome to discuss the crisis facing the Catholic Church over sexual abuse scandals. It is likely to produce a new round of public apologies, expressions of concern for victims and pledges of reform. But recent statements by leading bishops and the Pope suggest that church officials are not ready to take an essential step in ending the scandal: providing a full and detailed accounting of their own role in concealing credible allegations of child sexual abuse (Walker, 2019).

This was shown recently again as yet another senior clergyman resigned over his role in covering up paedophile priests' sexual abuse. Martin Shipperlee, abbot of Ealing Abbey, resigned after appearing before the UK independent inquiry into sexual abuse in early February 2020. The inquiry has written to the Pope's representative in Britain, Archbishop Edward Adams, requesting him to disclose details of his handling of complaints against staff in Catholic schools, but he has declined to cooperate (IICSA, 2019).

Pope Francis told reporters that the Vatican summit would include a penitential liturgy to ask forgiveness for the whole Church, testimony from victims to make bishops become aware and the establishment of new protocols for handling abuse cases. This agenda for the current summit fits the now-familiar pattern of apologising, expressing concern for victims and pledging reform, but failing to disclose evidence for use in criminal court action. The Pope also indicated in his remarks that the summit would focus on the need for sex education that adheres to Church doctrine. This plan for reform promoting Church doctrine on sexuality, calling out priests who have perpetrated abuse and pledging to clean house in the future is missing a key ingredient necessary to quell the crisis: until church officials provide a full accounting of their concerted efforts over decades to hide crimes from civil authorities, parishioners and the public, the clergy sexual abuse scandal will not go away (Walker, 2019b).

From the late 1980s, allegations of sexual abuse of children associated with Catholic institutions and clerics in several countries started to be the subject of sporadic, isolated reports. In Ireland, beginning in the 1990s, a series of criminal cases and Irish government enquiries established that hundreds of priests had abused thousands of children over decades. Six reports by the former National Board for Safeguarding Children in the Catholic Church established that six Irish priests had been convicted between 1975 and 2011. This has contributed to the secularisation of Ireland and to the decline in influence of the Catholic Church. Ireland held a referendum to legalise same-sex marriage in 2015 and abortion rights in 2018. Like the Catholic sex abuse cases in the United States, Australia and numerous other countries, the abuse in Ireland included cases of high-profile Catholic clerics. In many cases, the abusing priests were moved to other parishes to avoid embarrassment or a scandal, assisted by senior clergy. By 2010 a number of in-depth judicial reports had been published, but with only a limited number of criminal convictions (Walker, 2019b).

A report into the cover-up of child sexual abuse within the Church of England in 2017 concluded that the Church establishment, colluded with paedophile priests, failed to investigate allegations and ignored the needs of traumatised young men over a period of 20 years. Peter Ball was first accused in 1993 by a 17-year-old man who took his own life in 2012 when the police accused him of lying during a botched investigation. Former senior judge and devout Anglican Lady Butler-Sloss published a report in 2011 into the way the Church of England handled previous allegations against two ministers in Sussex who had sexually abused young boys. Eight months after her report was published, Butler-Sloss had to issue a six-page addendum in which she apologised for inaccuracies which, she admitted, arose from her failure to corroborate information given to her by senior Anglican figures as part of the inquiry. She had failed to test the evidence presented to her by senior Anglican figures (Walker, 2017).

In 2014 the Archbishop of York apologised for previous cover-ups of child sexual abuse by Robert Waddington, a former dean of Manchester Cathedral, who was once in charge of Church schools. The then Archbishop of York, Lord Hope, admitted he did not report the matter to the police or other child protection agencies even when evidence was shown him in 1999 and again in 2003. Waddington had begun abusing boys in the 1960s when he was headteacher at a school in Australia. In 2015, the Methodist Church made a very public apology after a wide-ranging independent investigation unearthed nearly 2000 reported cases of child sexual abuse dating to 1950. Evidence reveals that ministers or lay employees had been involved in a quarter of the cases, which included sexual, physical, emotional abuse as well as neglect. In the 200 cases concerning ministers, 102 were of a sexual nature (The Times, 2013).

The Church of England is the largest Christian denomination in the country, with over a million regular worshippers. Convictions for sexual abuse of children by people who were clergy or in positions of trust associated with the Church date back to the 1940s. The total number of convicted offenders associated with the Church from the 1940s until 2018 is 390. In 2018, 449 concerns were reported to the Church about recent child sexual abuse, of which more than half related to church officers (IICSA, 2020). Latterly, concerns included a significant amount of offending involved the downloading or possession of indecent images of children. The IICSA examined a number of cases relating to both convicted perpetrators and alleged perpetrators, many of which demonstrated the Church's failure to take seriously disclosures by or about children or to refer allegations to the statutory authorities. These included:

- » Timothy Storey, was a youth leader in the Diocese of London from 2002 to 2007. He used his role to groom teenage girls. Storey is currently serving 15 years in prison for several offences against children, including rape. He had admitted sexual activity with a teenager to diocesan staff years before his conviction but they did nothing.

- » Victor Whitsey, was Bishop of Chester between 1974 and 1982. Thirteen people complained to Cheshire Constabulary about sexual abuse by Whitsey and the Church of England is aware of six more complainants. The allegations included sexual assault of teenage boys and girls while providing them with pastoral support. He died in 1987.

- » Reverend Trevor Devamanikkam, was a priest until 1996. In 1984 and 1985 he allegedly raped and indecently assaulted a teenage boy, Matthew Ineson, on several occasions when the boy was living in his house. From 2012 onwards, Reverend Matthew Ineson made a number of disclosures to the Church and has complained about the Church's response. Devamanikkam was charged in 2017 and took his life the day before his court appearance.

Between 2003 and 2018, the main insurer of the Church of England (the Ecclesiastical Insurance Office) managed 217 claims relating to child sexual abuse in the Church. However this represents a small number of actual criminal acts against vulnerable children. The culture of the Church of England facilitated it becoming a place where abusers could hide. Deference to the authority of the Church and to individual priests, taboos surrounding discussion of sexuality and an environment where alleged perpetrators were treated more supportively than victims presented barriers to disclosure that many victims could not overcome. Another aspect of the Church's culture was clericalism, which meant that the moral authority of clergy was widely perceived as beyond reproach, and the confessional in the Catholic tradition was a place where crimes could be admitted but not disclosed to prosecuting authorities. There are bishops today who defend the practice of not disclosing crimes against children to the police (Walker, 2018).

# The inner world of the abused child

Research findings that explored the concept of spirituality with several groups of school-age children, some of whom held deep religious convictions and others who belonged to no formal religion, discovered that it is rare to come across a child who does not have at least an implicit spirituality.

*Even in the most resolutely secular child evidences of spiritual sensitivity emerge, sometimes through self-contradiction, or allusive metaphor, or through Freudian slips of the tongue. The task is not to detect the presence or not of spirituality, but to understand how and why it may become suppressed or repressed during the process of growing up.*

(Hay, 1990)

Four core qualities of spiritual experience have been identified: awareness, mystery, value and meaningfulness/insight. They are often assumed to be consistent with positive life-affirming experiences. However, children who experience wonder, awe and mystery can quickly become distressed and fearful, even terrified, if a secure and stable main carer is not available to contain those negative feelings. Many religions contain concepts of hell and punishment which could trigger profound feelings of despair that are experienced as completely overwhelming physically and psychologically. Church officials used the innocence of children, their vulnerability and wonderment at a higher authority to exploit and sexually abuse them at will, often blaming children or threatening them with damnation if they spoke out (Walker, 2013).

Sin is defined variously in different religions, and for a child or young person it comes with the sense of failing to be satisfactory, for example, from early toileting experiences through to exam performance or adolescent sexuality. The sense of sin and failure is quickly transformed into guilt and shame, resulting in feelings of depression, distress and despair unless there is some balancing influence.

*Children and young people without this balancing experience and with deficits in their environment and personal temperament are likely to develop mental health problems at the time or later on in life. It is easy for children to feel that they are failing or cannot fit easily into the world. This is the opposite of spiritual experiences of value, insight, and relatedness. A persistent sense of sinfulness or failure prevents the development of healthy relationships.*

(Crompton, 1996)

This is illustrated in the story of the Hindu god Krishna who was very naughty as a small boy. When he was accused of eating dirt, his foster mother Yasoda ordered him to open his mouth. When he did so she became terrified at the sight she beheld revealing as it did the eternal universe. Krishna understood that such knowledge would be harmful to Yasoda so he erased her memory of all she had witnessed. This tale illustrates how awareness and closeness to the divine can be potentially overpowering or harmful (Miller, 2016).

Children involved in war as victims or forced combatants are deprived of the enjoyment of spiritual rights. Research demonstrates the severe and enduring mental health problems experienced by refugee and asylum seekers from areas of conflict (Hodes, 2000). Carers and professionals supporting children can utilise spiritual beliefs in helping children recover from dehumanising and traumatising war atrocities by enabling the expression of terror and fearfulness through reconnecting them with the prevailing religious constructs that may have been abandoned. Some of these children will perhaps have a strong sense of guilt inherited from a religious belief system that blamed humanity for the death of Jesus.

The death of parents, siblings or close relatives will probably have resonated with these inherent guilt feelings compounding them into a persecutory frame of mind. In working with such children great care needs to be taken with evoking a religious construct that could inadvertently exaggerate already troubling feelings. Church staff abusing children could use their power and authority to select those most vulnerable and open to manipulation, ensure their silence, knowing that their Establishment leaders would cover up their crimes. The testimony of those children abused so cruelly when they have the courage and strength to do so as adults later in life, is a measure of the everlasting harm abuse leaves, but also a model for those who have held onto painful experiences all their lives and seek justice and perhaps a chance to achieve closure (Walker, 2019).

## Chapter 3 | Defining child abuse

*The trust of the innocent is the liar's most useful tool.*

Stephen King

# Introduction

Since child abuse was rediscovered in the latter half of the twentieth century, and researchers could trace a long unbroken history of child abuse back to ancient times, questions have been raised about why the phenomenon has proved so resilient. Laws have been formulated to define child abuse and in adversarial legal systems the aim is to assemble evidence, prosecute and find guilt before punishment is applied. Legislation in the UK was codified in 1989 under the Children's Act to improve child protection, encourage inter-agency cooperation and try public health/public awareness campaigns with children's charities in the forefront. This followed a series of high-profile child deaths which gripped media attention and dominated public discourse for a while.

The UK Parliament nudged by sensational tabloid stories and some truly shocking cases, however, follows a monotonous, regular pattern. First a public inquiry, fault finding and blame are the key ingredients, usually followed by hastily put together legislation or wholesale changes in the child protection arrangements between agencies involved with children. Even though such tragedies as child killings are extremely rare, such disruptions to procedures and protocols are disconcerting for child protection staff and disproportionate to the rare cases that end in a child's death. But at least the government of the day can be seen to be doing something, even though children are rarely made any safer as a result. Measures have been taken to try to improve the safety of children with the Children's Act 1989, the Children Act 2004, as amended by the Children and Social Work Act 2017, and *Working Together to Safeguard Children* guidance (2018), attempting to strengthen this already important relationship by placing new duties on key agencies in a local area. Yet still child abuse endures.

Specifically, the police, clinical commissioning groups and the local authority are now under a duty to make arrangements to work together, and with other partners locally, to safeguard and promote the welfare of all children in their area. The United Nations Convention on the Rights of the Child (commonly abbreviated as the CRC or UNCRC) is a human rights treaty which sets out the civil, political, economic, social, health and cultural rights of children. The Convention defines a child as any human being under the age of 18, unless the age of majority is attained earlier under national legislation. The UN General Assembly adopted the Convention and opened it for signature on 20 November 1989 (the 30th anniversary of its Declaration of the Rights of the Child). It came into force on 2 September 1990, after it was ratified by the required number of nations. As of 8 September 2020, 196 countries are party to it, including every member of the United Nations, except the United States.

# Types of abuse

Definitions of what constitutes child abuse vary among professionals, between social and cultural groups, and across time. The terms *abuse* and *maltreatment* are often used interchangeably in the literature. *Child maltreatment* can also be an umbrella term covering all forms of child abuse and child neglect. Defining child maltreatment depends on prevailing cultural values as they relate to children, child development and parenting. Definitions of child maltreatment can vary across the sectors of society which deal with the issue (Walker, 2006) such as child protection agencies, legal and medical communities, public health officials, researchers, practitioners and child rights advocates. Since members of these various fields tend to use their own definitions, communication across disciplines can be limited, hampering efforts to identify, assess, track, treat and prevent child maltreatment. This lack of common narratives and professional training paradigms means that when communication breakdowns occur, tragedies can and do follow. As of 2006, the World Health Organization distinguishes four types of child maltreatment: physical abuse, sexual abuse, emotional (or psychological) abuse and neglect (WHO, 2006).

# Physical abuse

Among professionals and the general public, there is disagreement as to what behaviours constitute physical abuse of a child. Physical abuse often does not occur in isolation, but as part of a constellation of behaviours including authoritarian control, anxiety-provoking behaviour and a lack of parental warmth. The WHO defines physical abuse as:

*Intentional use of physical force against the child that results in or has a high likelihood of resulting in harm for the child's health, survival, development or dignity. This includes hitting, beating, kicking, shaking, biting, strangling, scalding, burning, poisoning and suffocating. Much physical violence against children in the home is inflicted with the object of punishing.*

(WHO, 2006)

Overlapping definitions of physical abuse and physical punishment of children highlight a subtle or almost non-existent distinction between abuse and punishment but most physical abuse is physical punishment '*in intent, form, and effect*'. In 2006, for instance, Paulo Sergio Pinheiro wrote in the UN Secretary-General's Study on Violence Against Children:

*Corporal punishment involves hitting ('smacking', 'slapping', 'spanking') children, with the hand or with an implement – whip, stick, belt, shoe, wooden spoon, etc. But it can also involve, for example, kicking, shaking or throwing children, scratching, pinching, biting, pulling hair or boxing ears, forcing children to stay in uncomfortable positions, burning, scalding or forced ingestion (for example, washing children's mouths out with soap or forcing them to swallow hot spices.*

(UN, 2006)

Most nations with child abuse laws deem the deliberate infliction of serious injuries, or actions that place the child at obvious risk of serious injury or death, to be illegal. Bruises, scratches, burns, broken bones, lacerations as well as repeated '*mishaps*' and rough treatment that could cause physical injuries can be physical abuse. Multiple injuries or fractures at different stages of healing can raise suspicion of abuse. The psychologist Alice Miller, noted for her books on child abuse, took the view that humiliations, spankings and beatings, slaps in the face etc are all forms of abuse, because they injure the integrity and dignity of a child, even if their consequences are not visible right away (Miller, 1985). Physical abuse as a child can lead to physical and mental difficulties in the future, including re-victimisation, personality disorders, post-traumatic stress disorder, dissociative disorders, depression, anxiety, suicidal ideation, eating disorders, substance abuse and aggression. Physical abuse in childhood has also been linked to homelessness in adulthood (Walker, 2019).

# Sexual abuse

Child sexual abuse (CSA) is a form of child abuse in which an adult or older adolescent abuses a child for sexual stimulation. Sexual abuse refers to the participation of a child in a sexual act aimed towards the physical gratification or the financial profit of the person committing the act. Forms of CSA include:

*asking or pressuring a child to engage in sexual activities (regardless of the outcome), indecent exposure of the genitals to a child, displaying pornography to a child, actual sexual contact with a child, physical contact with the child's genitals, viewing of the child's genitalia without physical contact, or using a child to produce child pornography.*

(Walker, 2012)

Effects of child sexual abuse on the victim(s) include guilt and self-blame, flashbacks, nightmares, insomnia, fear of things associated with the abuse (including objects, smells, places, doctor's visits etc), self-esteem difficulties, sexual dysfunction, chronic pain, addiction, self-injury, suicidal ideation, somatic complaints, depression, post-traumatic stress disorder, anxiety, other mental illnesses including borderline personality disorder and dissociative identity disorder, propensity to re-victimization in adulthood, bulimia nervosa and physical injury to the child, among other problems.

Children who are the victims are also at an increased risk of sexually transmitted infections due to their immature immune systems and a high potential for mucosal tears during forced sexual contact. Sexual victimisation at a young age has been correlated with several risk factors for contracting HIV including decreased knowledge of sexual topics, increased prevalence of HIV, engagement in risky sexual practices, condom avoidance, lower knowledge of safe sex practices, frequent changing of sexual partners, and more years of sexual activity.

In the United States, about 15–25 per cent of women and 5–15 per cent of men report they were sexually abused when they were children (National Center for Victims of Crime, 2020). Most sexual abuse offenders are acquainted with their victims: approximately 30% are relatives of the child, most often brothers, sisters, fathers, mothers, uncles or cousins; around 60% are other acquaintances such as friends of the family, babysitters or neighbours; strangers are the offenders in approximately 10% of child sexual abuse cases. In over one-third of cases, the perpetrator is also a minor. In a survey of child sexual abuse in India in which 76 per cent of respondents said they had been abused as children, 40 per cent stated the perpetrator was a family member (Chouhdrey, 2018).

# Psychological abuse

In 2013, the American Psychiatric Association (APA) added child psychological abuse to the DSM-5 manual of psychiatric disorders and their assessment, describing it as *'non-accidental verbal or symbolic acts by a child's parent or caregiver that result, or have reasonable potential to result, in significant psychological harm to the child'.*

In 2014, the APA stated that:

*Nearly 3 million U.S. children experience some form of psychological maltreatment annually. Psychological maltreatment leads to the production of psychological and social defects in the growth of a child as a result of behavior such as loud yelling, coarse and rude attitude, inattention, harsh criticism, and denigration of the child's personality. Other examples include name-calling, ridicule, degradation, destruction of personal belongings, torture or killing of a pet, excessive criticism, inappropriate or excessive demands, withholding communication, and routine labeling or humiliation. Given the prevalence of childhood psychological abuse and the severity of harm to young victims, it should be at the forefront of mental health and social service training.*

(APA, 2014)

Victims of emotional abuse may react by distancing themselves from the abuser, internalising the abusive words or fighting back by insulting the abuser. Fighting back in this way can lead to physical abuse as the abuser runs out of ways to harm the child. Emotional abuse can result in abnormal or disrupted attachment development, a tendency for victims to blame themselves (self-blame) for the abuse, learned helplessness and overly passive behaviour (Walker, 2019).

# Neglect

Child neglect is the failure of a parent or other person with responsibility for the child to provide needed food, clothing, shelter, medical care or supervision to the degree that the child's health, safety or well-being may be threatened with harm. Neglect is also a lack of attention from the people surrounding a child and the non-provision of the relevant and adequate necessities for the child's survival, which could be lack of attention, love, and nurturing. According to Lansford et al (2010), some observable signs of child neglect include: the child is frequently absent from school, begs or steals food or money, lacks needed medical and dental care, is consistently dirty or lacks appropriate clothing for the weather. Featherstone et al (2017) conclude:

*Neglected children may experience delays in physical and psychosocial development, possibly resulting in psychopathology and impaired neuropsychological functions including executive function, attention, processing speed, language, memory and social skills. Researchers investigating maltreated children have repeatedly found that neglected children in the foster and adoptive populations manifest different emotional and behavioral reactions to regain lost or secure relationships and are frequently reported to have disorganised attachments and a need to control their environment.*

Such children are not likely to view caregivers as being a source of safety, and instead typically show an increase in aggressive and hyperactive behaviours which may disrupt healthy or secure attachment with their adopted parents. These children seem to have learned to adapt to an abusive and inconsistent caregiver by becoming cautiously self-reliant, and are often described as glib, manipulative and disingenuous in their interactions with others as they move through childhood. Teachers often fail these children by quick judgmental reactions. Children who are victims of neglect can have a more difficult time forming and maintaining relationships, such as romantic or friendship, later in life due to the lack of attachment they had in their earlier stages of life.

It is worth bearing in mind that the fear which often accompanies emotional abuse can be just as traumatic as physical violence and not only affects a child psychologically but can delay their development and physical growth. Some of the effects on the child may not initially be linked to abuse; rather the child is seen as the individual who has problems, especially when linked to behavioural problems or disruptive difficulties.

## Munchausens syndrome by proxy

This particular form of child abuse was first described by John Money and June Faith Werlwas in a 1976 paper titled '*Folie à deux*' in the parents of dwarfs (Money, 1986). In 1977 a UK paediatrician, Dr Roy Meadow, called it '*the hinterland of child abuse*' in which a parent repeatedly presents a child for medical care. The pattern results in a child being investigated and subjected to unnecessary procedures for a medical condition which does not actually exist. Dr Meadow advocated that the term *Munchausen syndrome by proxy* (MSBP) be reserved for the situation of abuse in which the perpetrator is motivated by the need to assume either the sick role by proxy or another form of attention seeking behaviour.

In recent years, the term has been changed to Factitious Disorder Imposed on Another (FDIA). The dangerous aspect is when descriptions of imagined illness are then accompanied by actual interventions by the parent to produce symptoms. Examples include deliberate suffocation to replicate breathing problems, administration of drugs or excessive amounts of salt to induce vomiting or diarrhoea. The motivations and explanations for this type of abuse focus mainly on mental illness of some form, the desire to gain attention/sympathy, extract charitable donations from well-wishers, gain admiration from other parents who champion the tenacity of such parents to do the best for their child and challenge medical opinion/orthodoxy.

MSBP first came to major public attention in the UK in 1993, during the sensational trial of Beverley Allitt, the nurse convicted of killing four babies, attempting to kill three others and causing grievous bodily harm to another three. Recent research has attempted to assess the prevalence of this form of child abuse. A population-based study by Ferrara et al (2013) evaluated the prevalence of factitious disorders, Munchausen syndrome, and Munchausen syndrome by proxy in a clinical setting. All children referred to the Pediatric Unit of the Department of Pediatrics of the Catholic University Medical School (Agostino Gemelli Hospital) in Rome were recruited between November 2007 and March 2010. An experienced interdisciplinary team of medical professionals analysed all suspected cases. A total of 751 patients were hospitalised. Factitious disorders were diagnosed in 14 out of 751 patients, resulting in a prevalence of 1.8%. Three of 14 (21.4%) patients fulfilled the criteria for Munchausen syndrome. Munchausen syndrome by proxy was identified in 4 of 751 patients, resulting in a prevalence of 0.53%.

# Reasons for abuse

When discussing child abuse and how to protect children and young people it is important to touch upon the variety of views as to why abuse occurs. There are three main groups of perspectives surrounding the theories of abuse (Corby, 2000; Wilson and James, 2002). The first, the psychological domain, suggests that certain individuals have a predisposition to take another's life or cause severe harm; for example, adults so cruelly deprived and harmed themselves during childhood seek to inflict the same experience on their own children. This perspective is used by psychotherapists especially to understand how disturbed adults, instead of self-harming, create a need to pour unacceptable feelings and inflict destructive actions onto vulnerable others such as children.

In good parenting, the child uses the caretaker as a poison container, much as it earlier used the mother's placenta as a poison container for cleansing its polluted blood. A good mother reacts with calming actions to the cries of a baby and helps it detoxify its dangerous emotions. But when an immature mother's baby cries, she cannot stand the screaming, and strikes out at the child. As one battering mother put it:

*'I have never felt loved all my life. When the baby was born, I thought he would love me. When he cried, it meant he didn't love me. So I hit him.' Rather than the child being able to use the parent to detoxify its fears and anger, the parent instead*

*injects his or her bad feelings into the child and uses it to cleanse his or herself of depression and anger.*

(De Mause, 1998)

Social psychological theories are those that focus on the dynamics of interactions between the abuser, the child and their immediate environment. This approach appears to be positioned between focusing on the individual and broader social factors. Therefore, how the individual is able to relate to their immediate environment is seen as the cornerstone for these perspectives. While explanations are given to the relationships within the family, individuals are often seen in isolation separated from the wider social influences and stresses. Therefore, the political and wider social implications in the deterioration of neighbourhoods or social networks is often ignored (Walker and Thurston, 2006).

Sociological perspectives are those theories that emphasise social conditions and the political climate as the principal reason for the existence of child abuse and neglect. Feminist theorists highlight the strong connection between abuse which is overwhelmingly perpetrated by males against females and the patriarchal gender power disparity in society (Dominelli, 2002). Exploring the sociological perspective of child abuse is unsettling as it raises the issue of safeguarding children and young people to the level of society rather than the individual. This includes professional childcare workers who when acknowledging this approach can feel that the daily intervention which they offer to families is often not enough to support family stress. This can lead to frustration as the worker cannot remove the family from poverty or the challenging social environment.

While all three main approaches have strengths and weaknesses, each approach alone is unable to fully encompass the reasons for the occurrence of child abuse. Corby (2000) cites the ecological framework as a four-level approach which recognises the different perspectives and how they interlink with each other. Children and families exist as part of an ecological system. This means that prevention strategies must target interventions at multiple levels: the individual, the family, the community and society.

*Primary responsibility for the development and well-being of children lies within the family, and all segments of society must support families as they raise their children. Assuring the well-being of all families is the cornerstone of a healthy society and requires universal access to support programs and services.*

(Belsky, 1980)

A compelling thesis advanced by radical thinkers such as Young-Bruehil (2012) expands the field of vision away from responding to the symptoms and impact of child abuse to include deep psychological explanations. These ideas form part of a framework which explains why people abuse children and their underlying unconscious motivations.

*Essentially this involves uncomfortable ideas about hatred of children, the genesis of which can be found in adults need to project those inner parts of themselves they find distasteful, and unacceptable onto children. So a person who finds feelings of anger, vulnerability, joy, guilt, and sorrow hard to bear will project these onto children and seek to punish them or stifle them. They can be rationalised as seeking compliance, good behaviour or abiding by social norms.*

(Young-Bruehil, 2012)

Young-Bruehill has coined the phrase *childism* in order to sit it alongside other *-isms* such as racism and sexism as another form of prejudice and societal discrimination. Modern progressive nations and UN declarations acknowledge the need to challenge and eradicate such prejudices but until *childism* is given the same high profile status, it is argued that the root causes of child abuse cannot be tackled. The term *childism* is also linked with a word coined in the 1970s: *misopedia*, which has fallen out of fashion. Like other general terms for group hatred such as misogyny and misanthropy, *misopedia* means a hatred or contempt of children. Parents, carers and childcare professionals will be upset and frightened by these ideas as they challenge the foundations of human behaviour and concepts such as natural instincts to look after children, protect them and nurture them. But they need to be included in any serious attempt at understanding why child abuse continues and, according to many clinicians, researchers and children's charities, is worsening.

# Prevention and early intervention

In 2020, nearly 4 million referrals were made to child protective services in the United States and over 3.5 million cases, a rate of almost 48 per 1000 children in the US population, were investigated out of concern for child maltreatment (Child Trends, 2020). Previous research shows that this number increases when children and young people are asked directly to report their experience of abuse and neglect to independent researchers (Finkelhor et al, 2009).

In other Western countries, the picture is much the same. According to one report from the United Kingdom, nearly 20 per cent of all young people between the ages of 11 and 17 experienced high levels of abuse and neglect prior to adulthood (NSPCC, 2010). In the past decade, the number of children on child protection registers has risen in all four jurisdictions of the United Kingdom. The Australian Institute of Health and Welfare (AIHW, 2016) reported a 35 per cent increase in the number of substantiated maltreatment reports between 2014 and 2015. This pattern is highly concerning because current levels of demand in statutory child welfare/protection systems surpass reasonable case load expectations and budgets as austerity measures follow global financial crises. Driven by awareness of the challenges experienced by child welfare agencies overwhelmed and unprepared to accommodate the demand for assistance, many in the social service sector and research community have called for a model of child welfare, one that places a much stronger emphasis on prevention.

An alternative to the current model of system engagement is one that positions public health prevention at the centre of all activities rather than at the periphery. The public health model offers a unique structure to address population-level or pervasive health problems in a coordinated manner. The present pandemic is a classic example where a universalist model of public health has come to the fore. The model relies on a large and multidisciplinary infrastructure to bring evidence-based primary prevention strategies to the public at a whole-of-population scale. At its core is a focus on early and comprehensive engagement (intervention) aimed at reducing child abuse risk factors and enhancing protective factors before problems first emerge (Herrenkohl et al, 2016).

Although universal public health preventive interventions are often conceptualised as meeting a different need within a population than those of a more targeted nature (as in selective or indicated approaches), programmes can be thought to exist along a continuum, with selective and indicated programmes connecting with, and augmenting, those geared more generically to the population as a whole.

*A critical success component is to equip universal service delivery platforms such as schools, early childhood education and care, maternal/child health, and broader health services with the skills and resources to tailor services to meet the variety of needs as well as being a referral to more intensive services. Integration between such primary and secondary service systems is sometimes referred to as progressive universalism or proportionate universalism.*

(Higgins, 2015)

# General risk factors

To explore how children and young people can be in danger of abuse, a clear understanding is required of risk and the factors involved. The media are sometimes responsible for encouraging the belief that all children and young people are at risk as soon as they emerge from their home environments. While it may be the case that some children are abused by strangers it should be acknowledged that children and young people are more vulnerable to all forms of abuse within their home environments by known male relatives than in the streets. However, Rogers (2003) highlighted in her report for the National Family and Parenting Institute, when commentating on government policy surrounding children and young people at risk, that there are difficulties in defining a child at risk whether in the street or in their home environment.

The child at risk may present in a similar fashion to their peers both in relation to physical appearance and mental well-being, and therefore may be difficult to assess. In reality, abuse usually occurs in an environment that the child is familiar with – either within the home, school or indeed their local community. Therefore, all professionals regardless of their work setting need to be aware of the risk factors involved. The child or young person is at risk of abuse by male family members or family friends.

*For some children and young people their peers may be the ones carrying out the abuse, the child or young person may be the abuser themselves, or they may place themselves in danger by willingly taking part in risk taking behaviour. It therefore becomes important to initially explore the risk factors which may produce circumstances within the family and local community that result in an inability to safeguard children and young people.*
(WHO, 2020)

## Specific risk factors

| Family violence/ abuse | Drug or alcohol abuse (child or parent) | Changes in family structure |
|---|---|---|
| Parenting difficulties | Poor parenting history | Unwanted pregnancy (difficult birth) |
| Family conflict | Child living away from home | Child or parent disabilities (including learning disability) |
| Child or parental mental illness | Changes in family finances | Physical environment and accommodation |
| Availability of services | Attitude of local community towards child and family | Child or family isolation (either geographically or culturally) |
| Poverty | Age of parents (both ends of the spectrum can find childcare difficult) | Unemployment |

These risk factors offer a broad outlook and only offer potential features which may lead a child or young person to be at risk of abuse, carrying out abuse to others or indeed undertaking risk-taking behaviour. When reflecting on the ways to safeguard children and young people a consideration of the accumulative effects is required. It is also worth noting that while risk and protective factors and clear assessment frameworks offer guidance to the childcare professional when supporting the child or young person, it is difficult to draw up a photo-fit picture of what the abuser may look like and their background. Some families who have accumulated a number of factors may in consequence be unable to fully care and support their children. But it is also the case that for other families there appear to be no predisposing factors. Kay (2003) comments:

*there are no prescriptions for detecting that child abuse will take place in any particular family, but it may be that these factors can be taken in conjunction with other information to help identify the vulnerable families who may need support.*

Some children and families may live through and survive emotional, physical or financial trauma with their family life intact, while other families may not be able to endure relatively minor changes in family circumstances. This can be due to a number of resilience factors an individual or family may have. Werner (2000) when exploring studies which have investigated the concept defines resilience '*as an end product or buffering process that does not eliminate risks and stress but that allows the individual to deal with them effectively*'.

She goes on to cite Garmezy et al (1984) who surmise that there are three main mechanisms which enable these protective factors to occur:

- » **Compensation** offers a framework where stress and protective factors counterbalance each other and personal qualities and support can outweigh the stress.

- » **Challenge** as a protective mechanism, highlights the strength that a moderate amount of stress can add to levels of competence.

- » **Immunity** as the protective factor within the child or their environment moderates the impact of the stress on the child, and the child adapts to the changing environment with less trauma.

These models are not mutually exclusive, rather they can work together or in sequence depending on the age and stage of the child's development. While there are a number of specific protective factors, these may vary over time depending on the child's age and resources available.

# Protective factors

| Low distress | Low emotionality |
|---|---|
| Sociability | Good self-help skills |
| Average intelligence or above | Impulse control |
| Strongly motivated | Keen interests or hobbies |
| Positive self-image | Self-confident |
| Independent | Good communication skills |
| Good problem-solving skills | Reflective learning style |
| Assertive | Positive set of values |

Protective factors can also come from within the family including the skills of the parent or caregiver to support and protect the child; this can include close family members and siblings who can also offer appropriate care to the child or young person. Within the home the encouragement of the child to develop independence, including undertaking chores in the house, can also support and protect the child. Werner (2000) also comments that having a strong faith or belief can give individuals a sense of stability even during personal, family or community crisis. Finally, the community itself can offer protective factors for children and young people. Bifulco and Moran (1998) comment that:

*this can include having a supportive person in the neighbourhood, who maybe a relative, family friend, or peer, someone they can go to for support, and in the school environment from teachers and mentors. This support through the teenage years enables the individual to create a secure and safe environment for themselves.*

Corby (2000) reminds professionals that while using predictive tools, which take into account these risk and resilience factors, is of value, when offering families services to prevent abuse their success rate is not guaranteed. This becomes especially true when the abuse is sexual rather than physical or neglect.

*In summary these studies demonstrate that it is possible to predict between 65 and 80 per cent of known future abuse. On the debit side, however, it is fact that in this process at least 20 per cent of any sample is likely to be wrongly thought to be likely to abuse or neglect their children.*

Conversely, a fifth to a third of all children being abused would still go undetected. Each child and young person is unique; therefore, so are his or her families. When exploring risk and resilience characteristics you cannot always predict the families' responses even when appropriately assessed. Key reasons for poor quality assessments and decision-making are an inability or failure to critically appraise information collected, random errors and our susceptibility to sources of bias such as observation bias (a tendency to see things and people in a particular way, based on certain features or on what we are told about them), the bias of *'cultural relativism'* (the tendency to exercise different standards across different cultures) and the dominance of first impressions. These, and other sources of bias, have consistently been implicated in serious case reviews and inquiries into child deaths. Research suggests that providing professionals with tools to help them organise and critically appraise information in a systematic way can minimise bias and error and improve decision-making (DFE, 2017).

## Signs of abuse

| Stress-related symptoms | Stomach aches | Eating disorders | Headaches |
|---|---|---|---|
| Sexually explicit play | Poor concentration | Regression to wetting and soiling | Panic attacks |
| Mental illness | Disruptions in sleep patterns | Clinging behaviour | Self-neglect |
| Nightmares | Aggression towards other children | Self-harm | |

The fear of abuse may lead young children to have frozen watchful awareness, where the child and young person watches everyone but remains perfectly still hoping not to be noticed. The child or young person may have sudden intrusive thoughts that lead to consequent actions including violence or aggression. The child may flinch for no apparent reason which may be a sign that the child is worried about being physically abused when someone moves close to them, while other children may wish to avoid talking about the events (Kay, 2003).

It is of paramount importance to ensure transparent and open lines of communication are pursued between the child or young person, their family and concerned professionals. Numerous inquiries scrutinising gaps in services have cited poor communication and inadequate cooperation as the main component for unsafe practice leading to severe child injury or death (Laming, 2003). Children are predominately cared for in families and therefore it seems right that support should maintain the family environment where the child is safe. However, if the family is assessed and parental involvement found unsuitable for the child, professionals have to make difficult judgments to ensure that intervention only supports the existing family unit while there is evidence for a positive outcome for the child. The child's well-being has to be seen as more important than any other factor in the family.

When assessing the abuse which may have occurred to children it is clear that this has to be placed in the context of what is inflicted on the child by the abuser rather than indicators that someone may believe that a child may have been abused. Some children are much more resilient to abuse than others, and where there are multiple risk factors this can sometimes be confusing. The rationale for this is that the signs and symptoms are often overlapping. It is also worth remembering that first impressions can be deceptive, not only in terms of what is abusive but also how the situation is affecting the child. Integrated thinking about why child abuse occurs and how it may manifest gives us the opportunity to view the whole of the child's world, rather than from the parent's or professional's perspective.

# Listening to children

It is only fairly recently that the views of children have been seriously taken into account when it comes to adult legislators, policymakers and various practitioners involved with their welfare. Some initiatives by progressive and imaginative researchers place children at the centre of their activity and scholarly work. Children's charities now have child representatives, or consultation groups, or even active groups of researchers composed of older teenagers assisted by experienced researchers. The concept is to place children at the centre of the research process and as much as possible put them in the driving seat of research topics, design and fieldwork. This approach ensures children and young people feel valued and respected and their concerns are taken seriously (Walker, 2001).

Alongside the general risk factors, individual circumstances for the child and young person also need to be considered when assessing child abuse. In the green paper *'Every Child Matters'* (DfES, 2003), children and young people commented that they wished to be fit and well, feel protected and secure, enjoy pleasurable experiences, reach their potential ability, give something back to society and not to be poor. The Commission for Social Care Inspection (2004) asked children and young people about the concerns they had about feeling safe. The report highlights the awareness of children and young people to the risks in communities and schools with regard to abduction, bullying and mugging. The report continues that *'most children do feel safe, however some issues raised included worrying about being believed if they spoke out and concerned that the offender would not be appropriately punished'*. This clearly shows the need to acknowledge any issues raised by children and young people and follow through their concerns.

While abuse is a concern for every child and young person with regard to their individual experiences, Bifulco and Moran (1998) argue that it is more complex as the effects of abuse are influenced by other factors:

*The type of the association between the child and the abuser will have an impact. For example if the child sees the person everyday and consequently develop a constant fear of abuse may be more harmful than a child who sees their abuser infrequently. When the abuse is brutal, it could be more damaging than if the abuse is perceived as more restrained.*

There are studies that show regular, sustained sexual abuse by a parent or older sibling after grooming can in later years lead the older abused person into extremely damaging and destructive lifestyles, including self-harm, and even suicide (Walker, 2019). The child's age and stage development has also to be taken into consideration; it may be argued that a young person who has already a clear picture of who they are may be less effected by abuse, no matter how severe, compared to a young child who is still discovering their own self-worth and value. Finally, it could be argued that the duration of the abuse and how often the abuse occurs may also have a bearing on the long-term outcome for the child or young person. However, each child and young person is unique and their level of resilience to the effects of abuse will also be individual to them. It is important to bear in mind that a child may have learned to appear calm, strong, coping and present a composed image on the exterior while inside living a nightmare, anguish and severe trauma.

# The ethics of consulting with children

One way to improve the safety of children and enable them to feel confident in disclosing abuse is to consult with them. In seeking to ascertain the perceptions of children and young people about protective services, the primary ethical consideration is to prevent any harm or wrongdoing during the process of research. While respecting children's competencies researchers need to also fulfil their responsibilities to protect children and young people. There is considerable uncertainty about the issue of children's consent to participate in research (Walker, 2001). The issue has yet to be fully tested in court.

This is linked to consent for treatment which was affected by the decision of the House of Lords in 1985 (Gillick 3 All ER) ruling that competent children under 16 years of age can consent. Since then further court cases by Judge Fraser have modified the Gillick principle so that if either the child or any person with parental responsibility gives consent to treatment, doctors can proceed, even if one or more of these people, including the child, disagree. While these rulings do not strictly apply to research they have implications for children's rights (Walker and Thurston, 2006).

Parents may have to sign the research consent form until their child is 16 or 18 for medical research. But non-invasive social and educational research may not require parental consent because of the lack of harm. Social research requiring answers to questions implies consent if the subject cooperates. But is a child cooperating under pressure, afraid to decline or to challenge adult authority figures? The onus should be on the adults to prove that the child does not have the capacity to decide, and the safest route is to ask for parental consent as well as the children's when they are able to understand. In the context of child and adolescent mental health, for example, the concept of informed consent requires sensitive explanation of the nature and purpose of research clearly and unambiguously, and at the very least, allow informed dissent from the children and young people themselves (Morrow and Richards, 1996).

There is growing evidence of researchers actively involving children to select topics, plan research or advise on monitoring research. Where this has been done the results demonstrate that young people value being asked to participate in this way, and have much to offer the development of the research process. It has been established that using teenagers as researchers with other young people, for instance, has certain advantages over using adult researchers (Walker, 2001). Properly supported and trained they can engage with younger children in ways adults are unable to achieve.

The timing of research with children and young people with mental health problems caused as a result of abuse, feedback provided to them and the dissemination of findings are further topics for ethical consideration. Attempting to interview during the course of treatment could be invasive or undermining of the therapeutic or supportive work being undertaken. In legal cases involving abuse, therapeutic work has been halted due to defence arguments of influencing child witnesses. Gaining access to the children and young people after the problem has resolved could be hampered by a need for the child and family to put their experiences behind them and avoid being reminded of painful issues. Children as a powerless group in society are not able to challenge the ways in which research findings about them are presented (Thomas and O'Kane, 1998).

The increasing trend towards including children and young people as active, rather than passive, recipients of health and social care means that the task of developing robust methods for obtaining children and young people's perceptions is important. Enabling them to collaborate in the design of research studies and to be consulted fully about the areas they consider important to research can only enrich these studies. The impact such research has in terms of the immediate effect on the child or young person, and on later service and practitioner development, is an area requiring attention from researchers involved in this area of work (Walker, 2019).

# The global context of child abuse

According to the World Health Organisation (WHO, 2020) violence against children includes all forms of violence against people under 18 years old, whether perpetrated by parents or other caregivers, peers, romantic partners, or strangers. Globally, it is estimated that up to 1 billion children aged 2–17 years have experienced physical, sexual or emotional violence, or neglect in the past year.

- » Nearly 3 in 4 children or 300 million children aged 2–4 years regularly suffer physical punishment and/or psychological violence at the hands of parents and caregivers.

- » One in 5 women and 1 in 13 men report having been sexually abused as a child aged 0–17 years.

- » Over 120 million girls and young women under 20 years of age have suffered some form of forced sexual contact.

- » Consequences of child maltreatment include lifelong impaired physical and mental health, and the social and occupational outcomes can ultimately slow down a country's economic and social development.

Experiencing violence in childhood impacts lifelong health and well-being. Target 16.2 of the 2030 UN Agenda for Sustainable Development is to end abuse, exploitation, trafficking and all forms of violence against, and torture of, children. Evidence from around the world shows that violence against children can be prevented if the political and cultural will is there. Children and young people who have been affected by sexual abuse have concerns that no one will believe them even if they are able to discuss what has occurred. Also they tend to have feelings of guilt because in some cases the perpetrator has groomed the child or young person over a number of years in a caring relationship and the sexual assault may not have been particularly painful. The child or young person may also have received gifts given as bribes in exchange for the abuse or financial rewards for the child and or his/her family and finally the physical act itself may have felt pleasurable.

The child or young person who has been groomed and manipulated physically and emotionally may have been led to believe that this is normal loving family behaviour, until they discover that someone touching their body in an inappropriate way is abuse. Further guilt and emotional trauma may potentially occur following disclosure to professionals:

*for example, it may be that not all abused children are traumatised by the sexual abuse in ways that continue to have an impact on their behaviour or to limit their outlook on life, however, it is also possible that children can be traumatised by the manner in which professionals react and attempt to address their experiences of abuse.*

(Trevithick, 2005)

Kay (2003) suggests that professionals and parents need to manage their own feelings when investigating abuse. Creating a warm, secure atmosphere and environment helps. Constant reassurance is required to facilitate conversation. Telling a child that they will be believed is crucial, even though police and other child protection staff have been attacked for believing the very rare example of false allegations. Often children and young people are frightened to disclose events because of the threats made by the sexual abuser.

It may take an incident or sudden awareness due to knowledge gained about sex from school or peers that leads to the realisation that abuse is occurring. Teachers are often in the front line of disclosures and they need high quality training and support to enable them to be of support to students. In the past, too many children were prevented from being safeguarded by teachers who refused to believe what they were told (especially about other teachers); often they accused children of lying or holding grievances against a teacher who had criticised them. Generations of children who had summoned the courage to disclose abuse were thwarted, silenced and left to cope alone with feelings of guilt and shame.

# Chapter 4 | Revealing child abuse

*Innocence eroded into nightmare. All because of very bad touch. Love, corrupted.*

Ellen Hopkins

# Introduction

The roots of post-1960s concerns about child abuse lay in the 1940s and in particular in research conducted by paediatric radiologists in America and Britain. This research was named *The Battered Child Syndrome* and, in doing so, directed concern to physical violence against young infants. It caused public outrage at the time with many suggesting the doctors were falsifying evidence to destroy families, while other doctors opened up about their long-held suspicions. Clashes between and within medical professions shaped this dynamic transnational research context. In debates between radiology, paediatrics, ophthalmology and dermatology, children and parents affected by abuse were primarily constituted as objects of study, and they were not directly engaged in discussion. Further, there was little analysis of the long-term effects of abuse.

To an extent, medical research drove the re-emergence of concerns around child protection in Britain and America in the post-war period. Descriptions of this time by historians and social policy theorists focus on the work of a series of pioneering male paediatric radiologists and the development of this profession. Significant, and publishing sporadically from the mid-1940s until the mid-1950s, were John Caffey, Frederic Silverman, Paul Woolley and William Evans, each of whom conducted research which utilised x-ray data to understand and to make visible the injuries of physically abused children.

*These men were working at a time when radiology itself was relatively new, with x-rays only discovered in 1895 and then patchily adopted throughout Britain and America as a profession developed through the 1920s and 1930s, overcoming initial industrial injuries.*

(Crane, 2018)

Conventional wisdom would suggest that in the UK and other developed countries we have really only become aware of the phenomenon of child sexual abuse since the early 1980s. Certainly at that time there was an upsurge of concern about it, brought into public consciousness by survivors and the second-wave Women's Movement.

This moment in time is also associated with some very strong criticisms of therapists discovering child sexual abuse accounts in their adult clients. The concept of recovered memories and experiences of patients in psychoanalysis were strongly resisted by the media and downgraded to fantasies based on Freud's ideas of infant sexuality and the Oedipus complex.

But the idea that agencies, professionals and governments did not know about sexual abuse or that there was a monolithic silence prior to the 1980s does a disservice to campaigners and feminists who, following the implementation of the Punishment of Incest Act in 1908 (Bailey and Blackburn, 1979), fought hard to extend the definition of adult–child sexual contact as harmful. Borrowing from Foucault's work on Victorian sexuality (1981), it might be more appropriate to question the assumption that there really was a silence over sexual matters of this kind, or, if there was a silence, to ask who was doing the silencing (Smart, 2000).

## Early signs and evidence

By the time historical records begin, the widespread sexual use of children is well documented. The Greek and Roman child lived his or her earliest years in an atmosphere of sexual abuse. Girls were commonly raped, as reflected in the many comedies that have scenes that were considered funny of little girls being raped. Both Greek and Roman doctors reported that female children rarely had hymens. Boys, too, were regularly handed over by their parents to neighbouring men to be raped. Child brothels, rent-a-boy services and sex slavery flourished in every city in antiquity. Children were so subject to sexual use by the men around them that schools were by law prohibited from staying open past sundown, so their pedagogues, slaves who were assigned to protect them against random sexual attack, could try to see that their teachers didn't assault them (Reeve, 1983).

By the thirteenth century in the West, abandonment via oblation, or the giving of young children to monasteries for sexual and other uses, was ended; the first disapproval of paedophilia appeared; the first childrearing tracts were published and some advanced parents began to practise what can be termed the ambivalent mode of childrearing, where the child was not considered to be born completely evil. The psychoanalytic interpretation of such adults' beliefs argues this was the concept of projection, whereby someone unable to bear certain uncomfortable feelings projects them onto, in this case, a child. So a child was seen as being still full of enough dangerous projections, and that the parent, whose task it was to mould it, must beat it into shape like clay. Church moralists for the first time began to warn against sexual molestation of children by parents, nurses and neighbours.

Childrearing reformers beginning in the eighteenth century began to try to bring this open sexual abuse under control, only it was the child who was now punished for touching his or her genitals and was put under threat of circumcision, clitoridectomy, infibulation and various cages and other genital restraint devices. These terrorising warnings and surgical interventions began to die out only at the end of the nineteenth century, after two hundred years of brutal and totally unnecessary assault on children's bodies and psyches for touching themselves. Despite the reformers' efforts, progress was so uneven that one British journalist could write in 1924 that:

*cases of incest are terribly common in all classes. Usually the criminal ... goes unpunished ... Two men coming out from an incest trial were overheard saying to a woman who deplored there had been no conviction, 'What nonsense! Men should not be punished for a thing like that. It doesn't harm the child'.*

(De Mause, 1998)

It goes without saying that the effects on the child of these physical and psychological punishments were immense. Adults remembered that as children they had had recurring nightmares and even outright hallucinations as they lay awake at night, terrorized by imaginary ghosts, demons, a witch on the pillow, a large black dog under the bed or a crooked finger crawling across the room. History is filled with reports of children's convulsive fits, dancing manias, loss of hearing and speech, loss of memory, hallucinations of devils and confessions of intercourse with devils (De Mause, 1998).

# Parenting under the spotlight

Infants were commonly swaddled by tightly wrapping them in cloth to restrict any movement from early times and into the twentieth century. This practice was not conducive to healthy development physically or mentally. In fact, it was harmful both physically and mentally. As parenting styles came under more scrutiny in the UK and elsewhere during the early eighteenth century, Hogarth's notorious illustration *Gin Lane* portrayed the link between cheap alcohol and child neglect, but skewed towards the poorer classes despite what we now know, that smart, middle- and upper-class children were also being systematically abused.

One of the first cases of child neglect and abuse in the United States (the case of eight-year-old Mary Ellen Wilson), which drew national attention to child abuse in the early 1870s, got through the legal arguments only after an attorney for the then well-established American Society for the Prevention of Cruelty to Animals (ASPCA) took her case to court and successfully argued for children as being, just like all humans, members of the animal kingdom, hence entitled for the right to be treated with the same legal protection from cruelty as are animals (Shelman and Lazoritz, 2005; Watkins, 1990). Mary had been beaten and neglected by her foster parents. This is rather telling in hindsight that in order to protect children, authorities had to rely on legislation designed to protect dogs from abuse (Regoli et al, 2014).

In July 1925, *The Lancet* carried a report which read: *'On Jan. 26th, 1924, 17 girls between 6 and 10 years old, living in an exceptionally well-administered home, were notified as suffering from gonorrhoeal vulvo-vaginitis'* (1925). It seems that such outbreaks were not uncommon because they were also mentioned in the Royal Commission on Venereal Diseases Final Report in 1916 where it was reported that such outbreaks were frequent. What is of interest of course is how the medical profession in the 1920s explained the appearance of gonorrhoea in babies and children (Smart, 2000).

It would seem that throughout this period, and even into the 1980s, the orthodox account relied on the idea of *'fomite'* transmission. Thus the source of infection was usually identified as lavatory seats, slipper baths, towels and later through rectal thermometers. The original source was seen as a precociously sexual and hence diseased child entering an institution who then infected all the other children. This was referred to as accidental or sometimes innocent transmission. Given that doctors knew perfectly well that adults contracted gonorrhoea through sexual contact, it required some fairly far-fetched theories to rely so heavily on ideas of innocent transmission. Thus *The Lancet* concluded:

*Many little girls are carriers of gonorrhoea as a result of infection by towels, w.c.'s, and lavatories, and the youth of a child by no means precludes the possibility of her having gonorrhoea ... No towels, baths, or bedroom chambers should ever be shared by girl children in institutions. ... A similar outbreak observed this year at a convent home for older girls in a home county was traced to infection from one or more imperfectly cured cases of gonorrhoea by towels and baths.*

(Porter, 1925)

Such outbreaks did not therefore seem to give rise to any suspicion that the children in an institution might be subject to sexual assaults. Although it was often conceded that a child who entered with the disease might have been assaulted prior to her admission, it was apparently unthinkable for abuse to be going on within the institution. The recently established IICSA has focused attention in recent years on the widespread sexual abuse of vulnerable children sexually assaulted by organised paedophiles attracted to working in children's homes. Children were also groomed and procured by men using children's homes as a source of victims who were already stigmatised, from chaotic abusive families, with histories of disturbed behaviour who could be easily threatened or coerced into being sexually abused. The Inquiry has revealed shocking evidence of systematic attacks on some of the most vulnerable children in society (Soares et al, 2019).

# Political action or inaction?

In the UK immediately after the ending of the First World War, feminists and child protectionists resumed the cause of protecting girls from sexual exploitation. They put various Private Members' Bills before parliament and subsequently a Joint Select Committee of both Houses was formed in 1918 to consider the common element of these bills, the main aim of which was to protect girls under 16 from indecent assault. Parliament was dissolved before the Committee reported and so a new Joint Select Committee was formed in 1920. After the Committee made its recommendations, a Private Member's Bill was introduced but it fell for lack of time, and so in 1922 the government introduced its own bill which was passed as the Criminal Law Amendment Act 1922 (Smart, 2000).

Subsequently, further pressure on the government resulted in the Home Office setting up the Departmental Committee on Sexual Offences Against Young Persons (1924–25) which made extensive policy recommendations on how to deal with the sexual abuse of young people. Although these recommendations were seen as too radical and too child-centred to be implemented, all this lobbying and government activity does show that there was intense concern about the sexual abuse of children between the wars. The main focus of the feminists and purity campaigners at this time was to extend protection to girls from forms of sexual assault that fell short of rape.

*As the law stood, before 1922 a man could engage in an act of indecency with a girl under the age of 16 years and then defend himself by claiming that she consented or by claiming that he thought she was over 16 years. It was recognised that many men were escaping conviction through these loopholes, and that charges of rape were often reduced to indecent assault and so even very serious offences were going unpunished.*

(Smart, 1980)

Campaigners' insight into the harm of sexual abuse appears to be very modern and it shows the extent to which some feminists in the 1920s held views which are very similar to their feminist granddaughters in the 1980s. The aim of the moral purity and the feminist campaigners was to convince parliament that young women were vulnerable to sexual exploitation and that there was little protection for them against men who defined children as sexually desirable. It is clear that they thought that to extend childhood (as some wanted, to the age of 18) would remove girls from this sexualising gaze. It is significant that they sought to explain sexual precociousness in young women as an outcome of sexual abuse, rather than following the patriarchal conventional view that saw precocious and immoral girls inviting sex and seducing older men.

However, there was extremely strong resistance to this discursive construction of men as dangerous and of young women as victims. The debates on the floor of the House of Commons were much more acrimonious than in the Committee chambers and it seems unlikely that the Criminal Law Amendment Act 1922 would ever have made it onto the statute book without government assistance. Reading the debates it is clear that this bill was seen as a major skirmish in the gender wars that had been running since the end of the previous century. A group of male MPs argued that '*it is legislation against one sex more than the other*' (Hansard, 5 July 1922 [156] 410). This set the basic focus of the argument, because the men wanted girls and young women to be punished equally alongside the offending men.

Attempts were made to exclude girls who were prostitutes under 16 years, thus showing the tenacity of the belief that children chose to be sexually immoral and having thus chosen should not be protected. A highly gendered and sexist concept that still prevails today as evidenced by the recent revelations of police attitudes to girls absconding from children's homes and engaged in prostitution. Girls were arrested and prosecuted, treated like criminals and subject to stereotyping as deliberate runaways, '*choosing this lifestyle*', rather than the fact they were subjected to grooming by gangs of organised men, plied with alcohol and drugs, raped and then pimped onto the streets to earn money (Bell, 2018).

The other main counter-argument in the 1922 House of Commons was the belief that the bill would be a blackmailers' charter, allowing unscrupulous girls to trick young men into believing they were over 16 years and then threatening to prosecute them. There was, on the part of some MPs, an absolute refusal to acknowledge harm done through the sexual exploitation of young women and an absolute unwillingness to acknowledge a power difference between young, working-class girls and older, middle-class men (Smart, 1980).

Subsequently, further pressure on the government resulted in the Home Office setting up the Departmental Committee on Sexual Offences Against Young Persons (1924–25) which made extensive policy recommendations on how to deal with the sexual abuse of young people. Although these recommendations were seen as too radical and too child-centred to be implemented, all this lobbying and government activity does show that there was intense concern about the sexual abuse of children between the wars. But it also reveals the mindset of the Establishment who had difficulties accepting the facts.

## Institutional resistance

There is evidence that many groups including moral purity, feminist and child protection organisations were rethinking all forms of sexual abuse of children between 1910 and 1960. A crucial part of these activities were their attempts to define adult/child sexual contact as a form of harm. Initially this harm was defined as moral, then it focused on physical harm as well, and ultimately concentrated more exclusively on psychological harm. In trying to define child sexual abuse as a moral harm the reformers encountered the argument that no moral harm was caused to children because they were not actually children (at least if they were over 10 or 13 years of age), and no harm was done because the girls were already considered immoral. The government established the Child Sexual Exploitation specialist unit in 2016, almost 100 years after the subject was first raised in Parliament. Resistance to the unpalatable truth is a hallmark of this narrative.

In defining child sexual abuse as a physical/health threat to children the reformers focused on venereal diseases. But the counter arguments from parts of the medical profession deflected this ultimately with debates on innocent transmission and also by de-sexualising sexual transmission by suggesting that men who engaged in this behaviour were misguidedly seeking a cure for VD (venereal disease). The shift to the psychological terrain had two aspects to it. The first was the focus on the damage done to children by the criminal justice system. This harm was either denied by the legal establishment or acknowledged but tolerated in the interests of justice for the accused. The second was the focus on direct psychological harm.

Opposition to recognising child sexual abuse as a form of harm, therefore, varied in content and over time but it is important to recognise that it was not always successful in totally defeating the argument. Moreover, it seems problematic to suggest that the issue itself was simply silenced. It seems there were no major campaigns on this issue during the war years and in the 1950s (as there had been in the 1920s and 1930s) but there were consistent calls to improve the criminal justice system to make it easier for children to give evidence. This focus by reformers reflected the fact that the criminal justice system remained a major obstacle to practical interventions where sexual abuse was occurring. It has been the legal system (although not necessarily individual judges and juries) that has consistently and unerringly failed to believe children throughout the twentieth century.

The modern criminal justice system is still failing children who manage to summon the courage to come forward and disclose sexual assault. Data reveals that very small numbers of children do so, very small numbers reach the Crown Prosecution Service threshold for initiating proceedings based on a calculation of the chances of securing a prosecution, and the tiny proportion of victims who get a court hearing are subjected to aggressive, abusive questioning by highly skilled, highly paid lawyers for the defendant (Walker and Thurston, 2006). The result is very, very few sexual abusers are prosecuted and those that do receive small custodial sentences, if at all.

It is also important to understand the nature and longevity of the power struggle involved in trying to define adult sexual contact with children as harmful (see Hooper, 1992). There was a multiplicity of different interests which emerged at different times in opposition to seeing child sexual abuse as a problem or as harmful, namely a male-dominated legislature, Victorian attitudes about children's status, powerful men fearful of exposure and a disbelief that such wickedness was happening at all. They were not a coalition but the effect of a range of these different forms of resistance was to stall radical change in the treatment of child sexual abuse for almost a century.

## Increasing awareness

Over the past several decades there has been a growing awareness of the extent of the abuse of children in general but especially in sexual abuse of children. The scale of regular revelations about institutions such as children's homes, churches, schools and youth organisations suggests an epidemic because of how many people have been and continue to be affected by it, either directly as victims or as those who know the victims or the victimisers. Sexual abuse is part of the continuum of abuse which includes physical and psychological cruelty, witnessing domestic violence, being humiliated regularly, bullied in person or online, abducted, trafficked and killed.

It is a symptom of the fact that most, if not all, organisations (secular and religious) are themselves legacies of educational principles and practices that go back to ancient Greece and, in particular, Plato, who advocated sex with children. To recognise that legacy is an essential first step in recognising just how deeply rooted sexual abuse of children is in our culture and thus why it has been, and is likely to remain, difficult fully to eradicate.

*The influence of Plato for over two thousand years is such that it would seem to be imperative that there be nothing less than a thorough reassessment of what underlies our political, educational and religious ideals, beliefs and practices and how that has fostered, directly or indirectly, and even legitimised a culture that sexually abuses children.*

(Dean, 2018)

The philosopher Thomas Hobbes' (Hobbes, 1651) famous and oft repeated aphorism '*the life of man, solitary, poor, nasty, brutish, and short*' is actually part of his treatise on how to avoid such occurrences. In his version he advocates for a strong, central authoritarian state to prevent society from descending into a kind of anarchy. Thus he exposes his ideas of a natural state of humankind being cruel, selfish and without regard to community cohesion. On the contrary, writing in the eighteenth century, Jean Jacques Rousseau (1762) advocated a people-led form of democracy with the power to unseat unpopular rulers. He believed that people were naturally inclined to support the common good, universal welfare and equality. These important philosophical ideas and debates were taking place in the context of industrialisation and population expansion and preceded revolutionary events challenging the conventional ruling order of the European monarchies and Church influence. Nowhere were the rights of children mentioned or deemed important or relevant.

The power of the Church in modernising eighteenth-century economies was still strong, and the Bible as a guide to life was replete with examples of child abuse.

> **Proverbs 13:24** *He who withholds his rod hates his son, but he who loves him disciplines him diligently.*
>
> **Isaiah 13:16** *Their little ones also will be dashed to pieces before their eyes; Their houses will be plundered; And their wives ravished.*
>
> **Ezekiel 9:6** *Utterly slay old men, young men, maidens, little children, and women, but do not touch any man on whom is the mark; and you shall start from My sanctuary. So they started with the elders who were before the temple.*
>
> **Joel 3:3** *They have also cast lots for My people, Traded a boy for a harlot; And sold a girl for wine that they may drink.*
>
> **Proverbs 29:15** *The rod and reproof give wisdom: but a child left [to himself] bringeth his mother to shame.*

# Understanding denial of child sexual abuse

According to Smart (2000), the shift to the psychological terrain in understanding child sexual abuse had two aspects to it. The first was the focus on the damage done to children by the criminal justice system. This harm was either denied by the legal establishment or acknowledged but tolerated in the interests of justice for the accused. The second was the focus on direct psychological harm. It is here that a specific interpretation of psychoanalytic theories became influential in denying harm by treating the original complaint as a fantasy. Opposition to recognising child sexual abuse as a form of harm therefore varied in content and over time but it is important to recognise that it was not always successful in totally defeating the argument. Moreover, it seems problematic to suggest that the issue itself was simply silenced.

Miller (1987) refers to the poisonous pedagogy of psychoanalysis (the tendency to disbelieve children) and, as she suggests, a part of our cultural heritage before psychoanalysis gave it a new form and mode of expression. It is problematic to identify psychoanalysis as one of the obstacles to understanding child sexual abuse. But this discourse cannot be isolated from the cultural context into which it was launched thus giving the impression that it was only the Freudian 'cover-up' (Rush, 1981) that stood between children and a proper recognition of sexual abuse. It is also important to understand the nature and longevity of the power struggle involved in trying to define adult sexual contact with children as harmful (see Hooper, 1992).

# Women who sexually abuse children

One of the aspects of society's difficulty in accepting that child sexual abuse is part of everyday life and has been with us for far longer than once thought, can be found in the revelations in ground-breaking work by, among others, Jacqui Saradjian (1996). She conducted research which revealed a sizeable minority of children who had disclosed abuse by female perpetrators. Widespread disbelief followed her work which can be accounted for in cultural terms. Socialisation of males tends to reinforce sexually aggressive behaviour, while for women it inhibits it. For women to sexually offend against children is to deviate greatly from the accepted schema/norms of femaleness. Feminists draw attention to gender stereotypes which inhibit women from participation in all aspects of life, and thus influence girls over their choices about work, relationships, careers and education.

When women are discovered to have sexually abused a child/ren, several reasons are submitted to explain why. These tend to deny the full, unconditional personal agency of the women involved. One is that such women do so while under the influence of alcohol, substance abuse, mentally ill or of very low intelligence. Another is that the women have been coerced by a man into the crime. A more subtle denial of women's responsibility in child sexual abuse is for it to be interpreted as a misguided extension of love. This fits with the stereotyping of women as natural carers and nurturing people. This concept is reinforced by assumptions by professionals and others that somehow the impact of sexual abuse by a female is somehow less traumatic for the victim. Finkelhor (1986) disproved this thesis in his research with victims which showed, if anything, it was more traumatic for a child to be sexually abused by a female than a man, because it went against cultural expectations and the very stereotypes of females, who they were conditioned into trusting as their carers and naturally protective, nurturing adults.

## Changing the narrative

The accumulation of research studies in the twentieth century began to draw attention to the idea that parents may have purposefully inflicted injuries on children, leading to discussing parental violence for the first time in the medical press. Researchers observed fractures and hypothesised they appeared to be of traumatic origin, that parents may permit trauma and be unaware of it, may recognise trauma but forget or be reluctant to admit it, or may deliberately injure the child and deny it. These assertions were relatively tentative and made years apart, but nonetheless significant in connecting physical injury to violence, and in pushing for social assessment to become a medical responsibility. Building on this small but important and growing body of literature, the paediatrician C. Henry Kempe and others were the first to explicitly detail and examine child battering at length in the medical literature.

The authors described the battered child syndrome as a clinical condition in young children, usually under three, though possibly of any age, who had been subject to serious physical violence. Emphasising that this was a frequent cause of permanent injury or death, the authors urged that physicians must consider this as a cause in children exhibiting symptoms such as fractures, soft tissue swellings and skin bruising. They also challenged the paediatric establishment to change their usual reluctance to get involved in investigating the criminal aspects of the injuries (Kempe et al, 1962).

The problem of battered children was conceptualised as a transnational or universal one from its inception, and later consciously so at the International Congress on Child Abuse, held in Geneva in 1976. Significantly, medical, social work and charitable communities in Britain and America exchanged and co-constructed knowledge about this syndrome. As a result, the NSPCC founded the Battered Child Research Unit in 1966, aiming to create an informed body of opinion about the syndrome and to devise methods of treatment (Crane, 2018).

Interest in the psychological and social contexts of violent parents continued apace in the late 1960s and the 1970s, led by the NSPCC and also by independent psychiatrists. Two separate key themes emerged in this research tensions about whether such parents were part of a social problem group and whether the parents had themselves been subject to violence in childhood.

*In terms of the first theme, numerous psychological studies emphasised that violent parents did not typically belong in any one demographic group, and that nor were they defined by social class, ethnicity, gender, or education. At the same time, clinical and media discussions of these parents echoed historic discussions of 'social problem groups' or 'problem families' which have reappeared in various forms since at least the Victorian period.*

(Smith, 1976)

The *British Medical Journal* in 1966 and 1967 explicitly characterised battering parents within a large group of social problem families, and as often already known to their general practitioners, health visitors and various social agencies as having many problems. This representation of families afflicted by low levels of personal responsibility, poor social environments and inadequate skills of home management was taken up enthusiastically by the tabloid press discussing battered children. Various narratives tended to overemphasise the number of working class families living in poor, overcrowded conditions, with multiple stressors including unemployment, financial problems and parental ill health.

Some clinicians, however, countered by revealing that comfortable, financially secure, middle-class homeowners were also abusing their children. But because they were not known to social services staff they largely remained undetected. While overtly denying that they perceived a class basis in battered child cases, irresponsible tabloid newspapers and some clinicians alike were explicitly, and not subtly, placing their discussions within a significant historical trajectory of a stigmatising and paternalist debate.

Drawing on research from the 1940s and 1950s, from the early 1960s a shift occurred in British society within which academic, medical, charitable and social work communities increasingly discussed the mistreatment of children in published works. While a shift took place over these years, the pace of change should not be overstated. By 1970, many practising medics and social workers continued to deny or ignore the existence of parental violence. Writing for the *British Medical Journal* in 1970, the paediatrician Bruno Gans described the case of a five-month-old infant repeatedly admitted into a southeast London hospital with injuries in his hand.

Despite x-ray evidence that a needle had been embedded in the child's heel, and the fact that the child's sibling had recently died in another hospital, Gans reported that his suggestions that this child may manifest the battered child syndrome were met with horror. When suggesting the diagnosis to his ward sister, Gans wrote, '*she was appalled at my even thinking of such a possibility*' (Gans, 1970). In 1969, the NSPCC's *78 Battered Children* survey emphasised that social workers and clinicians alike struggled to believe that parents could or would hurt their children. The report also emphasised that some social workers pushed parents towards alternative explanations of childhood injury. In one reported case, a social worker suggested all kinds of accidents may have caused a child's injuries and even suggested the dog being one (Skinner and Castle, 1969).

Thus, a change took place in the mid-twentieth century in terms of medical and social work discussions of abuse. From the late 1960s, the NSPCC's Battered Child Research Unit became significant in conducting research around the syndrome, and seeking to characterise and understand families. Work exchanged among transnational communities of radiologists, paediatricians, social workers and charities in Britain and North America thus sought to direct further resources to the study of battered children which, from early discussions, became conversations about physical, emotional and neglectful forms of maltreatment more broadly.

The growing awareness of child abuse in this period was complex. There was no simple shift in the management of violent families from public health doctors to social workers, or from the medical to the social. Rather, medical concerns about child protection were always inflected by social anxieties, developed alongside the strengthening of social medicine in the 1940s and 1950s, and shaped by clinical collaboration with social work agencies (Crane, 2018).

Paediatric radiologists and other clinicians tended to express their concerns about abuse in emotional language. Collaboration between social and medical actors did not yet extend to including children, parents or survivors in debate. Indeed, much research was framed in paternalist and stigmatising terms, and research was often driven by a primary fixation on family maintenance. This is still the problem at the heart of child protection today: to what extent is it possible to maintain family cohesion where abuse is suspected or proved? Are abusive parents able to change their behaviours when the underlying inequalities, psychological issues, and deprivation affecting their behaviours are left unchanged? Nonetheless, these shifts in thinking about the inner lives of children and parents did, at the same time, set the stage for the developing significance of experiential and emotional expertise.

Like most public inquiries, those into child abuse or child killings benefit from the wisdom of hindsight and tend to degenerate into a blame game in an attempt to apportion responsibility especially where child protection agencies are engaged. Yet it is a sobering reality that despite over 140 years of specific legislation in the UK and elsewhere, the same rhetoric accompanies detailed and often obscure inquiry reports. Apart from a blame culture there are regular calls for better interagency collaboration, communication and information systems to reduce the chances of abuse and murder of children. The funding issue features in the context of the prevailing economic context, enabling political arguments about the cost benefits of more investment in protective services and early intervention, against the libertarian and more Conservative concepts of individual responsibility, the need for less interference in family matters and punishment for offenders.

Research linking increased prevalence of child abuse with economic downturns, poverty, unemployment, poor housing, parental mental illness and low wages is cited as evidence that more government spending on children's services can reduce child abuse (Walker, 2012). Others argue for more surveillance of families deemed at risk and targeting services at them. Such families can feel persecuted, stigmatised and ostracised which paradoxically may make them even more vulnerable to child abuse. They can turn on their children blaming them for causing more stress and pressure. The typical knee jerk reaction from politicians under a wave of tabloid newspaper sensationalism has caused swings in legislative and policy directives confusing social workers who are ever mindful of the complexities and unintended consequences of highly interventionist policies. Removing a child from parents, even very abusive parents, can feel more traumatic than the original abuse and make it harder to rehabilitate families. This is as much an indictment of the poor quality child care system in the UK as it is a reflection of social work practice.

## Legislative inertia

Legislation to prosecute people accused of child cruelty has been in force since the 1880s but it has taken a series of high profile child abuse deaths and subsequent inquiries to establish the child protection system we have today. In 1945, the first formal child death inquiry in England was the Curtis Committee Report into the death of Dennis O'Neill, who was killed at the age of 12 by his foster father. In 1973, the death of seven-year-old Maria Colwell led to the establishment of our modern child protection system. Further changes were prompted partly by the inquiries into several other child deaths, including that of four-year-old Jasmine Beckford in 1984.

The Children Act 1989 established the legislative framework for the current child protection system in England and Wales. The Children (Northern Ireland) Order 1995 and the Children (Scotland) Act 1995 established the legislative framework for the current child protection systems in Northern Ireland and Scotland. The death of eight-year-old Victoria Climbie led to Lord Laming's report (2003) which led to sweeping changes to the way children's services were structured in England and Wales. The Children's Commissioner for Wales Act 2001 created the first children's commissioner post in the UK. The deaths of ten-year-olds Holly Wells and Jessica Chapman in Soham in 2002 led to the strengthening of legislation across the UK to protect children from adults who pose a risk to them.

The Children Act 2004, informed by Lord Laming's report (2003), established a Children's Commissioner in England (the last of the UK nations to appoint one); created Local Safeguarding Children's Boards (LSCBs) in England and Wales; and placed a duty on local authorities in England to appoint a director of children's services and an elected lead member for children's services, who is ultimately accountable for the delivery of services. In Scotland the Minister for Children published a review of the Children's Hearing System, entitled '*Getting It Right for Every Child*' (Creegan, 2006). In 2008, the death of one-year-old Peter Connelly led to further reviews of social service care in England by Lord Laming, with the House of Commons debating the case. Lord Laming's *The Protection of Children in England: A Progress Report* (2009), ordered following the Peter Connelly case, made 58 recommendations for child protection reforms.

In 2010, the new Secretary of State for Education, Michael Gove, commissioned LSE Professor Eileen Munro to conduct an independent review of child protection in England. Her recommendations highlighted the way social workers and others with child protection responsibilities had drifted into mechanical, poor quality risk assessments, losing sight of the child and resorting to a tick box mentality rather than engaging in more direct work with vulnerable families. The Minister for Children and Families, Tim Loughton, announced that Local Safeguarding Boards in England should publish the overview report and executive summary of all case reviews initiated on or after 10 June 2010. The Safeguarding Board Act (Northern Ireland) 2011 set out the law for the creation of a new regional safeguarding board for Northern Ireland and the establishment of five safeguarding panels.

In 2013, a new version of *Working Together to Safeguard Children* was published in England, informed by the Munro review. The Social Services and Well-being (Wales) Act 2014 provided Wales with its own legislative framework for social services for children and adults. Under Section 145 it gives powers to Welsh Ministers to issue codes of practice providing guidance, objectives and requirements on local authorities' provision of social services.

In 2015, the IICSA was officially launched in England and Wales to consider the growing evidence of institutional failures to protect children from child sexual abuse. The Children's Services Co-operation Act (Northern Ireland) 2015 requires public authorities to contribute to the well-being of children and young people in regards to physical and mental health, learning and achievement and living conditions. In 2016, the Football Association (FA) launched an internal review into child abuse following allegations of child abuse. The Scottish FA announced an independent inquiry. The Digital Economy Act 2017 extended protection from online pornography by allowing sites which display pornography to children to be blocked in the UK. An updated version of *Working Together to Safeguard Children* (Department for Education, 2018) was published for England, replacing LSCBs with safeguarding partner arrangements.

## Child abuse and the link with poverty

The relationship between poverty, child abuse and neglect is an area of child protection where there has historically been contention, debate and scholarship. However, in recent years in the UK, there has been less attention paid to understanding this relationship and to developing systematic research in this area, by contrast with a fairly substantial body of research in the USA (Featherstone et al, 2017). Indeed, in England, although with increasing divergence across the other UK countries, this debate is particularly evident with a strong political message that there is no relationship between poverty and the likelihood of a child being harmed or neglected. It is argued that it is irresponsible on the part of social work educators (and others) to suggest such a link (Gove, 2013).

Furthermore, there has been little attention paid internationally to the relationship between child abuse and neglect and levels of inequality within society apart from some notable exceptions (Eckenrode et al, 2014). This is despite a growing, well-publicised and robust evidence base in the last decade on the relationship between inequalities and a host of social concerns such as addiction and mental health problems, problems that are highly pertinent to understanding and dealing with harms that children experience (Wilkinson and Pickett, 2009).

Failure to thrive in very young children is an example where the debate about poverty and child neglect intersects. Health visitors and GPs in primary care are alert to spotting children who are underweight and not developing along normal expectations. However, the causes can relate to feeding difficulties, a child's temperament, parental lack of confidence or an underlying organic medical problem. Maternal depression, social isolation, alcohol use and substance abuse, domestic violence, poverty and a history of problematic parental childhood can make it harder for parents to have good relationships with their young children, which can lead to feeding difficulties or disordered mealtimes with poor nutritional value meals (Drotar and Robinson, 2000).

Definitions of poverty are much debated. Some of the debates tend to revolve around whether to use measures of absolute or relative poverty and whether to focus on material resources or to include broader measures of what allows for acceptable living standards and social inclusion. In recent years, the government in England has proposed a radical departure from either approach, with its proposals to uncouple any link with income. This is out of line with the vast majority of organisations working in this field and other countries, most of whom incorporate approaches to income measurement which have a relational component (Featherstone et al, 2017). Currently, for example, the Child Poverty Action Group uses the definition advanced by one of its founders, Peter Townsend, in 1979:

*Individuals, families and groups in the population can be said to be in poverty when they lack resources to obtain the type of diet, participate in the activities and have the living conditions and amenities which are customary, or at least widely encouraged and approved, in the societies in which they belong.*

(www.cpag.org.uk/content/what-is-poverty)

A recent report for the Scottish government on poverty and inequality stresses the importance of using relative poverty figures and demonstrates the huge impact that housing costs can have in exacerbating poverty and inequality (Eisenstadt, 2016). While shortage of material resources is at the heart of the hardships experienced by families, definitions also have to engage with rights and relationships, how people are treated and how they regard themselves. Shame has been described as the irreducible absolutist core in the idea of poverty. Shame forms an integral part of the public discourse that directly shapes how poverty is perceived and responded to in policy and practice (Chase and Walker, 2015). The belief that poverty is shameful and a reflection of individual failings is a central feature of media and policy constructions of poverty (Gupta, 2018; Walker, 2019). Stereotyping poor, vulnerable families as feckless scroungers or skivers rather than strivers is as inhuman as it is cruelly misleading. While these constructs retain their prominence and political advocates, they act as a hindrance to efforts to reduce the prevalence of child abuse.

## Chapter 5 | Children as labour

*Children are the living messages we send to a time we will not see.*

John F. Kennedy

# Introduction

Child labour refers to the exploitation of children through any form of work that deprives children of their childhood, interferes with their ability to attend regular school and is mentally, physically, socially or morally harmful (ILO, 2017). It is child abuse and a type that comes with the cruel economic necessity stemming from inequalities, poverty and the stark divide between the richest and poorest nations. Expectations in poor families give children no choice about whether to work or not; it is a matter of routine, normalised culture in some parts of the world and pressure can be subtle. But there are places where there is pressure, enforced labour and recruitment into psychologically damaging work activity.

Such exploitation is prohibited by legislation worldwide, although these laws do not consider all work by children as child labour; exceptions include work by child artists, family duties, supervised training and some forms of child work practised by Amish children, as well as by indigenous children in the Americas.

*Child labour has existed to varying extents throughout history especially in military campaigns. During the 19th and early 20th centuries, many children aged 5–14 from poorer families worked in Western nations and their colonies alike. These children mainly worked in agriculture, home-based assembly operations, factories, mining, and services such as news boys some worked night shifts lasting 12 hours. With the rise of household income, availability of schools and passage of child labour laws, the incidence rates of child labour fell.*

(World Vision, 2020)

In the world's poorest countries, around one in four children is engaged in child labour, the highest number of whom (29 per cent) live in sub-Saharan Africa. In 2017, four African nations (Mali, Benin, Chad and Guinea-Bissau) witnessed over 50 per cent of children aged 5–14 working. Worldwide agriculture is the largest employer of child labour. The vast majority of child labour is found in rural settings and informal urban economies; children are predominantly employed by their parents, rather than factories. Poverty and lack of schools are considered the primary cause of child labour. Globally the incidence of child labour decreased from 25 per cent to 10 per cent between 1960 and 2003, according to the World Bank (2020). Nevertheless, the total number of child labourers remains high, with UNICEF and ILO acknowledging an estimated 152 million children aged 5–17 worldwide were involved in child labour in 2017, of which 73 involved hazardous work (ILO, 2017).

# The Industrial Revolution

With the onset of the Industrial Revolution in Britain in the late eighteenth century, there was a rapid increase in the exploitation of child labour. Industrial cities such as Birmingham, Manchester and Liverpool rapidly grew from small villages into large cities and saw improving child mortality rates. Increased numbers of children provided opportunities by industrialists to tempt parents to send their children to work in order to increase family incomes needed to keep pace with inflation and to buy basic necessities. These cities also drew in the population that was rapidly growing due to increased agricultural output. This process was replicated in other industrialising countries.

The Victorian era in particular became notorious for the conditions under which children were employed. Children as young as four were employed in production in factories and mines working long hours in dangerous, often fatal, working conditions. In coal mines, children would crawl through tunnels too narrow and low for adults.

*Children also worked as errand boys, crossing sweepers, shoe blacks, or selling matches, flowers and other cheap goods. Some children undertook work as apprentices to respectable trades, such as building or as domestic servants (there were over 120,000 domestic servants in London in the mid-18th century). Working hours were long: builders worked 64 hours a week in the summer and 52 hours in winter, while servants worked 80-hour weeks.*

(British Library, 2020)

Child labour played an important role in the Industrial Revolution from its outset, often brought about by economic hardship. In nineteenth-century Great Britain, one-third of poor families were without a breadwinner, as a result of death or abandonment, obliging many children to work from a young age. In England and Scotland in 1788, two-thirds of the workers in 143 water-powered cotton mills were described as children. Despite fierce resistance from mill owners, the UK Cotton Factories Regulation Act of 1819 set the minimum working age at 9 and maximum working hours at 12 for children; The Ten Hours Bill of 1847 limited daily working hours to 10 for children (House of Commons, 1819).

A high number of children also worked as prostitutes. The author Charles Dickens worked at the age of 12 in a blacking factory, with his family in the debtor's prison. His works are among the most read in the world and capture the harsh brutal reality of life for the poorest and most vulnerable children in the UK at the time he grew up. Child wages were often low, being as little as 10–20 per cent of an adult male's wage. Karl Marx (1868) was an outspoken opponent of child labour, saying British industries could but live by sucking blood, and children's blood too, and that US capital was financed by the capitalised blood of children.

Letitia Elizabeth Landon castigated child labour in her 1835 poem 'The Factory', in which she describes the harsh, unyielding atmosphere of factory towns (Emerson, 2020), portions of which she pointedly included in her sarcastic 18th Birthday Tribute to Princess Victoria in 1837:

> *That smoke shuts out the cheerful day,*
> *The sunset's purple hues,*
> *The moonlight's pure and tranquil ray*
> *The morning's pearly dews.*
> *Such is the moral atmosphere*
> *Around thy daily life;*
> *Heavy with care, and pale with fear,*
> *With future tumult rife.*
> *There rises on the morning wind*
> *A low appalling cry,*
> *A thousand children are resigned*
> *To sicken and to die!*

Child labour whether in Poor Law England workhouses, orphanages, or industry brutalised children. The German physician Johann Frank, recognised as the founder of public health, was shocked by the agrarian child labour used in continental viticulture, which resulted in children becoming physically deformed and misshapen.

*The Guilds of the Middle Ages previously had regulated the work of children, not out of compassion but to prevent competitive cheap labour. Children were transported to the American colonies to be apprenticed until they were 24 years old. Pauper children were sold by almshouses to apprenticeships in a form of slave trade. As late as 1866 a Massachusetts legislative report hailed child labour as a boon for society and the economy.*

(Helfer et al, 1997)

On 4 July 1838, a mine disaster at Huskar colliery in Silkstone, England, killed 26 child mineworkers: 11 girls and 15 boys aged 7–16 (Mining Accident Database, 2021). These kinds of accidents were very common at the time; however, this case was unusual in that details were reported in London newspapers thanks to a campaigning local journalist. In small mining communities, without mass communication, mine owners were able to cover up such outrages, safe in the knowledge that local villages wouldn't complain or protest in fear of losing their livelihoods. Public outcry eventually forced an enquiry into conditions in British mines. However, young children continued to be forced to work down mines until into the twentieth century.

In the second half of the nineteenth century, child labour began to decline in industrialised societies due to regulation and economic factors and because of the growth of trade unions. The regulation of child labour began from the earliest days of the Industrial Revolution. The first act to regulate child labour in Britain was passed in 1803. As early as 1802 and 1819, Factory Acts were passed to regulate the working hours of workhouse children in factories and cotton mills to a maximum of 12 hours per day. These acts were largely ineffective and after radical agitation by, for example, the Short Time Committees in 1831 who were organized workers mostly in textile mills, and Quakers, a Royal Commission recommended in 1833 that children aged 11–18 should work a maximum of 12 hours per day, children aged 9–11 a maximum of eight hours and children under the age of 9 were no longer permitted to work.

This act however only applied to the textile industry, and further agitation led to another act in 1847 limiting both adults and children to ten-hour working days. Lord Shaftesbury was an outspoken advocate of regulating child labour. As technology improved and proliferated, there was a greater need for educated employees. This saw an increase in schooling, with the eventual introduction of compulsory schooling. Improved technology and automation also made child labour redundant to a large extent (Humphries, 2016).

## Early twentieth century

In the early twentieth century, thousands of young boys were employed in the USA in glass-making industries. Since furnaces had to be constantly burning, there were night shifts from 5pm to 3am. Many factory owners preferred boys under 16 years of age.

*Glass making was a dangerous and tough job especially without the current technologies. The process of making glass includes intense heat to melt glass (1723 °C). When the boys were at work, they were exposed to this heat. This could cause eye trouble, lung ailments, heat exhaustion, cuts, and burns. Since workers were paid by the piece, they had to work productively for hours without a break.*

(Hindman, 2009)

An estimated 1.7 million children under the age of 15 were employed in American industry by 1900. In 1910, over two million children in the same age group were employed in the United States. Children worked in toxic environments, for long hours with less pay than adult men. They could be bullied and physically abused by overseers without redress due to the desperate need for family income. Ironically, as regulation of factory conditions helped improve health and safety, this merely prompted an expansion of home-based working.

*Home-based manufacturing across the United States and Europe employed children as well. Governments and reformers argued that labor in factories must be regulated and the state had an obligation to provide welfare for the poor. Legislation that followed had the effect of moving work out of factories into urban homes. Families and women, in particular, preferred it because it allowed them to generate income while taking care of household duties.*

(Cunningham, 2005)

Families used their children in these income-generating home enterprises. In many cases, men worked from home. In France, over 58 per cent of garment workers operated out of their homes; in Germany, the number of full-time home operations nearly doubled between 1882 and 1907; and in the United States, millions of families operated out of home seven days a week, year round to produce garments, shoes, artificial flowers, feathers, matchboxes, toys, umbrellas and other products. Children aged 5–14 worked alongside their parents.

*Home-based operations and child labour in Australia, Britain, Austria and other parts of the world was common. Rural areas similarly saw families deploying their children in agriculture. In 1946, Frieda S. Miller then Director of the United States Department of Labor told the International Labour Organisation that these home-based operations offered low wages, long hours, child labour, unhealthy and insanitary working conditions.*

(Prugl, 1999)

# Twenty-first century

Child labour is still common in many parts of the world. Estimates vary between 250 and 304 million if children aged 5–17 involved in any economic activity are counted. If light occasional work is excluded, the International Labour Organisation estimates there were 153 million child labourers aged 5–14 worldwide in 2017 (ILO, 2017). Some 60 per cent of the child labour was involved in agricultural activities such as farming, dairy, fisheries and forestry. Another 25 per cent of child labourers were in service activities such as retail, hawking goods, restaurants, load and transfer of goods, storage, picking and recycling trash, polishing shoes, domestic help and other services. The remaining 15 per cent laboured in assembly and manufacturing in informal economy, in home-based enterprises, factories, mines, packaging salt, operating machinery and such operations. Two out of three child workers work alongside their parents in unpaid family work situations. Some children work as guides for tourists, sometimes combined with bringing in business for shops and restaurants. Child labour predominantly occurs in the rural areas (70%) and informal urban sector (26%).

Contrary to popular belief, most child labourers are employed by their parents rather than in manufacturing or formal economy. Children who work for pay or in-kind compensation are usually found in rural settings as opposed to urban centres. Less than 3 per cent of child labour aged 5–14 across the world work outside their household, or away from their parents.

*Child labour accounts for 22% of the workforce in Asia, 32% in Africa, 17% in Latin America, 1% in the US, Canada, Europe and other wealthy nations. The proportion of child labourers varies greatly among countries and even regions inside those countries. Africa has the highest percentage of children aged 5–17 employed as child labour, and a total of over 65 million. Asia, with its larger population, has the largest number of children employed as child labour at about 114 million. Latin America and the Caribbean region have lower overall population density, but at 14 million child labourers has high incidence rates too.*

(ILO, 2017)

China has enacted regulations to prevent child labour, yet the practice of child labour is reported to be a persistent problem within China, generally in agriculture and low-skill service sectors as well as small workshops and manufacturing enterprises. In 2020, the US Department of Labor issued a List of Goods Produced by Child Labor or Forced Labor, where China was attributed 12 goods, the majority of which were produced by both underage children and indentured labourers. The report listed electronics, garments, toys and coal, among other goods.

The Maplecroft Child Labour Index (CLI) 2012 survey reported that 76 countries pose extreme child labour complicity risks for companies operating worldwide. The ten highest risk countries in 2012, ranked in decreasing order, were Myanmar, North Korea, Somalia, Sudan, DR Congo, Zimbabwe, Afghanistan, Burundi, Pakistan and Ethiopia. Of the major growth economies, Maplecroft ranked Philippines 25th riskiest, India 27th, China 36th, Vietnam 37th, Indonesia 46th and Brazil 54th, all of them rated to involve extreme risks of child labour uncertainties to corporations seeking to invest in developing world and import products from emerging markets.

According to the latest CLI research, 23 countries have shown a significant increase in risk of child labour over the last year, but the issue is set to worsen in other territories over the months ahead as the economic impacts of the coronavirus pandemic take hold.

The latest annual edition of the Child Labour Index (CLI, 2020) released to coincide with World Day Against Child Labour, 12 June 2020, measured the risk to business from association with the employment of children in 198 countries. The significant increase in risk witnessed in over 10 per cent of countries worldwide has also swelled the extreme risk category of the index, which has jumped from 27 countries in 2019 to 31, due to the addition of Belize, Myanmar, Guinea and Lebanon. Africa remains the highest risk region, with seven of the ten worst performing countries.

Millions of children worldwide face the prospect of working through their formative years, sometimes in the most hazardous occupations, such as mining, manufacturing and agriculture. From a global perspective, over 81 per cent of the world's population live in countries with a high or extreme risk of child labour, with the impact of the COVID pandemic expected to worsen the situation for children as cheap labour to reduce the prices of goods for developed countries is demanded due to the global economic effect.

## The impetus behind child labour

Poverty is the single biggest cause behind child labour. Lack of meaningful alternatives, such as affordable schools and quality education, according to ILO, is another major factor driving children to harmful labour (ILO, 2017; UNICEF, 2017). Children work because they have nothing better to do. Many communities, particularly rural areas where between 60 and 70 per cent of total child labour is prevalent, do not possess adequate school facilities. Even when schools are sometimes available, they are too far away, difficult to reach, unaffordable or the quality of education is so poor that parents wonder if going to school is really worth it.

In European history when child labour was common, as well as in contemporary child labour of the modern world, certain cultural beliefs have rationalised child labour and thereby encouraged it. Some view that work is good for the character-building and skill development of children. In many cultures, particularly where the informal economy and small household businesses thrive, the cultural tradition is that children follow in their parents' footsteps. Child labour then is a means to learn and practise that trade from a very early age. Similarly, in many cultures the education of girls is less valued or girls are simply not expected to need formal schooling, and hence these girls are pushed into work such as providing domestic services.

Biggeri and Mehrotra (2002) have studied the macroeconomic factors that encourage child labour. They focused their study on five Asian nations including India, Pakistan, Indonesia, Thailand and Philippines. They suggest that child labour is a serious problem in all five, but it is not a new problem. Macroeconomic causes encouraged widespread child labour across the world, over most of human history. They suggest that the causes for child labour include both the demand and the supply side. While poverty and unavailability of good schools explain the child labour supply side, they suggest that the growth of low-paying informal economy rather than higher paying formal economy is amongst the causes of the demand side. Other scholars too suggest that inflexible labour market, growing size of informal economy, inability of industries to scale up and lack of access to modern manufacturing technologies are major macroeconomic factors affecting demand and acceptability of child labour (Cannon, 2014).

Systematic use of child labour was commonplace in the colonies of European powers between 1650 and 1950. In Africa, colonial administrators encouraged traditional kin-ordered modes of production. This involved hiring a whole household for work, not just the adults. Millions of children worked in colonial agricultural plantations, mines and domestic service industries. Sophisticated schemes were promulgated where children in these colonies between the ages of 5 and 14 were hired as an apprentice without pay in exchange for learning a craft. A system of Pauper Apprenticeship came into practice in the nineteenth century where the colonial master neither needed the native parents' nor the child's approval to assign a child to labour, away from parents, at a distant farm owned by a different colonial master.

*Other schemes included earn-and-learn programmes where children would work and thereby learn. Britain for example passed a law, the so-called Masters and Servants Act of 1899, followed by Tax and Pass Law, to encourage child labour in colonies particularly in Africa. These laws offered the indigenous people the legal ownership to some of the native land in exchange for making labour of wife and children available to colonial government's needs such as in farms and as picannins.*

(Helfer et al, 1997)

This period also saw a transition in the raising of orphans. Because of the importance of children to the continuation of a family's fortunes, European colonial countries established elaborate laws regulating guardianship, responsibilities and remuneration for taking care of orphans, and dowries or other arrangements for future marriages. In Western countries, prior to the nineteenth-century changes, the primary concern of national and local governments responsible for the care of poor orphans was to protect state assets (Marten, 2018). In such cases, children were placed in a family and required to work. The greatest concern was that such children did not become a drag on community resources. This led directly to the recruitment of such children from orphanages by English and Spanish colonists invading the Americas, taking with them fit young men often as indentured servants, or otherwise kidnapped and deceived into becoming cheap sources of labour in the New World.

Australia and New Zealand provided examples of how colonial economics could affect indigenous and settler children. Children of colonists experienced the same dislocation, disorientation and anxieties as children in other parts of the British Empire, but these colonies included another set of children who were orphans and juvenile offenders from the poorest backgrounds.

*By the 1830's children accounted for 20 per cent of the transported felons moving from England. The needs for cheap labour in an economy short of workers for domestic and farm use was more paramount than child protection. The colonial project in Australia and New Zealand also included the regular and long-standing practice of removing indigenous children from their families.*

(Marten, 2018)

Beyond laws, new taxes were imposed on colonies. One of these taxes was the head tax in the British and French colonial empires. The tax was imposed on everyone older than eight years, in some colonies. To pay these taxes and cover living expenses, children in colonial households had to work. In southeast Asian colonies, such as Hong Kong, child labour such as the Mui Tsai was rationalised as a cultural tradition and ignored by British authorities (Yuen, 2004). The Dutch East India Company officials rationalised their child labour abuses suggesting that it was better than a worse fate. '*Christian mission schools in regions stretching from Zambia to Nigeria too required work from children, and in exchange provided religious education, not secular education*' (Bass, 2004). Elsewhere, the Canadian Dominion Statutes, in the form of so-called Breaches of Contract Act, stipulated jail terms for uncooperative child workers (Charnovitch, 1996).

## Children deported as labour

For several decades, the UK sent children across the world to new lives in institutions where many were abused and used as forced labour. This policy is having repercussions still now. Thousands of British children in the decades immediately following World War II were sent abroad from childcare institutions supposedly to enjoy a better life. The astonishing scandal of the British child migrants was the first subject for which the UK Independent Inquiry into Child Sexual Abuse (IICSA) held full public hearings. It was first because the migrants are now nearing the end of their lives. One destination for these already dislocated and frightened children was the Catholic institution known at one point as Bindoon Boys Town in Australia. It is now notorious as a place of hidden horrors. Based around an imposing stone mansion in the Australian countryside, 49 miles north of Perth, are buildings child migrants were forced to build, barefoot, starting work the day after they arrived safely (Bean and Melville, 1989). The Christian Brothers ruled the place with the aim of upholding order and a moral code. However, it was only until years later as the story of child migrants began to be heard that the reality was revealed.

*Boys were systematically beaten and sexually abused by those supposedly caring for them. Britain is perhaps the only country in the world to have exported vast numbers of its children. An estimated 150,000 children were sent over a 350-year period to Virginia, Australia, New Zealand, Canada, and what was then Southern Rhodesia, now Zimbabwe. Australia was the main destination in the final wave between 1945 and 1974. There were twin purposes - to ease the population of orphanages in the UK and to boost the population of the colonies.*

(BBC, 2009)

The children were recruited by religious institutions from both the Anglican and Catholic churches, or well-meaning charities including Barnardo's and the Fairbridge Society. Hundreds of migrant children have given accounts of poor education, hard labour, physical beatings and sexual abuse. In 2009, the Australian government apologised for the cruelty shown to the child migrants. Britain also made an apology in 2010. The pressure for answers and reparations had been growing. Questions might never have been asked had it not been for a formidable and tenacious social worker.

In the early 1980s, a Nottingham social worker, Margaret Humphreys, came across Australian former migrants who had suddenly started to realise they might have living relatives in the UK. Many had been told, as children, their parents were dead. It wasn't true. She said: '*It was about identity, being stripped of it and being robbed of it*'. Her life's work has been about reuniting lost children with their lost relatives. Having reinstated their sense of identity, she went on to build a lifelong bond with many former migrants, and they began to disclose the physical and sexual abuse they had suffered.

*As you go along, you're learning more and more about the degrees and the awfulness of the abuse. That's been incremental because people can really only talk about it over a longer period of time when there is trust. There's a lot of trauma involved here.*

(Humphreys, 2019)

Australian law firm Slater and Gordon successfully claimed compensation on behalf of 215 former Fairbridge children, of whom 129 said they had been sexually abused. For the Christian Brothers the figures are even higher. The Australian Royal Commission on child abuse recently revealed 853 people had accused members of the order.

The Australian Royal Commission is examining child migration closely. In 1998, the UK's Health Select Committee also held hearings, in which the Child Migrants Trust described the Christian Brothers institutions as *'almost the full realisation of a paedophile's dream'*. But the committee did not get to the bottom of it, concluding: *'The Christian Brothers were very insistent that the abuses were not known to those who controlled these institutions. We cannot accept this'*. The IICSA produced new and startling revelations about the scale of sexual abuse abroad, and attempts by British and Australian institutions to cover it up. This will include an examination of the claims of some child migrants that they were sent abroad weeks after reporting sexual abuse at their children's home in the UK. The allegation is that they were hand-picked either to get them out of the way, or because they were of interest to paedophiles. Three former Fairbridge boys have claimed that the then Australian Governor General, Lord Slim, sexually molested them during rides in his chauffeur-driven Rolls Royce while visiting the home. These allegations were considered by the Inquiry (Daily Telegraph, 2014).

Margaret Humphreys is adamant the British government knew it was sending children abroad to be mistreated: *'We want to know what happened, we want to know who did it, and we want to know who covered it up for so long'*. In fact, government files reveal that there was a time when the migration programme could have been stopped. It came in 1956 when three officials went to Australia to inspect 26 institutions which took child migrants. There was enough warning of this fact-finding mission to allow a Fairbridge official to warn the manager of the Molong farm: *'It would be advisable to see [the children] wore their socks and shoes'*. Even in a land where it was easy to encounter poisonous wildlife, that wasn't standard practice at many of the institutions (BBC, 2017).

The resulting report, delivered back to the British government, was fairly critical. It identified a general lack of expertise in childcare and worried that children were living in institutions in remote rural areas, whereas the trend in Britain was towards fostering them into urban families. However, the report had a second secret section, never published, which went a little further. This named names, including those of five institutions which were not up to standard. When the UK's Home Office saw the report, it wanted five more added to create what became an infamous blacklist, places which should not receive more children because of poor standards of care. Fairbridge, Molong and Bindoon were all on the list. The Australian Royal Commission recently estimated that 7 per cent of the country's Catholic priests were involved in child abuse (BBC, 2017). The IICSA investigation will be able to seize the records, not just of the British government but also the migration institutions themselves, including the archives of the Fairbridge Society.

## Children used as soldiers

The earliest mentions of minors being involved in wars come from antiquity. It was customary for youths in the Mediterranean basin to serve as aides, charioteers and armour bearers to adult warriors. Examples of this practice can be found in the Bible, such as David's service to King Saul, in Hittite and ancient Egyptian art, in ancient Greek mythology (such as the story of Hercules and Hylas), philosophy and literature. In a practice dating back to antiquity, children were routinely taken on a campaign, together with the rest of a military man's family, as part of the baggage (Wessels, 1997).

*The Roman Empire made use of youths in war, though it was understood that it was unwise and cruel to use children in war, and Plutarch implies that regulations required youths to be at least sixteen years of age. Despite this, several Roman legionaries were known to have enlisted aged 14 in the Imperial Roman army, such as Quintus Postunius Solus who completed 21 years of service in Legio XX Valeria Victrix, and Caecilius Donatus who served 26 years in the Legio XX and died shortly before his honorable discharge.*

(Cowan, 2013)

Young boys often took part in battles during early modern warfare. When Napoleon was faced with invasion by a massive Allied force in 1814, he conscripted many teenagers for his armies. Orphans of the Imperial Guard fought in the Netherlands with Marshal MacDonald and were between the ages of 14 and 17. Many of the conscripts who reported to the ranks in 1814 were referred to as Marie Louises after Empress Marie Louise of France; they were also known as The Infants of the Emperor. These soldiers were in their mid-teens (Pope, 2000). One of their more visible roles was as the ubiquitous drummer boy. During the age of sail, young boys formed part of the crew of British Royal Navy ships and were responsible for many essential tasks including bringing powder and shot from the ship's magazine to the gun crews. These children were called powder monkeys.

During the American Civil War, a young boy, Bugler John Cook, served in the US Army at the age of 15 and received the Medal of Honor for his acts during the Battle of Antietam, the bloodiest day in American history. Several other minors, including

11-year-old Willie Johnston, have also received the Medal of Honor (US Army Center of Military Citations, 2007). By a law signed by Nicholas I of Russia in 1827, a disproportionate number of Jewish boys, known as the cantonists, were forced into military training establishments to serve in the army. The 25-year conscription term officially commenced at the age of 18, but boys as young as eight were routinely taken to fulfil the quota.

The youngest known soldier of World War I was Momčilo Gavrić, who joined the 6th Artillery Division of the Serbian Army at the age of eight, after Austro-Hungarian troops in August 1914 killed his parents, grandmother and seven of his siblings (Wayback Machine Večernje novosti, 2013.) In the West, boys as young as 12 were caught up in the overwhelming tide of patriotism and in huge numbers enlisted for active service. Others enlisted to avoid harsh and dreary lives. Typically, many were able to pass themselves off as older men, such as George Thomas Paget, who at 17 joined a Bantam battalion in the Welch Regiment. The last surviving combat veteran of the War was Claude Choules, who enlisted in the Royal Navy at age 14 and saw his first action at the Battle of Jutland at 15.

In the Gallipoli campaign, otherwise known as Çanakkale, children as young as 15 fought in the trenches. One hundred and twenty children fought in a special company, with no known survivors. According to George Orwell (1938), who fought in the Spanish Civil War on the Republican side:

*The centuria was an untrained mob composed mostly of boys in their teens. Here and there in the militia you came across children as young as eleven or twelve, typically refugees from Fascist territory who had been enlisted as militiamen as the easiest way of providing for them. At Monte Pocero I do not think there was anyone younger than fifteen, but the average age must have been well under twenty.*

Children on every side of all twentieth-century conflicts have been mobilised to fight by means of propaganda, family pressure, political policies or force. Soviet Bolsheviks sought to forge state loyalty among children to replace family loyalty. World War II especially enabled governments to mobilise children. In the USA, children's magazines painted enemies as less than human, urging children to find a role in the conflict. This would include scavenging for scrap metal or other salvageable material, or growing vegetables.

*Tens of thousands of children fought with partisan units in Eastern Europe in direct, dangerous combat or sabotage missions. In Germany children were recruited into the Hitler Youth Movement resulting in 70 per cent of the country's 16 year old boys enlisted in 1944. An estimated 5,000 children as young as 12 defended Berlin during the last years of the Reich. In Japan it meant serving the emperor by preparing to die for him in a last ditch defence against the allied invasion and nuclear bombing of Hiroshima and Nagasaki. It is estimated that 300,000 boys and girls served in the Soviet military during World War 2.*

(Marten, 2018)

According to Human Rights Watch (2013), although there are no exact figures, hundreds of thousands of children under the age of 18 serve in government forces or armed rebel groups. Some are as young as eight years old. Since 2001, the participation of child soldiers has been reported in 21 ongoing or recent armed conflicts in almost every region of the world. Children are uniquely vulnerable to military recruitment because of their emotional and physical immaturity. They are easily manipulated and can be drawn into violence that they are too young to resist or understand. Technological advances in weaponry and the proliferation of small arms have contributed to the increased use of child soldiers. Lightweight automatic weapons are simple to operate, often easily accessible, and can be used by children as easily as adults. Poverty, lack of education, combined with economic or social pressure or being abducted force children into army units. In some countries, a third of child soldiers are girls recruited after being raped and used by military commanders as sex slaves (Human Rights Watch, 2013).

Children are sometimes forced to commit atrocities against their own family or neighbours. Such practices help ensure that the child is stigmatised and unable to return to his or her home community. In some countries, former child soldiers have access to rehabilitation programmes to help them locate their families, get back into school, receive vocational training and re-enter civilian life. However, many children have no access to such programmes. They may have no way to support themselves and are at risk of re-recruitment. In 2000, the United Nations adopted an *Optional Protocol to the Convention on the Rights of the Child* on the involvement of children in armed conflict. The protocol prohibits the forced recruitment of children under the age of 18 or their use in hostilities. To date, it has been ratified by more than 110 countries. The ILO Convention on the Worst Forms of Child Labor prohibits the forced or compulsory recruitment of children under the age of 18 for use in armed conflict. It has been ratified by over 150 countries.

## Myths about child soldiers

According to the campaigning organisation War Child (2018), there are several myths perpetuated about this issue. Not all are used as soldiers. They can also be used as porters, cooks, messengers, spies or for sexual purposes. It's important to recognise that children do not have to take part directly in hostilities to be severely affected by them. There is a misconception that this all happens in Africa. While it is a serious issue in many African nations, it is a worldwide problem. In 2016, the UN estimated that there were 20 conflict situations around the world involving children in armed groups. The risks to children in armed groups are huge. Even if they're released or escape, the after-effects can last a lifetime. Children can face stigma, exclusion and the consequences of their traumatic experience. They may find their families have been killed in conflict, or sometimes they are rejected by their own communities.

In the UK, recent revelations about recruitment practices and the use of children in combat roles surprised many people. However, the media treated the story more as a sign of recruitment difficulties rather than a child abuse story. The MoD constantly admits that it is understrength. With an increasingly poor image, the army has never been seen as a more unattractive career choice. The adverse publicity over the culture of bullying and suicides at military training establishments, such as Deepcut, revealed a tiny, previously hidden glimpse of what many vulnerable young people may also be subjected to on a routine basis once they enter the service. While supposedly toughening young solders up for what lies ahead, the cost to their self-esteem and emotional well-being is very high.

Research in recent years revealed that the army has a problem dealing with mental illness among soldiers, which manifests as full-blown post-traumatic stress disorder (PTSD), or less-documented depression and anxiety (Madigan et al, 2020). The majority of army recruits are from poorer socio-economic groups, where a higher proportion of children and young people are at greater risk of developing mental health problems. The British Army recruits in low-income, high-unemployment and disadvantaged areas where children with few academic or career prospects are able to sign up to six-year minimum service contracts at 16 years of age captivated by glamorous images of travel, adventure, machismo, national pride and employable skills training (Walker, 2018).

Films, video games and literature that emphasise war as fun, exciting and a professional activity are widely distributed in schools, youth clubs and military recruitment offices. The MoD's current social media campaigns are aimed at GCSE results times, suggesting to 16-year-olds that an army career is open to them if they did not get the grades they wanted. Rachel Taylor of Child Soldiers International says: *'Using Facebook to target the country's young people unwittingly and exploiting the anxiety of those who may be disappointed with their GCSE results with idealised and unrealistic advertising is shameful'* (Guardian, 2018).

What potential recruits will not realise is that since 1971, 24 under-18s died and 10 were seriously injured while on active military service in the British Army. Young recruits will also not be told about the increasing levels of PTSD and other mental health problems in older veterans, who feature in disproportionate numbers among the homeless population.

*Young recruits under 18 years of age are still legally defined as children even though in the context of uniforms, regiments and all the paraphernalia of the armed forces, these young people may look a lot older than they are. The evidence suggests that, paradoxically, they may be psychologically and emotionally immature due to earlier childhood neglect and deprivation and thus more at risk of developing mental health difficulties under the strain of intense combat.*

(Walker, 2018)

According to an MoD research (MOD, 2014), young soldiers are three times more likely to commit suicide than their civilian counterparts. Britain recruits 16-year-old children to all three branches of the military, the only European country to do so. There are clear contradictions in the British government's use of minors with its legal obligations under the UN Convention on the Rights of the Child (CRC) and the Children Act 1989 to protect and safeguard children. The MoD has ensured that the needs of military power and political control override the best interests of those under-18s in the armed forces. Article 38 of the CRC emphasises the particular vulnerability of children as civilians and soldiers and recommends signatories refrain from sending children into battle.

It recognises that children's rights are particularly vulnerable to violation during armed conflict and lays down specific obligations on the state to protect children caught up in situations of war. The World Health Organisation recognises that young soldiers exposed to conflict situations can more easily develop PTSD leading to persisting patterns of problematic behaviour and functioning. While the MoD says under-18s are not deployed to combat zones, ministers' responses to parliamentary questions over the past two decades have shown that around 50 under-18s were involved in peacekeeping missions, while the BBC (2002) reported that under-18s had to be removed from a contingent in Afghanistan.

# Eliminating child labour

Following the success of various children's charities campaigning to end child labour, public interest and knowledge about where and how cheap garments were produced gathered momentum in the UK and elsewhere. Concerns have often been raised over the buying public's moral complicity in purchasing products assembled or otherwise manufactured in developing countries with child labour. However, others have raised concerns that boycotting products manufactured through child labour may force these children to turn to more dangerous or strenuous professions, such as prostitution or agriculture.

For example, a UNICEF (2017) study found that after the Child Labour Deterrence Act was introduced in the US, an estimated 50,000 children were dismissed from their garment industry jobs in Bangladesh, leaving many to resort to jobs such as stone-crushing, street hustling and prostitution, jobs that are more hazardous and exploitative than garment production. The study suggests that boycotts are blunt instruments with long-term consequences, which can actually harm rather than help the children involved.

One of the biggest challenges in tackling child labour in the fashion supply chain is the complex supply chain for each garment. Even when brands have strict guidelines in place for suppliers, work often gets sub-contracted to other factories that the buyer may not even know about. Tackling child labour is further complicated by the fact it is just a symptom of larger problems. Where there is extreme poverty, there will be children willing to work cheap and susceptible to being tricked into dangerous or badly paid work (Moulds, 2020).

The Fair Wear Foundation (2012) has a list of over 120 brands that have signed up to its code of labour practices, which do not allow for the use of child labour. They suggest that accredited brands must ensure with regular audits that all of the suppliers in the early stage of production meet these standards. Other accreditation schemes exist, such as the Fairtrade Label Organisation, the Global Organic Textile Standard and the Ethical Trading Initiative, but all of them struggle with the lack of transparency in the textile and garment supply chain. The cruel irony is that the cheapest suppliers of children's clothing in the UK are used by some of the poorest families in the UK who cannot afford anything more expensive. So cheap clothing produced by child labour is worn by poor children in the UK and elsewhere.

## Chapter 6 | Child sexual abuse becomes public

*Innocence does not find near so much protection as guilt.*

Francois de la Rochefoucauld

# Introduction

There is a popular perception among professionals involved in children's services, paediatrics and child protection agencies that child sexual abuse was discovered in the 1980s. There was a flurry of activity as certain cases hit the tabloid headlines in the UK and elsewhere in the world. Evidence of paedophile rings operating in and around children's homes was exposed, and the taboo area of child sexual abuse within the family started to filter through to public consciousness. Yet, like so much of child abuse, the truth is it has been happening since ancient times.

One of the first notorious cases in the UK involved the Kincora Boys' Home in Northern Ireland which appeared as a news story in the Belfast Telegraph in 1980 (McKenna, 1980). This was subsequently investigated and found to involve a cover-up involving high-profile Unionist politicians and the British Secret Service. The effect of this and other revelations led to adults sexually abused as children coming forward with their personal stories. More recently, in November 2016, former professional footballers waived their rights to anonymity and talked publicly about sexual abuse they suffered as youngsters by former football coaches in the 1970s, 1980s and 1990s. The initial allegations centred on Crewe Alexandra and Manchester City.

In the mid-1980s, a social worker Alison Taylor reported allegations made to her by former residents in children's homes. The subsequent North Wales child abuse scandal led to a three-year, £13-million investigation into the physical and sexual abuse of children in care homes in the counties of Clwyd and Gwynedd, in North Wales, including the Bryn Estyn children's home at Wrexham, between 1974 and 1990 (DOH, 1999). It has led to numerous other investigations and exposed how the whole institutional care system for vulnerable children was open to sexual abuse.

In 2012, allegations of child sexual abuse were made to 13 British police forces, against the national television personality and charity fundraiser Jimmy Savile after his death. This led to the inquiries into employment practices at the BBC and within the National Health Service where he gained access to disabled children as a charity fundraiser. The Metropolitan Police launched a formal criminal investigation,

Operation Yewtree, into historic allegations of child sexual abuse by Savile and other individuals, some still living, over four decades. The police pursued over 400 lines of inquiry, based on the claims of 200 witnesses. It described the alleged abuse as being on an unprecedented scale, and the number of potential victims as staggering. The total number of alleged victims was 589, of whom 450 alleged abuse by Savile (Walker, 2019c).

The report of the investigations undertaken jointly by the police and the National Society for the Prevention of Cruelty to Children (NSPCC), *Giving Victims a Voice*, was published in 2013. It reported allegations covering a period of 50 years, including 214 alleged acts by Savile which, though uncorroborated, have been formally recorded as crimes, some involving children as young as eight. The report states *'within the recorded crimes there are 126 indecent acts and 34 rape/penetration offences'*. Alleged offences took place at 13 hospitals as well as on BBC premises, according to the report. In October 2013, it was announced that inquiries had been extended to other hospitals. The findings revealed that Savile had sexually assaulted victims aged between 5 and 75 in NHS hospitals. Further investigations, in hospitals and elsewhere, led to additional allegations of sexual abuse by Savile. It is widely believed that such a high-profile public figure, and someone who the BBC relied upon to generate large audience viewing figures, was known among TV producers and executives for his paedophile activities but they did nothing to report him to the police. He had even been knighted by Prime Minister Margaret Thatcher, a rare honour.

## Sexual abuse in modern times

The high profile cases above and the sensationalist tabloid media reportage shocked many people outside social work. But they perpetuated the idea that this was something modern and that child sexual abuse was relatively rare and perpetrated by outsiders and strangers. The plethora of subsequent reports and disclosures by adults abused as children demonstrated that most child sexual abuse occurs in the family home by a parent, sibling or close relative.

The historic record shows that concerns about the sexual abuse of children go much further back, and attempts to tackle the problem faced resistance and opposition from powerful legal and political institutions. Immediately after the ending of World War I, feminists and child protectionists resumed the cause of protecting girls in particular from sexual exploitation. They put various Private Members' Bills before Parliament and subsequently a Joint Select Committee of both Houses was formed in

1918 to consider the common element of these bills, the main aim of which was to protect girls under 16 from indecent assault.

In America, modern studies led by researchers keen to develop a knowledge base and understand the scale of the problem of child sexual abuse, using the most accurate methodological studies, based on lengthy interviews, report that once people are actively asked to recall childhood adverse events they invariably turn up historic sexual abuse:

*30 percent of men and 40 percent of women remember having been sexually molested during childhood defining molestation as actual genital contact, not just exposure. About half of these are directly incestuous, with the family members, the other half usually being with others, but with the complicity of caretakers in at least 80 percent of the cases.*

(Williams, 1994)

These experiences of abuse are not just pieced together from fragmentary memories but are remembered in detail, are usually for an extended period of time and have been confirmed by follow-up reliability studies in 83 per cent of the cases, so they are unlikely to have been fantasies. The abuse occurred at much earlier ages than had been previously assumed, with 81 per cent occurring before puberty and 42 per cent under age seven. As high as these abuse rates may seem, however, they represent only a portion of the true rates, because the populations studied excluded those marginalized and very vulnerable groups such as sex workers, juveniles in homeless shelters, seriously mentally ill people and young people in care.

*Adjusting statistically for what is known about these additional factors, it has been concluded that the real sexual abuse rate for America is 60 percent for girls and 45 percent for boys, about half of these directly incestuous.*

(Finkelhor, 1994)

In England, a recent BBC *ChildWatch* program asked its female listeners if they remembered sexual abuse as children, and, of the 2530 replies analysed, 83 per cent remembered someone touching their genitals, with 62 per cent recalling actual intercourse (BBC, 1986). In Germany, the *Institut fur Kindheit* recently carried out a survey asking school children about their experiences, and 80 per cent reported having been abused by an adult (2006). Stop Educator Sexual Abuse Misconduct & Exploitation (S.E.S.A.M.E.) is an organization in the USA that describes itself as a national voice for prevention of abuse by educators and other school employees. It has compiled alarming statistics on the incidences of sexual abuse in schools nationwide, reporting that just under 500 educators were arrested in 2015.

*Of children in 8th through 11th grade in the USA, about 3.5 million students (nearly 7%) surveyed reported having had physical sexual contact from an adult most often a teacher or coach. The type of physical contact ranged from unwanted touching of their body, all the way up to sexual intercourse.*

(S.E.S.A.M.E., 2017)

The Crime Survey for England and Wales (CSEW, 2019) estimated that 7.5 per cent of adults aged 18 to 74 years experienced sexual abuse before the age of 16 years (3.1 million people) this includes both adult and child perpetrators. The abuse was most likely to have been perpetrated by a friend or acquaintance (37%). The majority of victims did not tell anyone about their sexual abuse at the time, with embarrassment being the most common reason. Shame and guilt are very common feelings experienced by children sexually abused. In the year ending March 2019, the police in England and Wales recorded 73,260 sexual offences, where there are data to identify the victim was a child.

As of 31 March 2019, 2230 children in England were the subject of a child protection plan (CPP) and 120 children in Wales were on the child protection register (CPR) for experience or risk of sexual abuse. Sexual abuse has become the most common type of abuse counselled by the children's online charity Childline in recent years and it was also the most commonly reported type of abuse by adults calling the National Association for People Abused in Childhood's (NAPAC) helpline in the year ending March 2019.

The IICSA reported in late 2020 that UK healthcare practitioners who committed child sexual abuse commonly did so under the guise of medical treatment, which went unchallenged by other staff even when unnecessary or inappropriate because of their position of trust, research has found. The report into abuse in healthcare settings between the 1960s and 2000s found that perpetrators were most commonly male GPs or healthcare practitioners with routine clinical access to children. Survivors spoke of attending health institutions seeking treatment, care and recovery from abuse, but were instead subjected to sexual abuse. This included fondling, exposing children to adult sexuality, and violations of privacy. More than half who shared their experiences described suffering sexual abuse by penetration. Only a quarter reported they were able to disclose the sexual abuse as a child. In some instances, children who told of abuse were dismissed by healthcare professionals as sick, lying or mentally ill.

Accounts describe sexual abuse in hospitals, psychiatric institutions and GP surgeries, and sometimes involved the use of medication or medical instruments. The report found that as well as the position of trust and authority held by healthcare professionals, other factors that enabled the sexual abuse to take place included physical isolation in private consultation rooms and victims' lack of knowledge about medical procedures. More than 20 per cent of victims and survivors experienced a direct impact such as pregnancy or a physical injury from the abuse. The majority described a significant impact on their mental health, such as anxiety and depression.

Similar to findings from participants sexually abused in other institutional contexts, they suffered lifelong impacts. Participants were fearful of healthcare professionals, leading to avoidance of contact with them in later life. They also reported feeling betrayed by perpetrators' colleagues who did not intervene to prevent or stop the sexual abuse, leading to subsequent broader distrust of authority, systems and adults. Of the 4295 people who shared an experience between June 2016 and July 2020, 3 per cent described sexual abuse that took place in a healthcare context (IICSA, 2020).

Teachers have lots of opportunities to sexually abuse children for whom they have a notional duty of care. Those so minded are adept at grooming children, misusing their power and can defend against accusations by claiming children are lying or have a grudge. In recent years, a regular trend of historic sexual abuse in schools is being revealed on news programmes. As more victims come forward, as adults they feel empowered to tell their stories. This encourages others to come forward. A third of teachers struck off in the UK in 2017 were involved in child sexual abuse; this was the highest number for three years, according to data obtained by *The Independent* (2017). More were banned for sexual misconduct alone than were forced out of the profession because of alcohol, drugs or violence in total during the last five years. Forty-two were convicted, which is a 20 per cent increase from three years earlier. The IICSA inquiry has reported via its disclosure Truth Project that of the 691 reports submitted about teacher abuse, males made up the majority of victims (55%). The proportion of males rose to 76 per cent and 78 per cent of those who experienced abuse in the context of independent and special schools, respectively, and fell to 45 per cent among state school pupils (IICSA, 2020).

The Indian subcontinent still has many groups, such as the Baiga, where incestuous marriage is practised between fathers and daughters, between mothers and sons, between siblings and even between grandparents and their grandchildren (Choudhry, 2018). In 2017, over 100 children were sexually abused every day in India (India Today, 2017).

Childhood in contemporary Japan still includes masturbation by some mothers to put them to sleep. And co-sleeping, with parents physically embracing the child, often continues until the child is 10 or 15.

*Historically Japan has been one of the most endogamous societies in the world, with incestuous marriages in court circles being approved in historical times and preferred sibling, cousin, uncle-niece and aunt-nephew marriages having been so extensive that genetics experts have discovered that the incestuous inbreeding has affected the size and health of the Japanese. There are still rural areas in Japan where fathers marry their daughters when the mother has died or is incapacitated, in accordance with feudal family traditions.*

(Tanaka et al, 2017)

The sexual use of children in the Near East is as common as in the Far East. Historically, all the institutionalised forms of child sexual abuse which were customary in the Far East are documented extensively for the Near East, including child marriage, child concubinage, temple prostitution of both boys and girls, parent–child marriage, sibling marriage, sex slavery, ritualised pederasty and child prostitution.

*Masturbation in infancy is said to be necessary to increase the size of the penis, and older siblings are reported to play with the genitals of babies for hours at a time. Mutual masturbation, fellatio and anal intercourse are also said to be common among children, particularly with the older boys using younger children as sex objects.*

(Polonko et al, 2011)

Girls are used incestuously even more often than boys, since females are valued so little. One report found 80 per cent of Near Eastern women surveyed recalled having been forced into fellatio between the ages of three and six by older brothers, cousins, uncles and teachers (Eldin et al, 2008). Female genital mutilation is still practised when girls are at a very early age. A 2008 survey of Egyptian girls and women showed '*97 percent of uneducated families and 66 percent of educated families still practiced clitoridectomy. Nor is the practice decreasing. UN reports estimate that more than 74 million females have been mutilated, with more female children mutilated today than throughout history*' (Eldin et al, 2008).

## Children's homes and other institutions

The UK's National Archives contain some appalling examples of abuse at children's homes and approved schools from decades past (BBC, 2014b). In 1952, the Home Office gave clear guidance to managers of these schools saying they had a duty to report allegations of crimes, including indecent practices, to the police. But the files show that often the managers were the perpetrators themselves. The files dealing with cases that the Home Office was alerted to years later by adult survivors, show how abuse was not taken as seriously as today. All of the cases in these files deal with attacks on boys at homes or schools. Approved schools somewhere between a children's home and a youth detention centre were disproportionately male. Here is a selection of some of the most significant cases in the National Archives files:

## Westfield Children's Home, Liverpool, 1965–66

Westfield was a local authority children's home with 26 children, aged 6–16, mostly from disturbed backgrounds. In September 1965, a young housemaster was found guilty of buggery (the offence of male rape did not exist then) and indecent assault against several of the boys, and was sentenced to four years in prison.

## The Ockenden Venture, 1965

In June 1965, Peter John Moor appeared in court in Leicestershire, and was found guilty of two offences against young boys who were resident at Donington Hall. They were refugee children, apparently aged 11 and 14. He had a long string of convictions for buggery, theft and indecent assault. He had first been convicted at the age of 15, in 1923, for assault on a male. In 1957, he had been sentenced to eight years in prison for a sexual assault on a 15-year-old boy.

## St Gilbert's, Christian Brothers school, 1963

The Christian Brothers, or De La Salle Order, ran several approved schools in England. The approved schools were the ultimate responsibility of the Home Office – children were sentenced to terms there by juvenile courts. They catered generally for boys who had committed relatively minor crimes. Their intention was reform. The files in the National Archives show that in 1963 a mother had complained to the police about the behaviour of one of the brothers. The name is redacted, but the context, and research by the BBC, indicates it was Brother Maurice. It shows that there had been earlier complaints about this monk – and the head of the order had moved him to Scotland. The order had also taken legal advice, indicating that they did not need to volunteer any information to the police. In January 1964, Brother Maurice pleaded guilty to six counts of indecent assault against boys at the school. He was sentenced to three years' probation, on condition he spent 12 months as an outpatient at St Bartholomew's Hospital.

## St Vincent's approved school 1948–49

St Vincent's was a junior school in Kent for boys as young as eight or nine. It was a small school run by nuns. In September 1949, several boys complained to the cleaning lady of *'rude behaviour'* on the part of one of the masters. When she asked more questions it was clear he had been sexually abusing them. She reported this to the police who gathered evidence from 10 boys that he had abused them and statements from a further 11 boys who were witnesses.

The police traced boys who had moved on to other approved schools. Nine boys said they'd been assaulted by a master who'd left the school in 1948, two said he had raped them. Five boys said they had been sexually assaulted by a housemaster who had also left the school. Charges were brought against all three masters and they were tried in early 1950. The current master confessed to five counts of indecent assault and two counts of buggery, and was sentenced to two-and-a-half years in prison.

## Danesford Approved School, 1965

Danesford was another school for younger boys, including many vulnerable children. The first allegation of sexual abuse came from a mother who had heard that another boy had been *'the subject of minor interference'* by a member of staff. *'She had expressed the hope that her son would not undergo the same treatment'*, the file says. The complaint was investigated, and a master questioned. It emerged that the man had previously been warned about spending too much time alone with individual boys. The master was suspended and interviewed by police. After first denying the allegations he broke down and confessed to offences against boys over a period of three years but mostly in the last few weeks, the file says.

## Lambeth Council, 1974

The Independent Inquiry into Historic Child Sexual Abuse heard testimony revealing hundreds of children in the care of Lambeth Council were subjected to prolonged sexual, physical and racial abuse. For decades, victims were targeted by paedophiles working at the council-run Shirley Oaks campus in Croydon. The inquiry heard that despite widespread mistreatment of children, the authority failed to investigate any allegations at the time. The Shirley Oaks abuse scandal is seen as one of the worst in British history.

Children were systematically abused by paedophiles who targeted jobs in the care system to give them access to young people, the inquiry heard. The inquiry also heard allegations of physical and sexual assault that took place at other Lambeth Council children's homes, including the South Vale Assessment Centre and Ivy House. Shirley Oaks was the oldest and largest residential care home for children, aged between 2 and 17, under the control of the council. The home allowed for members of the public, known as social aunts and uncles, to volunteer to spend time with children by taking them away on day trips or on holiday, the inquiry heard. Lambeth Council admitted that during the operational period of Shirley Oaks, which could house up to 350 children, there were no requirements for staff to hold social work qualifications or to be police checked. In 2016, the council started a £100-million redress scheme offering a payment and apology to any child at Shirley Oaks, regardless of whether they had been abused.

## Parliament and the powerful

As the Independent Inquiry into Child Sexual Abuse trained its focus on the Houses of Parliament, it became obvious that accurate historic information would never reach the public gaze due to the power of the political establishment to close ranks and cover up child abuse. Liberal Lord David Steel was suspended from the Liberal Party after he testified to the Inquiry that he did not report Liberal MP Cyril Smith's open admission that he was being investigated by the police for sexually abusing children in the 1970s; this is indicative of the attitude at Westminster. Steel resigned from Parliament in early 2020. In March 2014, *Smile for the Camera: The Double Life of Cyril Smith* was published, an exposé of child sexual abuse committed by former Rochdale MP Cyril Smith, written by Labour MP Simon Danczuk along with researcher and campaigner Matthew Baker (2014). Danczuk was the new Rochdale MP and had become aware of Cyril Smith's activities. The book was serialised in the *Daily Mail* and was named Political Book of the Year for 2014 by the *Sunday Times*.

During a Home Affairs Select Committee hearing in July 2014, Danczuk called for Leon Brittan, Home Secretary between 1983 and 1985, to make public what he knew about a dossier of allegations against politicians presented to him by Geoffrey Dickens an MP until 1995, which could identify several historic child sex abusers within parliament. The Home Office stated the dossier had not been retained in their files. Former Director of Public Prosecutions Lord Macdonald said the circumstances in which the dossier had gone missing were alarming, and recommended an inquiry into what happened.

Prime Minister David Cameron subsequently asked the Home Office Permanent Secretary to investigate what happened to the missing dossier. The same month Danczuk wrote to the Director of Public Prosecutions asking for a review of the decision not to investigate certain historical allegations of sexual abuse made against senior Westminster politicians. Danczuk's investigation significantly contributed to the decision of the government to set up the Independent Inquiry into Child Sexual Abuse, a statutory inquiry under the Inquiries Act 2005, which opened on 9 July 2015. For his investigative work on child abuse, Danczuk was named Campaigner of the Year by the Political Studies Association in November 2014 and won the Contrarian Prize in June 2015.

The scandal goes back several decades. In 2016, at the inquest of a woman who ran the Elm Guest House, evidence was submitted at the Coroners Court that MPs including members of the Tory right-wing Monday Club, judges, a bishop, a Local Authority Children's Services director and a prominent businessman all used the Elm Guest House to rape children who had been procured from Grafton Close children's home in Richmond.

A former Scotland Yard commander admitted he knew of an alleged paedophile ring at Westminster. John O'Connor, once head of the Flying Squad, confirmed there were rumours of a sex scandal and he had been on standby for a major investigation. O'Connor said: *'I remember when this was first flying about. I think it was in the early 1980s but then it just seemed to die a natural death'*. A former army intelligence officer has said he was ordered to stop investigating allegations of child sexual abuse at the Kincora Boys' Home in Northern Ireland in the 1970s. Brian Gemmell said a senior MI5 officer told him to stop looking into claims of abuse at the home in East Belfast because people of the highest profile were involved in paedophile activity. Gemmell presented a report on the allegations to the police in 1975 but nothing happened (Walker, 2017).

In 2015, the focus of attention switched to Dolphin Square in Pimlico, a complex of flats used almost exclusively by MPs due to its proximity to Westminster. One of the VIPs who sexually abused boys at Dolphin Square has been identified as a former deputy director of MI6, Peter Hayman. The disclosure of his identity had been provided to Scotland Yard for its investigation into historical allegations that MPs and other prominent people carried out child sex abuse at Dolphin Square. Havers was the Attorney General under the Thatcher government when many of the allegations were made. In the early 1980s, Havers was accused by campaigning MP Geoffrey Dickens of a cover-up when he refused to prosecute Sir Peter Hayman, a diplomat, former MI6 deputy director and member of the Paedophile Information Exchange (PIE) (Walker, 2018).

The Metropolitan Police were accused of participating in the cover-up of high-profile paedophile crimes and investigated by the Independent Police Complaints Commission (IPCC) for corruption relating to historical child sex abuse. The allegations by retired police officers included claims that investigations in the 1970s were halted by high-ranking officers and Special Branch after it was discovered MPs were involved. The latest investigations are in addition to 17 inquiries previously announced. They all relate to claims about the suppressing of evidence, officers hindering or halting investigations, and claims offences were covered up.

The National Archives recently released a file prepared for Prime Minister Margaret Thatcher which detailed the paedophile activities of Sir Peter Hayman (The Guardian,

2015). He was named by Geoffrey Dickens, MP in the House of Commons, when his name along with many other MPs and government officials was discovered in another dossier Dickens had collated. The Director of Public Prosecutions at the time did nothing despite correspondence within the dossier showing Hayman's link to the Paedophile Information Exchange and evidence of his interest in the sexual torture of young children (Walker, 2019).

In 2014, the former head of the Bryn Alyn Community in Wrexham was jailed for the sexual abuse of children placed in his care. Wrexham is the area where paedophile Tory MP Peter Morrison, a former top aide to Margaret Thatcher in the 1980s, preyed on vulnerable children. He was known to other MPs as a dangerous paedophile, and several warned the Tory leadership about him: they were Edwina Currie and Gyles Brandreth. In 2013, the Metropolitan Police launched Operation Cayacos to investigate claims that Righton was part of an establishment paedophile network. A former Special Branch police officer, Tony Robinson, is on record saying a historic dossier packed with information about Cyril Smith's sex crimes was actually in the hands of MI5 despite officially having been '*lost*' decades earlier in the Home Office while led by former Home Secretary Leon Brittan. The security services were again charged with the cover-up of a Westminster paedophile ring as it emerged that files relating to official requests for media blackouts in the early 1980s were destroyed.

Two newspaper executives told *The Observer* that their publications were issued with D-notices, warnings not to publish intelligence that might damage national security when they sought to report on allegations of a powerful group of high profile men engaging in child sex abuse in 1984. Don Hale, the editor of the *Bury Messenger*, said he had been accosted in his office by 15 uniformed and 2 non-uniformed police over a dossier on Westminster paedophiles passed to him by the former much-respected Labour cabinet minister Barbara Castle. Officers citing national security confiscated the file which listed 16 MPs along with senior policemen, headteachers and clergy. In 1984, Hilton Tims, editor of the *Surrey Comet*, was issued with a D-notice, an official warning not to publish intelligence that might damage national security, when he sought to report on a police investigation into the notorious Elm Guest House (IICSA, 2019a).

In June 2017, the group Survivors of Organised and Institutional Abuse (SOIA) announced '*with deep regret*' that it was formally withdrawing from the current national inquiry, saying that the investigation was not fit for purpose. They said that survivors had been totally marginalised and that the inquiry had descended into a very costly academic report writing and literature review exercise. There is highly credible testimony that crimes committed by high profile men were covered up by the Secret Intelligence Service, Special Branch and senior police officers.

# Child abuse in sport

Of the 3939 survivors of sexual abuse who came forward to the Truth Project, as part of the Independent Inquiry into Historic Child Sexual Abuse, and shared experiences occurring between June 2016 and March 2020, 64 described child sexual abuse that took place in a sporting environment. Fifty-eight (91%) of those 64 participants reported being sexually abused by a sporting coach or volunteer in a sports organisation. All perpetrators spoken about by this group were adult males, while sports clubs were most frequently reported as the location of the abuse (39 out of the 64 cases). In building the latest report the Truth Project (2020) analysed 9 of the 64 cases in greater detail to include a range of characteristics and circumstances, such as the time period, victim age and victim sex.

This is the fourth study released by the Truth Project with the first three focusing on abuses suffered by children in religious institutions, children's homes and residential care, and custodial institutions. '*In contrast to the cases of child sexual abuse in sport involving high-performing or elite athletes that have garnered media attention in recent years, the experiences shared with the inquiry by participants through the Truth Project reflect more diversity and more "grassroots" contexts*', it explains.

The report found that there are many factors associated with the enabling of abuse that also feature in other areas of life (perpetrators approaching parents outside sports to look after children unsupervised, arranging overnight stays, oversight of adults working in sport) but reported that sport provides a more conducive environment for physical contact, with the primary perpetrators being coaches, both of clubs and privately, and other adults working in sporting facilities (Truth Project, 2020).

Children in sport are open to both physical and emotional abuse, but recent events have focused attention on the issue of child sexual abuse. Sport offers a potentially high risk environment. The care of children is entrusted to coaches, officials, development officers, helpers and other adults who may not may be well known to parents. In training, there can be close contact in teaching technique and free access to changing facilities. Coaches or other adults may also be involved in transport to and from training and, as young athletes become successful, they travel to events and training camps further afield with relatively little supervision.

To a child the coach or official is a very important figure, a mentor, father figure and authority. They may pick the team, set the training and have a major influence on their success in the sport. Children also see how their parents react to, and often bow to the wishes of these officials or coaches, so they may perceive them as a higher authority than their parents. There is a huge conflict of emotion when a person of importance, influence and authority does something which they recognise as inherently wrong. And in most cases of child abuse, the victim feels guilty that it is their fault in some way.

*Children, however, seldom initiate malicious gossip and they are often quick to sense when things are not as they should be. Rumours may be kept initially among themselves at pool or trackside, but hints or comment that are overheard should raise suspicion. It is easy to dismiss these as idle gossip, and indeed at times this may seem the easier option, but we have a duty to listen and report any concern. The issue of child abuse in sport may also place medical personnel in a particularly challenging position.*

(MacCauley, 1996)

## Football: The beautiful game?

A child sexual abuse scandal involving the abuse of young players at football clubs in the United Kingdom began in mid-November 2016. The revelations began when former professional footballers waived their rights to anonymity and talked publicly about being abused by former coaches and scouts in the 1970s, 1980s and 1990s. This led to a surge of further allegations, as well as allegations that some clubs had covered them up. This follows a similar pattern when brave survivors come forward as adults which ennobles others to disclose crimes against them as children.

Echoing similar revelations in the 1990s, the initial 2016 allegations centred on abuse of young players at Crewe Alexandra and Manchester City due to the clubs' associations with Barry Bennell (previously convicted of sexual abuse offences in the UK and US) who, on 29 November 2016, was charged with new offences. Allegations were also made against George Ormond, a former Newcastle United youth coach and scout (who also had previous convictions), former Chelsea scout Eddie Heath and former Southampton and Peterborough coach Bob Higgins. In early December 2016, allegations about former youth coaches and scouts in Northern Ireland and Scotland also started to emerge.

Within a month of the initial reporting, the Football Association, the Scottish Football Association, several football clubs and over 20 UK police forces had established various inquiries and investigations and over 350 alleged victims had come forward. By July 2018, 300 suspects were reported to have been identified by 849 alleged victims, with 2807 incidents involving 340 different clubs. By the end of 2019, 15 men had been charged with historical sexual abuse offences, 14 of whom were tried. Among them, 13, namely Bennell, Ormond, Higgins, William Toner, Michael

Coleman, Jim McCafferty, Robert Smith, James Torbett, Gerald King, Frank Cairney, Norman Shaw, David Daniel Hayes and Dylan Lamb were convicted; all, except King (given a three-year probation order) were jailed. Paul McCann was cleared. Michael Carson took his own life before his trial opened. Other allegations involve individuals who had died prior to the revelations or died before charges could be brought (BBC, 2018).

At least 80 sports coaches have been convicted of child sexual abuse in the UK in the two years since the Offside Trust was set up, the body has claimed. The body was set up *'by survivors for survivors'* after child sexual abuse in football was revealed in 2016. According to Offside Trust research (2018), drawn from media reports, almost half of the cases involved crimes that have been committed since 2006. More than a third of cases have taken place in the last five years. The most high-profile case involved former Crewe coach Barry Bennell, who was jailed for 31 years at Liverpool Crown Court for 50 counts of child sexual abuse between 1979 and 1991. Football Association chairman Greg Clarke called the scandal one of the biggest crises in the history of the governing body.

Police have received more than 2800 referrals relating to their investigation into historic sex abuse in football, part of a wider investigation called Operation Hydrant. Those referrals and reports came via police forces and an NSPCC helpline which was set up in November 2016 in response to the allegations made by Walters and others.

## Gymnastics: Bending to the truth

The USA Gymnastics (USAG) sex abuse scandal relates to the sexual abuse of female athletes, primarily minors at the time of the abuse, over two decades in the United States, starting in the late 1990s. More than 368 persons alleged that they were sexually assaulted by gym owners, coaches and staff working for gymnastics programmes across the country. Particularly, long-time USAG national team doctor Larry Nassar was named in hundreds of lawsuits filed by athletes who said that Nassar engaged in sexual abuse for at least 14 years under the pretence of providing medical treatment. Since the scandal was first reported by *The Indianapolis Star* in September 2016, more than 265 women, including 20 former USAG national team members, accused Nassar of sexually assaulting them. It is one of the largest sexual abuse scandals in US sports history (Guardian, 2019).

In 2017, Nassar pleaded guilty to federal child pornography charges and was sentenced to 60 years in prison. He later pleaded guilty to several charges of first-degree sexual assault. An investigation by *The Indianapolis Star* found that the abuses were widespread because predatory coaches were allowed to move from gym to gym, undetected by a lax system of oversight, or dangerously passed on by USA Gymnastics-certified gyms. Besides Nassar, other coaches across the country were also involved in sexual abuse, in localities such as Michigan, Pennsylvania, California, Rhode Island and Indiana.

Commonwealth silver medallist and former Australian national champion Mary-Anne Monckton in July 2020 detailed a normalised culture of emotional abuse, including being body shamed and *'yelled at until I cried'*. Monckton's story reads familiar after similar revelations started emerging from the sport in the UK. Olympic bronze medallist Amy Tinkler revealed she retired because of her negative experiences in the British elite programme. Team GB gymnasts Becky and Ellie Downie concurred that they also suffered in abusive coaching environments. Just as British Gymnastics has been engulfed by allegations of a culture of fear, so too has there been a trickle-down effect to other parts of the world. Monckton became the first of the Australian elite contingent to speak out, and very recently the Swiss Gymnastics Federation suspended its head of elite sport amid an independent investigation into abuse claims, after two of their top coaches were fired in June (Daily Telegraph, 2020).

## Children's voices not heard

In late 2020 as the IICSA resumed its work, a formal criticism was made by a senior QC who, on behalf of several victim/survivor groups, felt that the voices of children were not being listened to at the expense of institutions and organisations attempting to ensure their side of the story achieved prominence. Another example of how children are so often relegated to the margins of narratives concerning their own protection from harm (Sky News, 2020).

Children's perspectives have rarely been explored in relation to the help they receive towards their emotional and mental well-being as a result of being sexually abused (Walker, 2012). The prevalence and upward trends of mental health problems in childhood, together with findings that young people with such difficulties are reluctant to make use of specialist services or quickly cease contact (Richardson and Joughin, 2000), indicate the importance of developing appropriate sources of help that are experienced as useful and relevant and therefore going to be accessible and used effectively. In order to do that, methods of consulting with children and young people need to be developed that are appropriate, accessible, effective and methodologically robust.

There is a growing literature on the subject of the rights of children and young people to influence decisions about their own health and healthcare (Alderson, 2000; Walker, 2019). However, this remains an area of contention for some professionals who believe that the notion that children can think, comment and participate in a meaningful way in evaluations of the help they receive, is at best misguided or at worst undermining parental and/or professional responsibility. There is added poignancy when this concept is applied to child and adolescent mental health, where the very emotional and behavioural problems of children give weight to the argument against seeking children's perceptions. Parents and those with parental responsibility might present powerful arguments for wanting to make exclusive decisions to enable them to cope with and manage sometimes worrying and disturbing behaviour, especially while in the course of empowering challenging young people, details of sexual abuse within the family may emerge (Walker and Thurston, 2006).

Despite years of training and much better data on child sexual abuse and how to spot signs and symptoms, professionals have an aversion to consider that a family member is committing this crime. It goes against years of beliefs, fantasies and instincts about caring that they cannot face up to facts. They also know the costs to them personally of accepting the crime is happening to a child they are responsible for or who they come into contact with. They fear blame, scepticism, legal action if the courts decide against the child witness, and sanctions against them from employers and professional/trades union membership.

They also know the emotional impact of knowing what is being done to a fragile, vulnerable child and this freezes them psychologically, overwhelming them with feelings of guilt and fear. Their line manager to whom they should report suspicions may be similarly emotionally limited and fearful about potential reputational damage to their organisation. So there are barriers to professional safeguarding action, limited training and little emotional support for those in the front line of trying to support and protect sexually abused children. Newly qualified staff are, due to shortages after years of local authority cuts and high vacancy rates, thrown headlong into complex child abuse work without regular sympathetic and psychodynamic supervision which would enable them to gain a better emotional and professional perspective. There is an urgent need for all staff, whether teachers, nurses and social workers, to be provided with much better training and support to enable them to carry out their duties competently and to better protect children from abuse.

## Chapter 7 | The contemporary picture

*For in every adult there resides the child that was, and in every child there lies the adult that will be.*

John Connolly

# Introduction

According to the global charity Oxfam (2020), wealth inequality impacts levels of child abuse and affects women and girls worse. In its latest report the charity revealed that 1 per cent of the richest people have twice the wealth of more than nine billion people. 258 million children are not able to access any education, while unpaid childcare work is estimated at over $10 trillion. Britain's total wealth grew by 13 per cent in the two years to 2018 to reach a record £14.6tn, with wealth among the richest 10 per cent of households increasing almost four times faster than those of the poorest 10 per cent. A study by the Office for National Statistics (ONS, 2019) also found that the poorest 10 per cent of households had debts three times greater than their assets compared with the richest 10 per cent who amassed a wealth pile 35 times larger than their total debts. In the UK, 2000 foodbanks have opened since 2010, handing out two million food parcels annually, where there are currently officially four million children living in poverty.

As long ago as 1996 a national commission of inquiry into the prevention of child abuse recognised the need for a more holistic approach. It included in its definition of child abuse not only direct and acute forms such as violence but also indirect forms such as poor housing, family health and poverty (1996 HMSO). There is a strong association between families' socio-economic circumstances and the chances that their children will experience child abuse and neglect. Evidence of this association is found repeatedly across developed countries, types of abuse, definitions, measures and research approaches, and in different child protection systems. However, there is no evidence for the portrayal of poor families as *inevitably abusive*; the irony is that wealthier, middle-class families are better at avoiding scrutiny for child abuse, leaving children in comfortable material circumstances at risk of any and every kind of abuse.

There are a variety of plausible explanatory models for the relationship between family socio-economic circumstances and the prevalence of child abuse. The most widely described suggest either a direct effect through material hardship or lack of money to buy in support, or an indirect effect through parental stress and neighbourhood conditions. Disadvantaging socio-economic circumstances may operate as acute or chronic factors, including their impact on parents' own childhoods (Bywaters et al, 2016).

## Housing and homelessness

The number of homeless children in the UK hit a 14-year high recently with 135,000 stuck in cramped and unsuitable multi-occupied B&Bs and temporary shelter. The number is up 3.1 per cent on 2018 and is the highest quarterly figure recorded since the summer of 2006. More than two-thirds of all people in temporary accommodation have dependent children living with them. Some 1550 parents with children are living for long periods in what are supposed to be short-term B&Bs. Overall the number of households in temporary accommodation soared 9.4 per cent from 2018 to 93,000 in 2019. Over 530 parents had been in B&Bs beyond the legal limit of six weeks. Research shows that children in temporary, overcrowded, insecure housing have lower levels of school attainment, greater risk of developing illness and are more likely to be living in a household suffering food poverty (Shelter, 2019). Multi occupancy bed and breakfast accommodation can be used by local authorities to house convicted paedophiles and other abusers. So vulnerable children end up in the same space using communal facilities such as toilets and bathrooms as dangerous sex abusers.

## Child health

Child health is an obvious indicator of the safety of children from child abuse and neglect. The UK infant mortality rate has risen significantly since 2014, and in the most deprived communities it stands as high as 5.2 deaths per 1000 (ONS, 2018). Overall 2636 babies died before their first birthday in 2017. While this is fewer deaths than in 2016, the birth rate has also fallen and that means the proportion of newborns surviving to age one has fallen. The infant mortality rate had been reducing since the 1980s, but since an all-time low in 2014 the rate has increased every year between 2014 and 2017.

Rickets was a scourge of dark, polluted, overcrowded Victorian slums. In 1855, Samuel Pearce, the Medical Officer of Health for St Matthew, Bethnal Green, East London, described the area as being densely filled by the poorest class:

*A labyrinth of streets where 'hundreds swarm like bees in close, un-sunned, low-lying courts. Rickets, not surprisingly, was rife: 21.4% of children's skeletons buried in a Bethnal Green cemetery between 1840 and 1855 showed evidence of rickets. An 1884 survey reported discovering signs of rickets in every child examined in Clydeside. As late as the 1930s, more than 80% of children in London and Durham showed symptoms of the disorder.*

(Gibbs, 1994)

Hospitalisations for rickets reached 17.8 children per million between 2007 and 2011. Most of these were children younger than five years of age. Rickets is not an isolated example of nutritional deficiency in infants. Despite living in the midst of plenty, infant malnutrition and malnourishment remain disturbingly common in the UK. A report for the British Association for Parenteral and Enteral Nutrition (BAPEN) and the National Institute for Health Research (NIHR) suggested that 15 per cent of children are malnourished when admitted to hospital (Elia, 2015). In general, malnutrition is synonymous with undernutrition. Obese people can be malnourished; they may consume more than enough calories, but from a poor-quality diet that is incapable of optimising health and well-being. Both infant malnutrition and malnourishment are linked strongly with poverty and food insecurity.

Almost 2,500 children have been admitted to hospital with malnutrition in the first six months of 2020, double the number over the same period in 2019, prompting fresh concern that families are struggling to afford to feed themselves and that the pandemic has intensified the problem. Statistics from almost 50 NHS trusts in England, representing 150 hospitals, show that more than 11,500 children have been admitted to hospital with malnutrition since 2015. Almost 1000 under-16s with malnutrition were admitted as inpatients to Cambridge University hospital's NHS foundation trust alone, suggesting the affluent city has wide disparities in wealth. Collectively the figures reveal 11,515 cases of hospital admissions of under-16s due to malnourishment. Fewer than two-thirds of all trusts responded, suggesting the real total figure is much higher (The Independent, 2020).

Data from the Food Foundation revealed in May 2020 that almost a fifth of households with children had been unable to access enough food in the preceding weeks, with children not getting enough to eat as already vulnerable families battled isolation and loss of income (Food Foundation, 2020).

# Youth justice

The example of the use of capital punishment on children is a stark reminder of the power of the state and legal apparatus over the life and death of children. Since 1642, in the Thirteen Colonies, the United States under the *Articles of Confederation* and the

United States under the *1776 Constitution*, an estimated 364 juvenile offenders have been put to death by the individual states (colonies, before 1776) and the federal government.

The earliest recorded state execution of a minor in the USA was that of Hannah Ocuish who was a Pequot Native American girl with an intellectual disability who was accused of killing six-year-old Eunice Bolles, the daughter of a wealthy farmer, after allegedly quarrelling with her about some strawberries. The primary evidence against her was her confession to the investigators. At her execution in 1786, she thanked the sheriff for his kindness as she stepped forward to be hanged at the age of 12 years and 9 months. The youngest person to be executed in the twentieth century was Joe Persons, an African-American boy, who was executed in Georgia in 1915 at the age of 14 for the alleged rape of an 8-year-old girl when he was only 13 (Hearn, 2015).

George Junius Stinney Jr. was another 14-year-old African American who was convicted, in a proceeding later judged to be an unfair trial in 2014, of murdering two white girls, Betty June Binnicker and Mary Emma Thames, ages 7 and 11, in his hometown of Alcolu, South Carolina. He was executed by electric chair in June 1944. A re-examination of the Stinney case began in 2004, and several individuals and the Northeastern University School of Law sought a judicial review. Stinney's conviction was overturned 70 years after he was executed, when a court ruled that he had not received a fair trial (Banner, 2005). Since 1990, juvenile offenders are known to have been executed in seven countries: China, Democratic Republic of Congo, Iran, Pakistan, Yemen, Nigeria, Saudi Arabia and the United States.

In the UK there are three types of youth imprisonment. Secure Children's Homes are run by local councils for children aged 10 to 14. Young Offender Institutions (YOIs) are for young people aged 15 to 21. Those under 18 are held in separate institutions. Many YOIs are also part of adult prisons. There have been repeated reports into conditions in these places especially since they were privatized. Bullying by other inmates or staff has occurred including the use of harmful and controversial restraint techniques, and 1000 reports of sexual abuse were made between 2009 and 2017 (Guardian, 2019). Several studies have revealed that 90 per cent of imprisoned young people have underlying and undiagnosed mental health problems stemming from childhood abuse (Walker, 2019).

In 2018–19, 73 per cent of those in UK youth custody were placed in a YOI, 17 per cent in a Secure Training Centre and 10 per cent in a Secure Children's Home. There was an average of 859 under-18-year-olds in youth custody at the end of any given month. Just over a quarter of the youth custody population in 2018 was being held on remand. The remainder had been sentenced to custody (House of Commons

Library, 2020). Concerns have been raised about the current provision of youth custody. These include:

- » lack of safety;
- » use of restraint and force including the use of pain-inducing techniques;
- » segregation of children away from others;
- » lack of purposeful activity and time out of cells;
- » disproportionate number of BAME children in custody;
- » distance away from home that children are sometimes held.

Hundreds of primary school-aged children are being needlessly criminalised because of the young age of criminal responsibility in England and Wales, according to experts who are calling for it to be increased (EHRC, 2019). Representatives from youth services, the justice system and politicians have urged the UK government to raise the minimum age a child can be convicted of a crime by at least two years from 10 to 12. Currently, a child aged ten can be convicted of a crime and subjected to a police investigation, potentially resulting in them having a criminal record for life. Despite repeated criticism and pressure from the UN and other groups to raise the age to at least 12, the internationally recognised minimum, the UK government has so far resisted. No other country in the EU criminalises such young children, with the age of criminal responsibility set at 14 in Germany, 15 in Sweden, 16 in Portugal and 18 in Luxembourg, for example.

# Exorcisms of young people

It might surprise many people to learn that exorcisms by established churches in the UK and elsewhere are still conducted on children today. In the 1970s, the Archbishop of Canterbury, Donald Coggan, voiced his approval of exorcism and required all 42 dioceses to have an exorcist. Former children at a Christian fundamentalist school in the UK reported they witnessed blood-curdling exorcisms on fellow students conducted by church leaders who encouraged students to speak in tongues (The Independent, 2016). Other testimonies from children subjected to exorcisms against their will recall horrific, abusive experiences often as a result of the increased evangelical trend in the Church of England where fundamentalist ideas hold sway. Children with mental health problems or a diagnosis of autism are especially at risk (Guardian, 2018).

Sometimes children are killed during attempts to heal them (The Cult Observer, 1987). A couple and two young, self-ordained preachers were indicted in 1985 in North Carolina for the choking to death of a four-year-old during a laying on of hands healing service at a store-front church. This attempt to rid the boy of a demon left him with abrasions and fingernail marks on his throat and a crushed windpipe. In Louisiana in 1987, an eight-year-old Downs syndrome girl was strangled to death, while her mother was present, in an attempt to exorcise evil spirits from her body.

In 1986, a ten-year-old boy was starved and beaten with sticks by a fundamentalist Christian cult, His Rest Christian Fellowship, which believed he was possessed by demons. Police said that the malnourished and abused child, who had never been to school, was probably one of many victims of the group's exorcism rites. Authorities also reported that the 19-year-old son of another member of the church was beaten and cut with knives in a purification ritual by other members when he tried unsuccessfully to run away and escape (Toronto Sun, 1986). News of several deaths of children during exorcisms regularly appear in the US media. In 2010, a 14-year-old boy in England was beaten and drowned to death by relatives trying to exorcise an evil spirit from him (Guardian, 2012).

Meanwhile The House of Bishops in the UK (2012) revised its 1975 guidelines to reiterate its willingness to train clergy and expect them to conduct exorcisms on children. Such beliefs in demonic possession and the violent exorcisms that may follow have a long history. The belief that demons can possess people is one of the most widely held religious beliefs in the world. The Vatican first issued guidelines on exorcisms in 1614 and revised them in 1999. As many as 250 priests from 50 countries arrived in Rome in 2018 to learn how to identify demonic possession, to hear personal accounts from other priests and to find out more about the rituals behind expelling demons. Exorcism remains controversial, in part due to its depiction in popular culture and horror films. But there have also been some cases of abuse linked to exorcisms in a range of religious sects. The week-long Vatican course was described as the only international series of lectures of its kind. Entitled *Exorcism and the Prayer of Liberation*, it first opened its doors in 2005 and the number of priests attending has more than doubled since then (BBC, 2018a).

Catholic priests in several countries have told the press that there has been an increase in the numbers of people reporting signs of demonic possession. In 2017 Pope Francis told priests that they must not hesitate to refer parishioners to exorcists if they suffer from genuine spiritual disturbances. Half a million people reportedly seek exorcisms every year in Italy, while a report by Christian think-tank Theos (2017) said that the practice was also on the rise in the UK, in part due to the spread of Pentecostal churches. Some dioceses have developed their own courses to meet the growing demand, including in Sicily and the US city of Chicago.

Child abuse linked to witchcraft and the notion that these concepts were somehow buried in an ancient past were starkly challenged by the revelations in the trial of two people accused of the murder of Victoria Climbie in London in 2000. Before her death, Climbié, originally from Sierra Leone, was burnt with cigarettes, tied up for periods of longer than 24 hours and hit with bike chains, hammers and wires. The couple charged with killing her were convinced by their local church that Victoria was possessed by a demon and the abuse was a form of exorcism (The Independent, 2019). Witchcraft called *Kindoki* is practised in some churches. Scotland Yard said it had conducted 83 investigations into faith-based child abuse since 2000 (Channel 4 News, 2012).

Child abuse linked to belief in witchcraft is a growing phenomenon, according to evidence submitted to a Commons Select Committee's inquiry into child protection set up in 2010. The UK government published an action plan to tackle faith-based child abuse in 2012. This plan aimed to address certain kinds of child abuse linked to faith or belief. This included belief in witchcraft, spirit possession, demons or the devil, the evil eye or djinns, dakini, kindoki, ritual or muti murders and use of fear of the supernatural to make children comply with being trafficked for domestic slavery or sexual exploitation. The beliefs which were the focus of this action plan were not confined to one faith, nationality or ethnic community. According to the Metropolitan Police, abuse linked to faith or belief is where concerns for a child's welfare have been identified, and could be caused by a belief in witchcraft, spirit or demonic possession, ritual or satanic abuse features; or when practices linked to faith or belief are harmful to a child (DOH, 2012).

In South Africa the murder of children for body parts with which to make muti, for purposes of witchcraft, still occurs. Muti murders occur throughout South Africa, especially in rural areas. Traditional healers or witch doctors often grind up body parts and combine them with roots, herbs, seawater, animal parts and other ingredients to prepare potions and spells for their clients. In the early twenty-first century, Uganda has experienced a revival of child sacrifice. In spite of government attempts to downplay the issue, an investigation by the BBC into human sacrifice in Uganda found that ritual killings of children are more common than Ugandan authorities admit. *'There are many indicators that politicians and politically connected wealthy businessmen are involved in sacrificing children in practice of traditional religion, which has become a commercial enterprise'* (Rogers, 2011).

# Child marriages

Child marriage is *'any formal marriage or informal union between a child under the age of 18 and an adult or another child'* (UNICEF). The UK Parliament has recognized the inherent abuse in this practice by raising the minimum age for leaving education or training to 18, that childhood should be safeguarded as a time for learning and personal development. Safeguarding children from child marriage will enable every child the opportunity to complete their education, make informed choices about their future and reach their full potential. Child marriage is both impacting children from the UK and is also being perpetrated by men from the UK against children overseas. It takes the form of registered marriages, which are recognised under British law and also religious or customary marriages, which can happen at any age and may or may not also be registered. An unregistered child marriage causes no less harm than a registered marriage.

Office of National Statistics (ONS, 2019) data shows that in the last ten years, for which data is available (2006–16), 3354 marriages involving children aged 16 and 17 were registered in England and Wales. Significantly, overall, the average age of marriage in England and Wales has continued to rise and the number of people getting married aged 17 and under has fallen (to 179 in 2016). This shows that as a society we have moved on and that most people no longer want child marriage. However, as the data shows, child marriage has continued and the damage that it causes to the children involved is so profound that the law is currently not fit for the purpose to protect children from this abuse.

Registered marriages are only part of the picture of the UK child marriage problem; the ONS statistics do not capture non-registered religious or cultural marriages or child marriages that take place abroad involving children or adults who have lived in the UK. Child marriage is a hidden form of child abuse, so it is important to look to a range of sources for prevalence. In 2018, a third of cases (33%, 574) dealt with by the UK's Forced Marriage Unit involved children aged 17 and under. The vast majority of victims (75%) were females, showing that this issue is disproportionately affecting girls. The cases relate to 110 countries demonstrating the breadth of the UK child marriage problem globally.

Since 2015, the national helpline for honour-based abuse received 852 child marriage cases involving under-18 year-olds, and many other charities working domestically have been supporting many more children at risk of child marriage within the UK and abroad (IKWRO, 2020). Many child marriages are never reported nor captured by statistics. Current ambiguity in the law is a barrier to protection and likely keeps the known numbers down. There is no explicit crime of child marriage, at any age (including under 16, the minimum age that a marriage can be registered). A child marriage that takes place involving a child aged under 16 is simply not legally binding, unless it qualifies as a forced marriage.

For a child marriage to qualify as a forced marriage, it is required to ascertain whether both parties are deemed to have consented and had the capacity to consent. The test for capacity to consent is defined under the Mental Capacity Act 2005 and, importantly, age is not a stand-alone factor in determining lack of capacity to consent. One or both parties being a minor does not automatically qualify a child marriage as being a forced marriage and, therefore, a crime. The onus is on the child to recognise the marriage is forced in order to get protection from it, which in practice leaves many vulnerable to child marriage.

## Honour killings

An honour killing or shame killing is the murder of a member of a family due to the perpetrators' belief that the victim has brought shame or dishonour upon the family, or has violated the principles of a community or a religion with an honour culture. Typical reasons include divorcing or separating from their spouse; refusing to enter an arranged, child or forced marriage; being in a relationship or having associations with social groups outside the family that are strongly disapproved by one's family; having premarital or extramarital sex; becoming the victim of rape or sexual assault; dressing in clothing, jewellery and accessories which are deemed inappropriate; engaging in non-heterosexual relations and so on.

Recent official figures revealed 11,744 incidences of these crimes between 2010 and 2014, consisting of data from 39 out of 52 police forces in the UK. They included forced marriage and female genital mutilation (FGM). Data show that police recorded 759 honour violence crimes and 265 forced marriages in London between 2015 and 2017, but just 138 people were charged with offences. The data also show that prosecution rates for both crimes have fallen in the past three years when national statistics revealed the number of women coming forward to make allegations was rising (Home Office, 2020). The majority of cases don't reach the courts because victims are afraid to prosecute their parents for fear of reprisals.

## Modern slavery

Referrals of suspected child victims of modern slavery made by councils in England have soared by 1400 per cent in five years, putting children's services under increasing and significant pressure, according to the Local Government Association (LGA, 2020). Latest statistics show the number of council referrals of suspected child victims of modern slavery in England to the National Referral Mechanism (NRM), the UK's framework for referring and supporting victims, has risen from 127 in 2014 to 1971 in 2019, a staggering increase of 1452 per cent.

The rate of these child referrals increased by 71 per cent in one year alone, with the number of referrals in 2018 standing at 1152. Children accounted for 91 per cent of all referrals (child and adults) made by councils in England in 2019. Estimates of the number of victims of modern slavery in the UK range from 13,000 to more than 130,000, with the overall costs to UK society of modern slavery estimated to be between £3.3 billion and £4.3 billion. The Local Government Association says that the spiralling rate of modern slavery referrals is further evidence of the huge pressures on children's services, and is being fuelled by both an increasing awareness of modern slavery and of the exploitation of young people by county lines drugs gangs.

## Sex education

Research by the Sex Education Forum (2020) found that young people's safety is being undermined by dramatic variations in what is taught in schools' sex and relationships education (SRE). The survey of over 2000 11–25-year-olds showed that across a range of topics that could protect children from harm, such as knowing where to turn to for help if they experience sexual abuse, or information about FGM or sexual consent, many young people are left in the dark by gaps in their SRE.

The survey of over 2000 young people found their safety may be at risk due to inconsistent sex and relationships education. Half (50%) of young people did not learn how to get help if they were abused. Over half (53%) did not learn how to recognise grooming for sexual exploitation. More than four in ten had not learned about healthy or abusive relationships. A third (34%) of young people said they learnt nothing about sexual consent at school. Campaigners have called for statutory sex and relationships education to help keep young people safe.

Half (50%) of those surveyed had not learnt from their primary school about how to get help if they experienced unwanted touching/sexual abuse, 16 per cent had not learnt the correct names for genitalia and even more (17%) had not learnt that the genitals are private, all key to recognising and reporting abuse. Young people were more likely to have learnt about the difference between safe and unwanted touch from discussions at home than at school, but even so, less than half of young people (45%) said they had learnt about this with a parent or carer. When asked about their school SRE as a whole, it was found:

- » over half of young people (53%) had not been taught to spot the signs of when someone is being groomed for sexual exploitation;
- » more than four in ten had not learnt about how to tell when a relationship is healthy (46%) or abusive (44%);
- » worryingly, given that sexual assault is something that a significant minority of young people experience, lessons about sexual consent are not routinely covered in schools;
- » half (50%) of young people had not discussed real-life scenarios about sexual consent;
- » a third (34%) had been taught nothing at all about sexual consent;
- » only a quarter (24%) of young people said they learnt about FGM, but the figure increased to four in ten (40%) among 11–13-year-olds, suggesting things are starting to change.

# Mental well-being

In 2009, a study revealed that Britain's 12 million children and teenagers are the unhappiest and unhealthiest of any wealthy European country (Children's Society, 2010). A league table of child well-being, compiled by academics at the University of York and comparing figures from all 25 member states of the European Union, ranked the UK 21st. Only children in Latvia, Estonia, Lithuania and Slovakia were worse off. These findings are seen as evidence for an independent inquiry into what makes a good childhood. York University researchers compared children's material wealth, housing, health, safety, education, well-being and relationships across the EU. They discovered that while those in the UK suffer average levels of poverty, more than 17 per cent live in households whose adult members are unemployed, the highest level in the EU. The UK came out worst in the EU when judged in terms of family structure. Researchers found that only 60 per cent of children spoke to their parents regularly and a third did not eat meals with them. Professor John Bradshaw, who led the study, said the Government's efforts to step up spending to tackle child poverty and improve education and healthcare could help transform the UK's very poor rating, but it had a huge challenge ahead.

According to a recent report from The Children's Society (2020), children in England are still, even ten years later, among the unhappiest in the world, behind countries such as Ethiopia, Algeria and Romania. Their research looked at 15 diverse countries, ranking England 14th for life satisfaction of its young people, ahead only of South Korea. More than a third of English children said they had been bullied in school, and half had felt excluded, it found. The University of York carried out the research in England, which was then drawn together for the Children's Worlds Project, and compared with data from 14 other countries. Researchers surveyed more than 53,000 children in total, aged between 8 and 12, from diverse cultures and places, from remote villages to large cities.

Levels of satisfaction with life as a whole were highest in Romania, where the mean level of satisfaction among 12-year-olds was 9.5 out of 10, followed by Colombia with 9.3 out of 10. England came 14th out of the countries surveyed, with 12-year-olds giving a mean satisfaction score of 8.4 out of 10, and 7.1 per cent reporting low levels of well-being and happiness. The survey also found that levels of unhappiness at schools in England grew as children got older, 61 per cent of ten-year-olds said they enjoyed school but the figure fell to 43 per cent by the age of 12. English children were the most likely of all the countries surveyed to say that they had been left out by other children in their class at least once in the last month, the survey found. More than a third (38%) aged between 10 and 12 reported being physically bullied in the previous month. English girls ranked second lowest for happiness with their body confidence, self-confidence and appearance, rating their satisfaction as 7.3 out of 10 on average. This places them just above South Korea, with a mean score of 7.1 (Children's Worlds Project, 2020).

# Cyber bullying

Being bullied online can have just as damaging an effect on a child as more apparently serious physical types of abuse. It can involve body shaming, transphobia, rejection, sexting, trolling, flaming, racism, homophobia and sexism. It is forming another part of the modern abusive context of children's lives. It is emotionally damaging leading to self-harm and in some cases suicide. Intimate photos taken by young teenagers can be posted by former boy/girlfriends to embarrass and humiliate a person instantly to a large peer audience.

Adults such as parents, other family members and teachers also bully children. They may do it by making a child feel bad/embarrassed or humiliated in front of other people, by shouting, teasing or poking fun at them. New research reveals that websites encouraging suicide and self-harm topped a list of teenagers' greatest worries about the internet. The findings have raised fears that growing numbers of young people are becoming vulnerable to the messages being put out by such sites (Li, 2006).

The widespread condemnation of internet trolling associated with the death of the cyber-bullying victim Amanda Todd captured worldwide attention as the potential fatal impact of cyber bullying was revealed in 2012. The Canadian teenager was found dead after she had posted a harrowing YouTube video in which she told of the online bullying she had suffered by holding up handwritten notes. Cyber bullying has been defined as:

*The use of information and communication technologies such as e-mail, cell phone and pager text messages, instant messaging, defamatory personal Web sites. 'Repetitive, wilful or persistent behaviour intended to cause harm, carried out by an individual or a group; inappropriate text messaging and emailing; sending offensive or degrading images by phone or via the internet; gossiping; excluding people from groups and spreading hurtful and untruthful rumours'.*

(National Society for the Prevention of Cruelty to Children [NSPCC], 2010)

Others include blogs, online games and defamatory online personal polling websites, to support deliberate, repeated, and hostile behaviour by an individual or group, that is intended to harm others (Belsey, 1999). Many school students involved in cyber-bullying can be unaware of what they are contributing to (Betts, 2008). Anti-bullying policies are not effective in stopping it because of the special nature of this form of bullying which allows those involved in passing on hurtful material to feel less responsible. '*It is as harmful if not more harmful than the usual forms of bullying due to the secret nature of the attack, and the invasion of personal space. Potentially harmful messages can be displayed to a large audience in minutes*' (Cowie and Jennifer, 2008). Nearly one third of all 11–16 year olds have been bullied online, and for 25 per cent of those the bullying was ongoing.

Research to date enables us to be quite confident about the specific problems that result from bullying as a consequence from the way an individual reacts to the chronic stress of being consistently involved in predictable, aggressive and humiliating situations. In latest research (Petrov, 2020) with young people showed that:

- » only 38 per cent of cyberbullying victims are willing to admit it to their parents;
- » 34 per cent of kids in the US have experienced cyberbullying at least once;
- » cyberbullying victims are 1.9 times more likely to commit suicide;
- » 210 out of 1000 victims of bullying are high school girls with different skin colour;
- » 68 per cent of children through online harassment have experienced mental health issues;

» 42 per cent of LGBT youth have experienced cyberbullying;

» 33 per cent of teenagers have sent explicit images or text to someone else at least once;

» 66 per cent of female victims have feelings of powerlessness because of cyberbullying.

# Sexual exploitation of children

First identified as a global concern at the Stockholm World Congress against Commercial Sexual Exploitation of Children (CSEC) in 1996, CSEC is a complex problem that requires very specific interventions and the full attention of the world community. CSEC can take many forms, each with equally devastating consequences for children and the communities in which it occurs. The main forms of CSEC are child prostitution, child pornography and trafficking of children for sexual purposes. One form of CSEC that has received considerable media and public attention over the past 15 years is child sex tourism (CST). It is also sometimes referred to as sexual exploitation of children in tourism (SECT). Child sex tourism occurs in multiple tourism destinations and even in places which do not have any real tourism infrastructure. It is one of the greatest tests of an increasingly connected world and an important challenge to the ever-expanding travel and tourism industries.

*There are many factors that make obtaining accurate data a challenge. Firstly, since child sex tourism is an illegal activity, it is mostly hidden or involves organised criminal groups. Secondly, it is a topic that is still regarded as a taboo subject: in many parts of the world, key stakeholders deny the existence of the issue or downplay it, fearing that highlighting it will produce a negative image of the destination and hinder tourism development. In addition, there is a general lack of understanding and confusion on the issue by the key actors in law enforcement, government, the media and the community as a whole.*

(ECPAT, 2008)

Countries in North, Central and South America have all experienced child sex tourism, albeit in different ways and to varying degrees. Often, CST in this region has followed the industrialised-to-developing-country pattern, with Canadian and American nationals travelling to countries in Central and South America in order to take advantage of their wealth and engage in CSEC. Some destinations have experienced the phenomenon of CST for over 20 years, while others, such as Colombia, have only recently begun to experience it. Many African countries have encouraged tourism to attract foreign investment and to fund infrastructure development. While this, coupled with a renewed focus on Africa from tourist-sending countries, has sparked tourism growth on the African continent, this growth has, predictably, been accompanied by an increase in CST. While the problem has been associated with several countries in West and North Africa, such as Morocco and Senegal, it seems that other countries and regions of the continent are experiencing an influx of tourists seeking sex with children, including those from within the region, as in the case of Kenya (Ecpat, 2008).

More than any other region, Asia, particularly Southeast Asia and certain countries in South Asia, has long been the target of child sex tourists. Thailand and the Philippines, partly due to their existing sex industries, have been frequently associated with child sex tourism. However, other countries have emerged as prime child sex tourist destinations: Cambodia and Vietnam are said to have suffered an influx of child sex tourists as a result of increased efforts to combat the issue in Thailand. Countries such as Mongolia have also witnessed a growth in the abuse of children by tourists, showing that sexual exploitation of children in tourism shifts as political, economic and social development occurs (Unodc, 2014).

According to the latest Home Office research into child sexual abuse during the pandemic (Home Office, 2021), there is evidence from third-sector partners to suggest that child sexual abuse may have increased during the pandemic. The NSPCC saw a threefold increase in Childline counselling sessions about child sexual abuse within the family between March and May 2020, from an average of eight sessions per week before the restrictions were imposed to an average of 23 per week. Over a quarter of Childline counselling sessions about sexual abuse within the family related to abuse that has happened recently. Between April and August 2020, NSPCC also saw an 11 per cent increase in Childline counselling sessions about online sexual abuse, as well as a 60 per cent increase in contacts from adults concerned about children experiencing online sexual abuse.

Offenders and potential offenders are likely to have spent more time online, with limited or no access to usual employment, recreation or social networks that may prevent harmful or abusive behaviour. The Lucy Faithfull Foundation have seen an increase in use of their preventative resources for child sexual abuse, which support those with concerns about their own or another's behaviour. Between spring and autumn 2020, the average number of weekly users of their offender-focused website, *Stop It Now!*, increased by 128 per cent. The risk to children of online sexual abuse, alongside other forms of online harm, is likely to have increased as a result of isolation measures, with children being educated and spending more time online. There was a sustained increase in public reports to the National Crime Agency's (NCA) Child Exploitation and Online Protection (CEOP) command in the summer of 2018 with 29 per cent more reports received compared with the same period in 2019.

In 2020, the Internet Watch Foundation also processed 16 per cent more reports containing child sexual abuse material compared to 2019, equating to millions of images and videos. Of these reports, there was an increase of 77 per cent in images and videos containing self-generated child sexual abuse content compared to 2019's total. This may indicate an increase in children being groomed or forced to perform sexual acts and/or an increase in sexting, which can constitute harmful sexual behaviour and make children and young people vulnerable to blackmail and abuse. Home is not the safe space it should be for all children and lockdown measures may have increased the risk around forms of intra-familial abuse.

*However, children may also have had some protection from intra-familial abuse because of the presence of non-abusing parents, carers or family members in the home. At the height of lockdown restrictions, the risks around contact child sexual exploitation outside of the home may be decreased due to children, young people and perpetrators being forced to stay at home. As restrictions are eased, risks around contact exploitation in the community may rise as children and young people spend more time in public spaces again.*

(Home Office, 2021)

## Viewing child sexual abuse

Online child sexual abuse and exploitation (CSAE) is the latest variation of a historic timeline of abuse of children. Indecent images of children (IIOC) are images of, or depicting, a child or part of a child which are judged to be in breach of recognised standards of propriety. Examples of images considered to be indecent are those depicting a child engaging in sexual activity or in a sexual manner, through posing, actions, clothing etc. IIOC includes photographs, videos, pseudo-photographs and tracings. Online CSAE offending can take a number of different forms which include:

» **Online grooming** – The act of developing a relationship with a child to enable their abuse and exploitation both online and offline. Online platforms, such as social media, messaging and live streaming, can be used to facilitate this offending.

» **Live streaming** – Live streaming services can be used by child sex offenders (CSOs) to incite victims to commit or watch sexual acts via webcam. CSOs also stream or watch live contact sexual abuse or indecent images of children with other offenders. In some instances, CSOs will pay facilitators to stream live contact abuse, with the offender directing what sexual acts are perpetrated against the victim.

- » **Online coercion and blackmail** – The coercion or blackmail of a child by technological means, using sexual images and/or videos depicting that child, for the purposes of sexual gain (eg to obtain new IIOC or bring about a sexual encounter), financial gain or other personal gain.

- » **Possession, production and sharing of IIOC and prohibited images** – CSOs can use online platforms to store and share IIOC and prohibited images. Online platforms can also be used to facilitate the production of IIOC, for example, screen-recording of CSAE perpetrated over live streaming.

Prohibited images of children are non-photographic images, for example, CGI, cartoons etc, which portray a child engaging in sexual activity, a sexual act being performed in the presence of a child, or focus on the child's genital or anal region. The Internet Watch Foundation annual report (2019) showed the amount of child sexual abuse material hosted in Europe has risen, with a vast amount of the world's worst material being hosted on servers in the Netherlands. The IWF is the UK-based charity responsible for finding and removing images and videos of children suffering sexual abuse from the internet. It takes such reports from more than 30 countries.

*IWF figures released in their annual report show that: In 2019, almost nine in 10 (89%) known URLs containing child sexual abuse material were hosted in Europe. This compares to eight in 10 (79%) in 2018. This is followed by North America, which hosted 9% of all known child sexual abuse URLs in 2019, a fall from 18% in 2018. The Netherlands hosts 71% of the child sexual abuse content found by the IWF. This equates to 93,962 URLs. This is an increase from 2018 when the Netherlands was found to be hosting 47% of all known child sexual abuse material.*

(IWF, 2019)

As societies worldwide respond to a more open culture about reporting and investigating child abuse, the true nature and scale of child abuse is slowly being revealed. But it also shows those countries that are a long way behind in protecting children. There are historic, cultural and religious complexities in less open societies where children's rights are a low priority, yet in the most liberal, progressive nations the very openness in communications or internet access is putting children at risk and in danger.

## Chapter 8 | Changing perceptions of children

*Violence against children (VAC) encompasses all forms of physical or mental violence, injury and abuse, neglect or negligent treatment, maltreatment or exploitation, including sexual abuse.*
Article 19, United Nations Convention on the Rights of the Child 1989

# Introduction

One of the modern innovations to understand children better and inadvertently combat child abuse was the development of the subject of childhood studies, but at only 30 years old it is still in its infancy. The concept behind this development was associated among some in safeguarding services with the growing acknowledgement that child abuse and the neglect of children was continuing unchecked and the voices of children still unheard in any meaningful sense.

The corresponding interdisciplinary field of children's studies was founded at Brooklyn College of The City University of New York in 1991. It followed the UN Declaration of the Rights of the Child in 1989 (still not signed by the USA). Its aim was to promote a unified approach to the study of children and youth across the disciplines in the arts, humanities, natural and social sciences, medicine and law. This new concept of children's studies emphasises an interdisciplinary and comprehensive approach of study to children from 0 to 18 years of age (Brooklyn College, 1991).

After 1991, other academic institutions established children's studies programmes. In subsequent years, the concept of childhood studies emerged alongside the field of children's studies. There are children's studies and childhood studies programmes at academic institutions worldwide. Whereas childhood studies claims as its major focus to understand childhood, the field of children's studies, from its beginnings, made the ontological claim that children must be viewed in their fullness as human beings, as a generational and social class in all their civil, political, social, economic and cultural dimensions. From a child protection perspective, this novel development heralded a concern about the human rights of children.

# Childhood studies

Explanations for child and adolescent problems, behaviours, mental health and their roots in child abuse can be located in a macro understanding of the way childhood itself is considered and constructed by adults. According to James and Prout (1990),

*Childhood is a social construction. It is neither a natural nor a universal feature of human groups but appears as a specific structural and cultural component of many societies. Childhood is a variable of social analysis. Comparative and cross-cultural analysis reveals a variety of childhoods rather than a single or universal phenomenon. Children's social relationships and cultures require study in their own right, independent of the perspective and concern of adults.*

By using a human rights, child-centred approach to their work, social workers and other professionals need to demonstrate and incorporate in routine practice an element of awareness of how abused children actually communicate indirectly that they are or have been harmed. This can be difficult when workloads are increasing and demands on time are enormous, or there appears to be a risky situation to deal with. Teachers especially feel overwhelmed with demands on their time and the profession has a high attrition rate. It is also hard to admit to not knowing or being confused or uncertain; these are not what managers, the public and policymakers expect. Yet they may be realistic and a more accurate picture than presenting a neat, coherent explanation for a child's behaviour in a short time scale. The competitive power dynamics in interagency meetings or high-pressured child protection conferences cannot tolerate ambiguity and demand clarity, brevity and certainty. However, hasty judgements made to prevent embarrassment, protect corporate image or personal vulnerability can have long-term consequences.

The Munro review of child protection completed ten years ago (Munro, 2011) urged UK ministers to back a set of reforms designed to cut bureaucracy and place more trust in professionals. Munro argued services needed to be freed from the grip of managerialism. A targets and terror culture, which Munro argued dominated public services, left social workers and directors obsessing over performance indicators and paperwork, not what really mattered which was direct work with families. Munro argued that in trying to improve child protection services after several high profile deaths of children where social workers were involved, the system was altered in the wrong kinds of ways for so long that it ended up taking away that focus on one human being creating a respectful relationship with another human being in order to help them. The amount of time social workers spent at computers using tick box forms disturbed her, as did the way some talked about families in a completely bureaucratic way. She was also alarmed that Ofsted used computer records alone to judge the quality of care, concluding that:

*Ofsted had no evidence on whether children were actually benefitting. A lot of families were not helped, and they were possibly even harmed, by a rather indifferent social work contact that scared them and made them reluctant to ask for help.*

(Munro, 2011)

## Philosophical understandings of childhood

Philippe Ariès (1962) argued powerfully that conceptions of childhood have varied across the centuries. The very notion of a child, we now realise, is both historically and culturally conditioned. But exactly how the conception of childhood has changed historically and how conceptions differ across cultures is a matter of scholarly controversy and philosophical interest (Kennedy, 2006). Thus Ariès argued, partly on the evidence of depictions of infants in art, that the medievals thought of children as simply little adults. Shulamith Shahar (1990), by contrast, finds evidence that some medieval thinkers understood childhood to be divided into fairly well-defined stages.

Any discontinuity at least in Western conceptions of childhood arises from the dominant view of children embodying a broadly Aristotelian conception of childhood which perceives the human child as an immature version of the adult. A *'work in progress'* if you will. Matthews (2009) argues that a Piagetian-type stage theory of development tends to support a deficit conception of childhood, according to which the nature of the child is understood primarily as a configuration of deficits, missing capacities that normal adults have but children lack.

This conception, he argues, ignores or undervalues the fact that children are, for example, better able to learn a second language, or paint an aesthetically worthwhile picture, or conceive a philosophically interesting question, than those same children will likely be able to do as adults. How childhood is conceived is crucial, not just the philosophically interesting questions about children, but crucial for questions about what should be the legal status of children in society and thus how vulnerable they are to exploitation and abuse by adults.

# Culture, ethnicity and prejudice

Child abuse is now recognised as a problem of significant proportions in most cultures and the emotional and psychological consequences are well documented in the literature (Trevithick, 2000; Al-Krenawi et al, 2001; Walker and Thurston, 2006; Hann and Fertleman, 2016). Yet despite compelling evidence, practitioners still persist in ascribing other explanations for the behaviour or emotional state of minority ethnic individuals and families, for example (Walker, 2005). Even within cultures there are marked differences based on gender. A recent study of Australian children who had been sexually abused found that boys were more likely to be in contact with public mental health services than girls. Abused boys and girls were more likely to be labelled as having conduct disorders or personality disorders (Spataro et al, 2004). If a child presents with disturbed behaviour that tends to the anti-social, it's likely they will be medicated and socially restricted, rather than assessed for being sexually abused, depending on the initial professional encounter.

In addition to assessing the relevance of the orthodox developmental theories for a culturally competent understanding of child and adolescent development, there are other, less prominent but as important resources to draw upon to help inform child protection practices. Sociology may be suffering from less emphasis in UK government policy and occupational standards guidance, but it still offers a valuable conceptual tool to enable a rounded, holistic process of assessment and intervention. Sociological explanations for child and adolescent problems can be located in a macro understanding of the way childhood itself is considered and constructed by adults.

An examination of the experience of childhood around the world today shows how greatly varied it is, and how it has changed throughout history. To understand child abuse better, we need to understand how adults think about children and young people. Contemporary children in some countries are working from the ages of 8 and independent from the age of 14, whereas in other countries some do not leave home or begin work until they are 21 (Alderson, 2000; Hendrick, 1997; Bilton et al, 2002). The conventional developmental norms show how adults construct childhood and therefore how to measure children's progress and detect problems. They are, however, set down as solid absolutes and are based on notions of adults' fears about risk, lack of confidence in children and rooted in adults' own childhood experiences. These theories have had positive effects but they have also restricted the field of vision required to fully engage with and understand children and adolescents from the diversity of cultures in a multi-ethnic society.

The evolution of childhood studies as an academic field has much in common with the development of other types of multidisciplinary scholarship such as

African-American studies and women's studies. Each was initiated for the purpose of bringing to the wider public points of view that had been underrepresented, if not repressed. New developments in the field of childhood studies include the founding of international childhood studies. This is interested in how global and international structures and processes shape children's lives and cultures of childhood. Karen Wells writes in *Childhood in a Global Perspective* (Polity Press, 2009) *'that global processes and structures especially the increasing influence of international law and international NGOs, are reshaping childhood'*.

# The slowly changing status of children

Abuse of children is inextricably linked to the status of children which has undergone changes since ancient times, yet still remains of less importance socially, legally and economically. There are still very strongly held beliefs about parental authority and control of their offspring, backed up by laws that enshrine parental rights and obligations. Resistance to state interference in family matters has been a long running narrative, often used against social workers in particular with recourse to the law courts to prevent interventions designed to protect children at risk of abuse or significant harm. It is only relatively recently that children's voices have been deemed important and relevant enough to be heard in disputed cases, despite fierce resistance from family rights campaign groups. Children's rights are still a controversial subject for many people in the UK and other countries.

Medieval works of art typically depict children as miniature grown-ups. In medieval Europe, the idea of childhood did not exist. Most people were not even sure of their own age. For much of that time newborns were considered intrinsically evil, burdened with original sin from which they had to be redeemed through instruction and education. That changed in the seventeenth century, when children instead began to be seen as innocents who must be protected from harm and corruption by the adult world. Childhood eventually and slowly came to be regarded as a separate stage of life. John Locke, a seventeenth-century English philosopher, saw the mind of a newborn child as a blank sheet, to be filled in by its elders and betters. A few decades later Jean-Jacques Rousseau, a Swiss philosopher, argued that children had their own way of seeing, thinking, feeling and reasoning and should be left to develop as nature intended (Walker, 2012).

Medieval European society did not think of childhood as an important period of development, so children were not cherished as individuals. In the Middle Ages, children had no status in society and were considered as miniature adults. Children were trained to become the future productive members of society or the community.

Moreover, the young children were not expected to need any special treatment. This placid attitude was reflected deeply in the lack of schools available. The possibility of having proper education was remote, and considered to be an extravagant luxury fit only for the boys coming from wealthy families.

Children's welfare and rights were not properly recognised or acknowledged. But society's conception of childhood changed gradually over time and continued to evolve. Eventually, children were stopped being considered as a source of additional contribution to their families' financial economy. Thanks to the initiative, efforts and work of influential international figures, new concepts of childhood were introduced. James Parkinson was one of those and is better remembered for his work which led to the discovery of the neurological condition named after him. But a lesser known fact is that he was a passionate advocate for children's welfare as he witnessed the squalor and poverty in the East End of London in the early nineteenth century (Gardiner-Thorpe, 2010).

New systems and reforms were established to give status to the child. Towards the twentieth century, education replaced child labour in developed economies. Unlike previous centuries, society acknowledged the assets of the child's educational contribution, rather than their financial input. Since then, education became the main element of childhood, and has become a necessity.

Before the emergence of a youth culture or concept of teenagers which tends to be dated to the post-Second World War period, boys and girls went directly from childhood to adulthood from school to work at a young age. They were often not able to express their unique identities until they were in a position which enabled free expression, by then most appeared to conform to their role in society and did not appear to openly rebel (Bee, 1992; Bannister and Huntington, 2002). Research has acknowledged the needs of older children and young people which gave rise to studies showing the complexities in the lives of young people and their lifestyle choices (Stokes and Tyler, 2001).

Yet as young people became more empowered and their voices listened to by adults during the twentieth century, there was no real shift in the attitudes of those who sought to harm or exploit young people. According to Kelly (1996), *'the self-serving construction of paedophilia as a specific, and minority, sexual orientation acts as a useful distraction to the problem. It obscures both the widespread sexualisation of children, and girls in particular, in western cultures and the prevalence of sexual abuse'*. In one US study, a significant proportion of 193 male college students reported that they could be sexually interested in children if they were guaranteed that there would be no legal consequences (Briere and Runtz, 1989). The representation of the ideal heterosexual partner for men continues to be younger, small, slim with minimal body hair. Across many cultures, sexual access to girls and young women is often the prerogative of powerful men: chiefs, priests and religious leaders (Kelly, 1996). The Western echo of this age-old patriarchal tradition can be seen in the prerequisite young girlfriend, occasionally underage, of older rich men such as Jeffrey Epstein.

Revelations about the convicted sex offender Jeffrey Epstein gained international media attention due to his association with many high profile celebrities. In 2005, police in Palm Beach, Florida, began investigating Epstein after a parent complained that he had sexually abused her 14-year-old daughter. Epstein pleaded guilty and was convicted in 2008 by a Florida state court of procuring an underage girl for prostitution and of soliciting a prostitute. He served less than 13 months in custody, but with extensive work release. He was convicted of only these two crimes as part of a controversial plea deal, though federal officials had identified 36 girls, some as young as 14 years old, whom Epstein had sexually abused.

There is an important theme here which links male power, economic power and social status with sexual access to girls and young women:

*The separation of paedophiles in much of the clinical literature on sex offenders from all men, but also other men who sexually abuse, has involved the presumption of difference. Similarities in the forms of abuse, in the strategies abusers use to entrap, control and silence children are ignored. In this way fathers, grandfathers, uncles, brothers who abuse are hardly ever suspected of being interested in the consumption, or production, of child pornography, nor are they thought to be involved in child prostitution. This in turn means that investigations of familial sexual abuse seldom involve either searches for or questions about these forms of abuse.*

(Kelly, 1996)

This contrasts with what we know from adult survivors who tell of relatives showing them pornography, expecting them to imitate it and being required to pose for it. Some also tell of being prostituted by relatives.

# Representations of children

In 1954, William Golding's seminal book *The Lord of the Flies* was published and it has since earned the status of a classic and features on a variety of school and university curricula. The central concern of *Lord of the Flies* is believed to be the conflict between two competing impulses that exist within all human beings: the good instinct to live by rules, act peacefully and value the good of the group, and the evil impulse to savagery, cause chaos and act violently to obtain supremacy. The latter seems to gain prominence as the story unfolds. The book provides an example of how children can be perceived to act when left to a *'natural state'*, which fuels moral discourses about the need to contain, control and punish children. The murder of two-year-old James Bulger in 1993 by two ten–year-old children unleashed a wave of tabloid-fuelled outrage and debate about whether the boys were *evil* or *disturbed* and whether they were cognisant of the enormity of their actions. The case enabled a focus on the nature of children, their potential for gross crimes and the underlying causes behind their behaviour.

The novel *Lolita* published in 1955 and later turned into a movie in 1962 features a 12-year-old girl who is portrayed as a seductress, reinforcing Victorian ideas about underage girls' ability to draw innocent men into statutory rape. Critics have further noted that, since the novel is a first-person narrative by Humbert, the novel gives very little information about what Lolita is like as a person, that in effect she has been silenced by not being the book's narrator. Not only is Lolita's voice silenced, her point of view is rarely mentioned and since it is Humbert who tells the story throughout most of the novel, the reader is absorbed in Humbert's feelings. Objectifying young women is another recurring theme in sexual violence against girls and women. Christine Clegg (2000) notes that this was a recurring theme in criticism of the novel in the 1990s.

In 1984, soon after the launch of Channel 4 in the UK, a programme called *Minipops* featuring pre-teen children dressed to look much older and singing contemporary adult-themed pop songs was televised. Though the series was a success for Channel 4 (gaining 2,000,000 viewers), little thought was given to the ethics of child performers singing songs originally written for older artists and dressing and dancing in a provocative style often influenced by the original performance. Whilst embraced by children who loved the idea of ordinary children singing and dancing as they did along with their favourite songs, the show sat uneasily with some adults. This was further capped by a performance from Joanna Fisher, who covered the Sheena Easton song '9 to 5' in nightclothes and included the lyrics 'night time is the right time, we make love'.

In response, the programme began attracting criticism from commentators in the British media, who suggested that portraying children in this manner (singing songs which often contained a subtext of adult content, often in unsuitable costumes and heavy make-up) was somewhat sinister. A 1983 article in *The Observer* said:

*Is it merely priggish to feel queasy at the sight of primary school minxes with rouged cheeks, eye make-up and full-gloss lipstick belting out songs like torch singers and waggling those places where they will eventually have places? The final act of last week's show featured a chubby blonde totlette, thigh-high to a paedophile, in a ra-ra skirt and high heels; her black knickers were extensively flashed as she bounced around singing the words 'See that guy all dressed in green/He's not a man, he's a loving machine'. Kiddie porn, a shop-window full of junior jailbait? And does the show thrust premature sexual awareness onto its wide-eyed performers?*

Miss Teen USA is a beauty pageant run by the Miss Universe Organization for girls aged 14-19. Unlike its sister pageant Miss Universe, which broadcasts on Fox and Miss USA, this pageant is webcast on the Miss Teen USA website and simulcast on mobile devices and video game consoles. The pageant was first held in 1983 and was broadcast live on CBS until 2002 and then on NBC from 2003 to 2007. In March 2007, it was announced that the broadcast of the Miss Teen USA pageant on NBC had not been renewed, and that Miss Teen USA 2007 would be the final televised event. This followed declining audience figures and concerns about the sexualisation of children.

In 1996, when footage of six-year-old Jon Benét Ramsey was broadcast on television across the US of her performing onstage wearing a skimpy outfit with full make-up and hair during a child beauty pageant, viewers felt as if they were watching child pornography. With popularity of similar child beauty pageant television shows like *Toddlers & Tiaras*, the public were concerned that young contestants were being displayed as sex objects on stage. Many viewed the child's appearance as obscene or inappropriate. Children develop a sense of sexual identity during the age of adolescence and sexualisation makes this task more difficult for youth. When parents enter their child into beauty competitions, they are encouraging their children to engage in behaviours and practices that are socially associated with sexiness. According to Vernon R. Wiehe, professor in the University of Kentucky College of Social Work:

*sexualization occurs through little girls wearing adult women's clothing in diminutive sizes, the use of makeup which often is applied by makeup consultants, spray tanning the body, the dying of hair and the use of hair extensions, and assuming provocative postures more appropriate for adult models.*

(Wiehe, 2011)

# Refugee and asylum seekers

According to The Children's Society (2020), there are 13 million child refugees worldwide, with 9000 unaccompanied children applying for asylum in the UK since 2016. In 2019, European countries recorded 672,935 new asylum seekers. Nearly a third of them (202,945) were children. This represents a slight increase of 6 per cent compared to the same period in 2018 (191,800). Among children, 17,735 were considered unaccompanied while claiming asylum in Europe, a number 13 per cent less compared to 2018 (20,440). In 2019, the Syrian Arab Republic continues to be the most common country of origin among child asylum seekers, yet it currently represents only 21 per cent of child asylum seekers (compared to 24% in 2018). Other common countries of origin among child asylum seekers include Afghanistan, Iraq, Eritrea, followed by Nigeria, Turkey, Colombia and Albania. Most unaccompanied children came from Afghanistan (28%), Pakistan (8%), Syrian Arab Republic (8%) and Iraq and Eritrea (6% each). In general, 45 per cent of all child asylum seekers in 2019 were female, and most of them originated from the Syrian Arab Republic, Afghanistan and Iraq.

Similar to previous years, Germany remained the top destination for refugee and migrant children, registering 35 per cent of all child asylum applications lodged in Europe between January and December 2019 (71,420 children). According to UNICEF (2020), other European countries that recorded large numbers of child asylum seekers include France (26,160,13%), Greece (25,165, 12%), Spain (21,715, 11%) and the United Kingdom (10,295, 5%). Health professionals working with these children report high levels of mental health problems, including anxiety, nightmares, depression and self-harm, sufficient in some cases to be diagnosed as PTSD (Walker, 2019). Many of these disturbed children have witnessed the murder of family members, parents, the rape of siblings, bombing of towns and villages, emergency evacuation and loss of education.

Palestinians represent the world's largest refugee population and one of its longest standing. Military conflict and political turmoil stemming from the Arab–Israeli dispute have forced millions of Palestinians to leave their homes and seek refuge elsewhere, many more than once. The great grandchildren of the original refugees are now parents to refugee children, testimony of the duration of the dispute. The socio-economic hardship in which the Palestinian people have been living, whether it is in the Occupied Palestinian Territory (OPT) itself or in the neighbouring countries of Jordan, Syria or Lebanon, is therefore likely to continue to be a serious challenge for the new generation in the foreseeable future (UNICEF, 2011).

The lives of Palestinian children in the West Bank, including East Jerusalem and the Gaza Strip, have been heavily affected by the presence of Israeli occupation forces, settlers and checkpoints since the Six-Day War of 1967 between Israel and the Arab states. The total population of the OPT was estimated at about 3.9 million as at mid-2009: 2.4 million in the West Bank (including East Jerusalem) and 1.5 million in the Gaza Strip. As elsewhere in the region, OPT population is youthful – 52 per cent are under the age of 18, and 42 per cent under 15. Population density in the OPT is high by world standards; the 2007 estimates were 439 people per square kilometre in the West Bank (including East Jerusalem) and 3881 people per square kilometre in the Gaza Strip. The West Bank includes large areas of arid and unproductive land, most of it under total Israeli control.

# Risk taking behaviour

Children thus face challenges to develop and adjust to their changing bodies and lives and society's perception of who the young person is, and should be, can be more problematic when other influences are involved in their decision-making. Risk taking is seen behaviour that may end up in disaster, damage or injury. This can be seen as a need by the young person to walk a fine line between fearfulness and exhilaration, even though the young person may only see the thrill and not the risk.

*Influences that may lead to difficulties include responses by the young person, their family and friends to the developmental responsibilities, and ambiguity in the role of the young person during this time. This is most significant when related to family and how the young person views their place and task with this, and also more broadly the environment the young person lives within including the local community, school and peer groups.*

(Visser and Moleko, 2005)

The types of risk taking behaviour can be seen to be on a continuum, from staying out late at night, to getting into fights, committing murder, self-harming or attempting suicide. A degree of risk taking is thought to be a normal transitional behaviour during adolescence; however, extreme risk taking can lead to self-destructive activities (Visser and Moleko, 2012).

Young people who lack boundaries set by their parents to supervise and challenge high risk behaviour have more potential to continue the risk taking. The positive influence of friends and peers in reducing the involvement in risky behaviour has stimulated peer support and even peer counselling in schools and universities. Some of the factors cited above such as powerlessness and conflict can be directly linked to previous abuse; however, concerns of sexually active young teenagers is not evidenced in research studies into the subject. It is rather the case that few young people have casual sex, and multiple partners are rare (Moules and Ramsey, 1998). It is society's perception of young people that that groups of young people are more likely to cause trouble (Gregg, 1995). A common belief is that the moral decline of young people who offend or engage in anti-social activity is due to poor parenting and the breaking up of families with the destruction of family values. This contrasts with more progressive and subtle ideas about the sense of hopelessness and despair among young people, exaggerated by social deprivation, discrimination, racism and poverty.

# Perceptions of young people

Society, on the whole, does not appear to have ever had a high opinion of teenagers, with evidence going back centuries to moral panics about rebellious, destructive teenage gangs. Garrett et al (1997) reflect that it is a common view that young people are always involved in crime, violence and/or drugs evidenced by the invention of anti-social behaviour orders (ASBOs) (Slack and Yoo, 2004). Young people can, however, be understood as an oppressed group, openly discriminated against in local and national politics, and who have to struggle, mostly unnoticed, in order to overcome adult prejudice. During adolescence, young people will experience change in a number of areas: from child to adult health services, school to higher education or work, and childhood dependence to adult autonomy. This dichotomy in society's negative view of young people and the needs they have unfulfilled can also affect the services offered, as individuals may not always be seen as deserving of services which are theirs by right.

One of the starkest examples of the way children were perceived in modern societies was illustrated by the actions of the National Council for Civil Liberties (now Liberty), an advocacy group and membership organisation based in the United Kingdom, which campaigns to challenge injustice, protect civil liberties and promote human rights through the courts, in parliament and in the wider community. The Paedophile Information Exchange (PIE), an organisation that campaigned to decriminalise sex with children as young as four years of age, was happily affiliated into the National Council for Civil Liberties (NCCL) in the 1970s. In 1976, the NCCL in a submission to the Criminal Law Revision Committee of the British Parliament argued against a blanket ban on child pornography and advocated the decriminalisation of incest: *'Childhood sexual experiences, willingly engaged in, with an adult result in no identifiable damage ... The real need is a change in the attitude which assumes that all cases of paedophilia result in lasting damage'*. The NCCL also sought to place the *'onus of proof on the prosecution to show that the child was actually harmed'*.

Organisations such as Paedophile Information Exchange, a pro-paedophile activist group, and Paedophile Action for Liberation became affiliated to the pressure group for eight years from 1975 to 1983. What is instructive is the context in which this supposedly liberal, progressive campaigning organisation operated in this way at a time when liberation movements formed part of the wave of social policy and legal challenges in the post-World War II supposedly enlightened times. Anti-colonial movements worldwide were enabling self-determination and independence from former colonies throughout the 1960s and 1970s. As women's rights, gay rights and anti-racist movements began to gain traction in public consciousness, eventually leading to significant change, concerns about children were missing from these discourses. Griffin (1993) argues:

*Stories about delinquency juggle the contradictory representations of young people as victims of other 'delinquent youth', environmental conditions, psychosocial and/ or psychological characteristics, and perpetrators of delinquent activities. Whichever viewpoint becomes the accepted belief, young people who offend can be seen as a group of vulnerable individuals who need guidance to develop into mature citizens.*

Youths who persistently offend may be problematic, but in many ways they often can be seen as a product of society rather than a problem for society to treat. A study by Wilnsnack et al (1997) found that adults suffering with alcohol abuse which began in childhood were found to have been sexually abused as children. Several epidemiological studies have shown that experiencing abuse as a child increases the risk for substance abuse later in life. Adults who were abused as children often turn to drugs and alcohol as a coping mechanism for dealing with their childhood trauma. Results from a long-term study following abused children up to the age of 24 showed that physical abuse during the first five years of life predicts subsequent substance use later in life (Dube, 2003; Lansford et al, 2010).

The fact that some youths persistently offend suggests that they still receive more benefit by committing the offence than if they were to become law abiding. The seriousness of the offence may reflect their position in their group and indeed may be the only way to stay part of the group. The law abiding youth would have a different method of attaining status, but for some troubled youths it is a way of bonding with their peers. Only by giving positive reinforcements to not commit further offences can it be hoped to break the link in their potential crime career. Community supervision, rather than custodial sentencing, in youth justice that is well resourced both financially and with experienced professionals has been a positive step forward.

# Needs of young people

When exploring the needs and requirements of young people, care has to be taken to acknowledge the variety of situations that may place young people at risk and requiring help from specific services. Some young people are preparing to leave care, others are working with youth offending teams due to criminal behaviour, and some young people are challenged by leaving school and deciding their future, while others are living with abuse or long-term health or social needs. Not every young person will be seen to be in need of specific services; however, opportunities should be available for all young people to access services which are universal. Issues such as disability, culture and religion also need to be acknowledged.

*One of the themes that often appears for children and young people at risk is the difficulties of transition from child/youth services to adult services, or indeed a complete discharge from services when they leave public care. Abused children often report feeling abandoned while in care, yearn to return to even abusive households and then left to their own devices when the state discharges its parental responsibilities. While the individual needs of young people within child and youth services seem to be more in focus and a clearer picture of the care that needs to be offered compared with the past, this is still not always ideal.*

(Wilson and James, 2002)

When preparing young people to transfer to adult services, a number of different options may need to be explored related to the specific assessment of the young person's needs.

Support for the young people should change as the transition occurs between child and adult services and once the young adult is receiving services from the adult teams. This includes the success of the communication between services. Child/young people-focused services appear on the whole to be able to coordinate care between agencies and the specialist services satisfactorily. This appears to be more problematic in the move to adult services. Other challenging issues can occur for young people coming of age and leaving care, and also young offenders leaving secure units. The need to support the young adult integrating into their local community, finding appropriate housing and work or education can be hampered by the lack of resources and planning for integration. The principal risk factors associated with teenagers who have been looked after and could also relate to young offenders include:

*socio-economic deprivation; limited involvement in education; low educational attainment; limited access to consistent, positive adult support; being ... a teenage mother; low self esteem; and experience of sexual abuse, which are to be found more often in the looked after population than among children and young people who are not in care.*

(Halsey and White, 2008)

# Children in care

Children in the care of public authorities have long been recognised as a particularly vulnerable group. Yet towards the end of her term of office in 2020, the Children's

Commissioner for England delivered a damning indictment of children's social care and accused the state of too often being a bad parent. Anne Longfield had become increasingly vociferous about the shortcomings of the care system, which she accused of failing thousands of vulnerable children who are falling through the gaps and into the clutches of criminals:

*The system is in need of urgent reform and additional funding if it is to survive and protect those in its care. She called for children to be more involved in the decisions made about their care, and challenged politicians to do more than simply apply a sticking plaster to a system in crisis. When the state steps in, it needs to help set up children for life, not increase their chances of ending up on the streets or in prison. The truth is while the state can be a great parent, it can also be a really bad one. In fact, sometimes so negligent that it would risk having its children taken into care if it was an actual parent.*

(Children's Commissioner, 2021)

The Rotherham child sexual exploitation scandal consisted of the organised child sexual abuse that occurred in the town of Rotherham, South Yorkshire, Northern England, from the late 1980s until the 2010s and the failure of local authorities to act on reports of the abuse throughout most of that period which centred on children in care. Researcher Angie Heal, who was hired by local officials and warned them about child exploitation occurring between 2002 and 2007, has since described it as the biggest child protection scandal in UK history (House of Commons, 2014).

Evidence of the abuse was first noted in the early 1990s, when care home managers investigated reports that children in their care were being picked up by taxi drivers. From at least 2001, multiple reports passed names of alleged perpetrators, several from one family, to the police and Rotherham Council. Yet the first group conviction only took place in 2010, when five British-Pakistani men were convicted of sexual offences against girls aged 12–16. Up until then the police viewed girls who had absconded from the care homes and found on the streets as prostitutes were choosing a lifestyle and were criminalised instead of being seen as vulnerable and the victims of criminal offences.

Taxi drivers had been picking the children up for sex from care homes and schools. The abuse included gang rape, forcing children to watch rape, dousing them with petrol and threatening to set them on fire, threatening to rape their mothers and younger sisters, and trafficking them to other towns. There were pregnancies, one at age 12, terminations, miscarriages, babies raised by their mothers, and babies removed, causing further trauma. The failure to address the abuse was attributed to a combination of factors revolving around race, class and gender; contemptuous and sexist attitudes towards the mostly working-class victims; fear that the perpetrators' ethnicity would trigger allegations of racism and damage community relations; the

Labour Council's reluctance to challenge a Labour-voting ethnic minority; lack of a child-centred focus; a desire to protect the town's reputation; and lack of training and resources. Rotherham Council's chief executive, its director of children's services, and the police and crime commissioner for South Yorkshire Police all resigned (Gladman and Heal, 2017).

The care system in England has regularly been described as unfit for purpose, currently buffeted by COVID-19 and overwhelmed by demand as the rates of unemployment, poverty and domestic violence increased during 2020. Referrals have gone up 100 per cent in the last decade while funding has declined by 16 per cent. According to the charity Become (2020), in 2019 in England, figures show that around 3570 children in care left the care system because they were adopted, and 20 per cent of children in care left the care system because they returned to live with parents or relatives with parental responsibility as part of the care planning process. Around a third of children will return home to their birth family after a period of time spent in care, if it's decided that this is in the best interests of the child.

Other children may find a permanent new home through adoption or a special guardianship order. But for those who are in care in their late teens, in 2019, 12,560 young people left care in England aged 16, 17, 18 or older. Removing a child from their parents is the most extreme intervention the state can make in family life. Once a child or young person is in care, responsibility for their well-being falls to their *'corporate parents'*: this refers to everyone who is elected to, or employed by, a local authority, and their partner agencies, who all share a collective responsibility to the children looked after by that local authority. There are seven corporate parenting principles set out in the Children and Social Work Act 2017. These state that corporate parents must:

» act in the best interests of and promote the health and well-being of children and young people in care;

» encourage children and young people in care to express their views, wishes and feelings;

» take into account the views, wishes and feelings of children and young people in care;

» help children and young people in care to access the full range of services provided by the local authority and partners;

» promote high aspirations, and secure the best outcomes, for children and young people in care;

- » ensure the safety of children and young people and provide stability in their home lives, relationships and education;
- » prepare children and young people for adulthood and independent living.

In 2019, 10 per cent of young people left the care system aged 16 or 17 and 32 per cent left on their 18th birthday. The number of children in care in the UK in 2018 was 99,672. Over a third of children come into the care system aged four or under. Three in four children in care live with foster carers. One in ten children in care have three or more care placements in a year. Around 11,000 young people leave care aged 16, 17 or 18 each year. Disrupted care, multiple placements and feeling abandoned after leaving care is not the way to prepare already abused and neglected children for adulthood, but a sure way to make them vulnerable to exploitation and further abuse. Care leavers have been the subject of concern for many decades and while some positive improvements have been made to their experiences after leaving care, and while they have been looked after in many cases, they still too regularly appear in the juvenile system, or mental health services, in highly disproportionate numbers. They deserve so much better.

## Chapter 9 | Children's rights and parent support

*Defend the children of the poor, punish the wrongdoer.*
Inscription at the Old Bailey in London

# Introduction

The wording above the Old Bailey in London, reproduced above, could be seen as rather cruelly ironic, given the way the British justice system has let children down over the years. Clever, highly paid defence lawyers have savaged and attacked children in court proceedings brought against child abusers. It was only very recently that the legal system began to listen to children's advocates, social workers and psychologists who had argued for decades that child witnesses were acutely vulnerable as they attempted to recall horrific attacks by their abusers. Changes brought about by pressure now enable testimony to be given remotely via video link, shielding children from their abusers.

The low conviction rate (as in rape cases brought by women and girls) was recognised as inconsistent with the facts revealed in countless research surveys among children and females of the veracity of their experiences (Walker, 2012). Children were accused in public courts by male lawyers of being liars, wicked and unreliable witnesses. Their cases were hampered by the lack of witnesses, corroboration or forensic evidence. Most paedophiles or family members abuse in secret and are careful not to leave forensic clues. Children reported feeling re-abused and traumatised by the experience of going to court and mocked by their abusers. In one study in the USA, researchers discovered that less than 20 per cent of cases went forward to trial and of those less than half resulted in a prosecution or guilty plea (Cross and Whitcomb, 2017). There were fewer prosecutions for child abuse-flagged cases in the latest year in the UK. In the year ending March 2019, the Crown Prosecution Service recorded 8814 defendants prosecuted in child abuse cases. This was a fall of 18 per cent from the previous year total of 10,704. The number of defendants proceeded against for child sexual abuse offences has fallen by 31 per cent in the latest year data available (ONS, 2019).

# The study of child abuse and neglect

The study of child abuse and neglect emerged as an academic discipline in the early 1970s in the United States. Elisabeth Young-Bruehl (2013) maintains that despite the growing numbers of child advocates and interest in protecting children which took place, the grouping of children into the abused and the non-abused created an artificial distinction that narrowed the concept of children's rights to simply protection from maltreatment, and blocked investigation of the ways in which children are discriminated against in society generally. Another effect of the way child abuse and neglect have been studied, according to Young-Bruehl, was to close off consideration of how children themselves perceive maltreatment and the importance they place on adults' attitudes towards them. Young-Bruehl writes *'that when the belief in children's inherent inferiority to adults is present in society, all children suffer whether or not their treatment is labelled as abuse'*.

Young-Bruehl places the roots of child abuse in a wider context of societal prejudice and discrimination and it is a clue to why it persists. Childism is the hardest form of prejudice to recognise because children are the one group that, many of us think without thinking, is naturally subordinate. The older term *misopedia* coined in the eighteenth century has fallen out of fashion; yet it originated in classical Greece where similar group-hatred terms originated such as *misanthropy* and *misogyny*.

The concept of obeying parents without question, or parents punishing the child who steps out of line, has the potential for wider implications, according to Miller (1985). She suggests such obsession with conformity and denial of a child's open feelings can produce later adults who are susceptible to authoritarian or totalitarian political regimes. These regimes demand unquestioning obedience and conformity to an ideology based on hatred towards free thinking, questioning and open-mindedness.

Childism takes many forms. In the half-century-old field called child abuse and neglect (CAN), four main types of child maltreatment have been identified: physical abuse, neglect, sexual abuse and emotional abuse. But these categories do not reflect how frequently the four types overlap in a given case.

*Thinking in terms of childism that intends to eliminate or destroy children, to make them play roles no child should play or to dominate them totally, reveals the dark inner world of adults narcissistically erasing their own identities. Survivors of child abuse make clear that the worst part of their experience the most difficult to heal from, the least forgivable was that no one protected them from it. They often make it clear, as well, that they have internalised the prejudice and direct it toward themselves. This explains the high rates of self harm among survivors of abuse.*

(Young-Bruehl, 2013)

# Legally sanctioned beating of children

The legality of corporal punishment of children varies by country. Corporal punishment of minor children by parents or adult guardians, which is any punishment intended to cause physical pain, has been traditionally legal in nearly all countries unless explicitly outlawed. According to Human Rights Watch (2010), 90 per cent of the world's children live in countries where corporal punishment and other physical violence against children is still legal. Many countries' laws provide for a defence of '*reasonable chastisement*' against charges of assault and other crimes for parents using corporal punishment. This defence is ultimately derived from English law. Only 65 countries worldwide out of a total of 195 have banned corporal punishment as of 2020, the first being Sweden in 1979.

In England, criminal law has a general prohibition against common assault and battery, but corporal punishment is legal through tradition and an implicit common law justification/defence (R v Hopley 2F&F 202, 186) to such charges for parents striking their children in the context of lawful correction where the act is '*moderate and reasonable*'. The Children Act 2004 effectively provides a statutory definition of '*immoderate*' by disallowing this justification for any act of punishment inflicting injuries or effects that amount to wounding, actual bodily harm (ABH), or any act considered cruelty to persons under 16 in violation of the Children and Young Persons Act 1933 and was described at implementation as criminalising visible bruising and rendering lesser injuries (comparable to not serious common assault) implicitly lawful/defensible. This legal quagmire explicitly disregards and appears immune to the idea that the act of being physically chastised is felt by the child as humiliation, frightening and triggering feelings of low self-esteem and potential depression (Walker, 2019).

The total abolition of corporal punishment has been discussed many times in the media and excites considerable debate. In a 2004 poll by the advocacy group Children are Unbeatable!, 71 per cent of respondents supported giving children the same protection against battery as for adults '*if it would not lead to parents being prosecuted for trivial or minor acts of physical punishment*'. In a 2006 survey, 80 per cent of the population said they believed in smacking, and 73 per cent said they believed that any ban would cause a sharp deterioration in children's behaviour. Seven out of ten parents said they themselves use corporal punishment. In a 2012 poll conducted by Angus Reid Public Opinion, 63 per cent of Britons voiced opposition to banning parents in the UK from smacking their children. However, in 2019 the Welsh assembly voted to end all corporal punishment in Wales which will take effect in 2022. Similar legislation came into full effect in Scotland in November 2020.

Use of force against young people in custody is at a five-year high (ONS, 2019). The average monthly rate in 2018–19 was 46.6 per 100 children. Pain-inducing techniques had been used 251 times (slightly down from 260 in 2017–18). Children suffered a total of 254 injuries as a result of use of force during 2018–19, of which 19 were serious and required hospital treatment. The European Committee of Social Rights, a body responsible for monitoring compliance with the European Social Charter, ratified by the UK government in 1962, has found the UK in breach of its obligations. The report concluded that children's rights to economic and social protection are systematically breached by the UK government in several ways. This includes lack of prohibition of all forms of corporal punishment, low age of criminal responsibility (which is 10 years in England and Wales) and the use of pain-inducing restraint techniques in child prisons. The Committee reminded the UK government that the use of pain-inducing restraint has been previously opposed by the UN Committee Against Torture, the European Committee for the Prevention of Torture and the UN Committee on the Rights of the Child, as well as labelled a form of child abuse by the Independent Inquiry into Child Sexual Abuse (IICSA).

## Prevention and response

Violence against children can be prevented and many children's services staff use non-violent techniques which parents can be taught in order to modify a child's behaviour and keep them safe. Preventing and responding to violence against children requires that efforts systematically address risk and protective factors at all four interrelated levels (individual, relationship, community, society). Under the leadership of WHO, a group of ten international agencies have developed and endorsed an evidence-based technical package called INSPIRE: Seven strategies for ending violence against children. The package aims to help countries and communities achieve targets on ending violence against children. Each letter of the word INSPIRE stands for one of the strategies, and most have been shown to have preventive effects across several different types of violence, as well as benefits in areas such as mental health, education and crime reduction. The seven strategies are:

» implementation and enforcement of laws, for example, banning violent disciplining and restricting access to alcohol and firearms;

» norms and values change, for example, altering norms that condone the sexual abuse of girls or aggressive behaviour among boys;

» safe environments such as identifying neighbourhoods which are 'hot spots' for violence and then addressing the local causes through problem-oriented policing and other interventions;

- » parental and caregiver support, for example, providing parent training to young, first-time parents;
- » income and economic strengthening such as microfinance and gender equity training;
- » response services provision, for example, ensuring that children who are exposed to violence can access effective emergency care and receive appropriate psychosocial support;
- » education and life skills such as ensuring that children attend school, and providing life and social skills training.

In May 2016, a World Health Assembly resolution endorsed the first ever WHO Global Plan of Action on strengthening the role of the health system within a national multisectoral response to address interpersonal violence against women and girls, in particular, and against children. According to this plan, WHO in collaboration with member states and other partners is committed to monitoring the global magnitude and characteristics of violence against children and supporting country efforts to document and measure such violence (WHO, 2016).

Maintaining an electronic information system that summarises the scientific data on the burden, risk factors and consequences of violence against children, and the evidence for its preventability is paramount. It is crucial to develop and disseminate evidence-based technical guidance documents, norms and standards for preventing and responding to violence against children. Regularly publishing global status reports on country efforts to address violence against children through national policies and action plans, laws, prevention programmes and response services provides external scrutiny. Countries and partners need support in implementing evidence-based prevention and response strategies, such as those included in INSPIRE: Seven strategies for ending violence against children. Finally collaborating with international agencies and organizations to reduce and eliminate violence against children globally, through initiatives such as the Global Partnership to End Violence against Children, Together for Girls and the Violence Prevention Alliance, is critical (WHO, 2016).

As the most widely adopted human rights treaty, the Convention on the Rights of Child (CRC) *'has had significant impact on domestic legal systems throughout the world and on domestic legislation in particular'* (Liefaard and Doek, 2015). A UNICEF study of child rights legislation in 52 state parties showed a trend, since the CRC was adopted, towards establishing additional legislation on child sexual exploitation in Asia, Latin America, Central, Eastern and Western Europe, as well as in some Middle

Eastern and African states. Such legislation includes the introduction of a legal age for children, the criminalisation of child prostitution and the use of child pornography, the recognition of child trafficking, and the introduction of protection measures for child witnesses (UNICEF, 2007).

Some states, such as Japan, also recognised the jurisdiction of their domestic courts over sexual offenses committed against children outside the state. By 2011, a UN survey of 100 states' progress on preventing and responding to child sexual abuse and exploitation (CSA/E) found that 90 per cent had specific legislation prohibiting child sexual exploitation, including in prostitution and child sexual abuse materials (pornography) (Radford et al, 2015). Dubowitz (2017) offers the most recent global assessment of state-level legal definitions and responses to CSA/E, based on surveillance data collected on 73 countries by the International Society for the Prevention of Child Abuse and Neglect (ISPCAN). Most respondent states (86%) were found to have a clear legal definition of child sexual abuse (CSA), with Asia being the only region to score lower than 80 per cent (75%), though definitions among states differ (Dubowitz, 2017).

Internationally, the most frequent legal responses to child sexual exploitation involve targeting perpetrators domestically. About 79 per cent of respondent states made an arrest of an adult in the previous year for child sexual exploitation (CSE), 72 per cent made an arrest in the previous year for child pornography and 69 per cent reported often or sometimes prosecuting citizens who engage in CSE in the home country (Dubowitz, 2017).

# Parenting support

Just as family therapists today find that child abuse often functions to hold families together as a way of solving their parents' emotional problems, so, too, the routine assault of children has been society's most effective way of maintaining its collective emotional homeostasis (Walker and Akister, 2004). In recent years, a growing body of evidence has demonstrated the effectiveness of parenting programmes in changing parenting attitudes and behaviours, improving parental mental health, and preventing or improving children's social, emotional and behavioural difficulties (Furlong et al, 2013; Walker, 2019). Three key strategic findings emerged from research led by Joseph Rowntree Foundation examining this issue (Bywaters et al, 2016):

> » There should be widespread recognition of the strong association between families' socio-economic circumstances and children's chances of being

subject to abuse or neglect. It is essential that this association is framed as a public issue and matter of avoidable social inequality, not as a further source of shame and pressure on individual disadvantaged families.

» Programmes should be developed and implemented to rectify the limited data and evidence base in the UK on the extent and nature of the association between families' socio-economic circumstances and child abuse and neglect (CAN), the consequences in adult life, and the economic costs, and to test explanatory models through research.

» Effective anti-poverty policies should be developed and connected with policies aimed at reducing inequities in child health and education, explicitly incorporating a focus on their relevance for CAN. In particular, the impact of anti-poverty policies on CAN for different groups of children should be considered and addressed, especially different age groups, disabled children, all ethnic groups and children living in particularly disadvantaged neighbourhoods.

It has been established that a confluence of several risk factors in childhood can create the conditions for adult psychosocial difficulty, including in particular socio-economic disadvantage, child abuse and parental mental illness. But there are protective mechanisms that can mitigate the chance of some children going on to develop anti-social behaviour or serious mental health problems. These can be obscured by the imperative for medical diagnosis or the overreactions of inexperienced child protection professionals or untrained volunteer family support workers. Feminist-informed practice can help women challenge these notions which in child protection cases can sometimes carry the double bind of making them feel at fault while insisting they are the only parent who can do the job (Walker, 2003).

The consequent lack of support and eventual mother-blaming highlight the importance of assessment methods in child protection contexts informed by systems theory that take account of not just individual characteristics within the child but equally within the family and broader social environment. It is unlikely this holistic level of assessment is available to unqualified family support workers or volunteers in charitable activity however well-intentioned. These tend to be the lowest paid, least supervised and lowest qualified employee or volunteer. A social model of family life incorporating the continental European heritage of social action could enlarge the panorama and depth of assessment activity. In combination, a sophisticated assessment process using systems theory identifying strengths and protective factors, together with a more explicit social mandate, could create a chain of indirect links that foster improved family functioning in a context of social inclusion (Walker and Thurston, 2006).

In a government policy consultation paper in 1999 'Supporting Families', the focus of attention emphasised better support and education for current and future parents as a preventive strategy. Key themes included the intention to improve advice and information to parents, and achieving a reduction in child poverty, while offering financial help for working parents. Yet 20 years later the UK's social safety net had been *'deliberately removed and replaced with a harsh and uncaring ethos'*, according to a senior UN official. Special rapporteur on extreme poverty Philip Alston said ideological cuts to public services since 2010 have led to tragic consequences after he visited numerous communities and witnessed devastating scenes of poverty (BBC, 2019).

Various initiatives aimed at children and their families living in disadvantaged areas such as the Sure Start programme (1998) were evidence of the practical implementation of the implicit preventive aspects of policies which were based on evidence of success from the USA Head Start scheme (Newman, 2004). This scheme demonstrated long-term reductions in anti-social activity, marital problems, child abuse, adult mental health difficulties and unemployment in later life, in a group of children who received the intervention with a comparison of children who did not receive the intervention.

Quantifying the impact of preventive family support work is complex and to achieve systematic results is expensive; therefore, there is little in the way of evidence of long-term effectiveness in Britain or elsewhere (Walker, 2012). However, there are signs that while outcome measures from various projects are intangible, small-scale social action projects can evidence changes in relationships between parents and professionals, how to work in partnership, how to engage positively with parents, and ways to reduce child abuse (Robbins et al, 2006). All of these contributed to supporting families better and were experienced as accessible and more user-focused.

## What helps protect children?

The lessons for child protection practice are for emphasising empowering strategies, searching hard for creative solutions beyond narrow service-led resources, and refining relationship-building skills. This challenges the service management orthodoxy and financial constraints for short-term focused assessments aimed at identifying risk and need according to a limited range of resources. A different approach based on long-term effectiveness does not fit with the short-term political imperatives based on legislature's calendars. It offers the opportunity to provide professionally qualified staff with more satisfying work over longer time periods, and provides service users the chance to feel respected, valued, contained and supported in a consistent and reliable way. The prospect is for combining the best features of welfare practice grounded in a solid psychosocial systems theoretical base.

Parent education or training programmes have expanded in the face of exponential demand for help from parents in modern times, to deal with a range of child and adolescent difficulties, ranging from toddler tantrums to suicide attempts, eating disorders, to cyber bullying and drug and alcohol addiction (Moran et al, 2004). This form of intervention is popular and is now expected to be offered as part of a repertoire of contemporary family support measures, with a desired reduction in child abuse. Studies of parent education programmes, which while they are limited in number, show they can be an effective way of supporting families and reducing child abuse. They highlight the impact group-based behaviourally oriented programmes have in producing the biggest subsequent changes and are perceived by parents as non-stigmatising. Programmes where both parents are involved and which include individual work with children are more likely to affect long-term changes (Walker, 2012a).

However, parent education/training programmes, while enjoying a growth in popularity in Britain and other European countries, are generally not subject to rigorous evaluation. Research shows that in a number of studies 50 per cent of parents continue to experience difficulties, and it is not clear to what extent changes are due to the format, the method of intervention, the group support or the practitioner's skills. *'High attrition rates from some programmes are attributed to practitioner variables such as their level of qualification and experience, and qualities such as warmth, enthusiasm, or flexibility'* (Lindsay and Totsika, 2017). There is also some evidence that by operating a gender-neutral format, meaning the service is offered without restrictions or eligibility, men find it difficult to attend and engage in groups where discussion of feelings and partner relationships is a focus. Equally women with abusive partners present can feel further disempowered in such contexts where they cannot open up to explain their domestic circumstances for fear of retribution. It may also be the case that some programmes are inappropriate for parents lacking motivation or feeling compelled to attend under the pressure of child protection concerns.

Few British studies have used randomised controlled trials which inhibit identification of the most beneficial elements of a programme, and because most provision is geared to rectifying problems in socially disadvantaged groups, the available research evidence reflects that bias. Those that have been conducted are nevertheless yielding important qualitative data from stakeholders' perspectives (Barlow et al, 2007).

It is argued that the tendency for the masculine managerialist preference for evaluating work on the basis of the three E's (efficiency, effectiveness, economy) reflects a limited agenda for quantitative outcome measures. These data need to be supplemented with the three P's (partnership, pluralism, process) which better reflect feminist-informed principles seeking to incorporate service users' perspectives (Dominelli, 2002). Further studies which pay attention to realistic models of parenting in the community would counter this bias by identifying skills that lead to successful parenting by focusing on what went right, rather than what went wrong.

It is also noteworthy that the views of parents and children are largely absent from the research, particularly in families with lone parents, gay and lesbian parents, and step-parents. There is also very little systematic incorporation of culture and ethnicity as factors influencing parenting styles, or on disability and the particular issues facing parents with disabled children who may have emotional and behavioural problems, and on gender influences within families and within professional groups. A systems approach offers a perspective that can incorporate and address every possible social, political, economic, psychological and relational influence on family experience. Families for whom parent education is unlikely to be a sufficient response to child management difficulties are those which feature maternal depression, socio-economic disadvantage and the social isolation of the mother (Quinton, 2004). Extra-familial conflict combined with relationship problems contribute to the problem severity and chronicity and therefore influence the ability of support staff to introduce change.

Parenting education or training programmes seem to be a response to a demand for a variety of support, including information, child development knowledge and skills development in managing children of all ages. The continuation of the fragmentation of families in the industrialised European economies corresponds with social and economic mobility and are a feature of everyday life. This results in unstable communities where friends, relatives, female and male networks become transient while traditional grandparent figures are often missing or live long distances apart. There is thus little in the way of a secure emotional and social base for vulnerable parents to use as a resource and increases the chances of child abuse and neglect as vulnerable parents are pushed to a breaking point. The concept of family support in Britain is currently perceived as an alternative to child protection, rather than part of a connected architecture of resources to be activated as different needs emerge. Therefore, the public policy to develop indirect voluntary provision of family support services in Britain can be better seen as a symptom of, rather than solution to, retrenchment in family support offered by professional workers using creative approaches.

## Developing progressive practice

One way that children's services can tilt the balance away from repressive child protection procedures and illustrate the pragmatic use of progressive practices, is reflected in the example of family group conferences (FGCs). Introduced some years ago and borrowing from New Zealand Maori traditional practices, they have challenged the orthodoxy in British social services planning which places primacy on the professional social worker's power, values and perceptions. The key idea in these conferences is that family meetings are convened where there are concerns about the welfare of a child or children. The family in these circumstances is defined widely and extended family members are encouraged to participate. Their task is to create their own plan for the child of concern by assuming responsibility in deciding how to meet the needs of the child (Morris and Tunnard, 1996).

Thus the social worker's role changes dramatically from an inspectorial/adversarial role largely prescribed by procedures and a restricted definition of their task, to one more consistent with the skills and knowledge of family therapy. In the context of family group conferences, social workers can emphasise communication, negotiation, mediation and facilitation skills that are better informed by a systems approach seeking to emphasise problem-solving and highlight the strengths within a family system. At the heart of the family group conference is a re-definition of social work practice with children and families. It puts into sharp focus a tangible example of the elusive and often ill-defined notion of empowering practice. It is a challenge to social work that is driven by a defensive culture and to social workers comforted by the ability to retreat into procedural safety when faced with complexity, uncertainty and the normal swings and roundabouts of family life (Morris and Tunnard, 1996).

## Children's rights

Children, like adults, also have the right, under the terms of the UN Convention, to be consulted with, and to express their views, about services provided for them (UN 1989 Article 12). In some public services in England there is a legal duty to consult them in order to ascertain their wishes and feelings (Children Act, 1989). An examination of some contemporary contributions on the subject of consulting with children and young people reveals a mixed picture in terms of effectiveness, inclusion, methodologies and ethical considerations.

Hennessey (1999) in a meta-review of a collection of research studies on this subject concluded that with the increasing interest in seeking children's views there need to be better developed instruments for measuring satisfaction and gaining children's evaluation of the services they receive, such as child protection/safeguarding. Only a minority of studies examined had presented information on the structure, reliability and validity of the instruments they used. Most of the studies concerned education contexts, the paediatric studies treated parents as the sole clients, while in mental health studies the correspondence between children's and parents' evaluations of services seemed to be greater.

The extent to which children's evaluations are similar to the evaluations of parents raises important questions about validity. It can be assumed that perceptions should be different, but in the area of child and adolescent mental health, for example, differences in perception of the help received can indicate that the underlying cause of the difficulty remains untreated as in child abuse cases. In the case of a child, this can result in symptom deterioration reinforcing parental perceptions that it is the child who has the problem. Or such a consequence can produce a resistance from the child at an older age to engaging with further help, thereby contributing to the development of mental health problems into adulthood.

It is important to explore the extent to which services are meeting the needs of differing groups of children in terms of age, gender, ethnicity, religion and socio-economic status. The research on the relationship between client satisfaction in mental health services is better developed than in any other service sector. Three types of outcome have been used: client-assessed, parent-assessed and therapist-assessed. There are inconsistent findings reported for the relationship between client satisfaction and therapist evaluation of treatment progress. The problem of practitioner power and status is regarded as influential in determining the ability of children and young people to express discontent with help offered. It is recognised that children and young people feel under pressure to say what they expect the practitioner to hear (Walker, 2012b).

A few studies have looked at the relationship with personal and/or family variables. Understanding these relationships is potentially important for understanding the way in which services may or may not be meeting the needs of various clients. The information currently available is limited. There have been relatively small numbers of attempts to do this and those that have, used different measures. The National Audit Office (NAO) and the House of Commons Committee of Public Accounts have reported local authorities' finances and services are increasingly under strain. In 2016, the Committee of Public Accounts concluded that:

*the Department seemed worryingly complacent that nothing could be done to improve children's services more quickly, and that it lacked a credible plan for how and by when it would make a difference and ensure that local authorities were intervening effectively to make a difference to children's lives. Until recently, the Department has not seen it as a central part of its responsibilities to understand drivers in demand for children's social care across all local authorities. Unless adequate and effective children's social care is in place, children in need of help or protection will be exposed to neglect, abuse or harm.*

Age is a particularly important variable in understanding and empowering young people because of the different cognitive, social and emotional needs and abilities of children of different ages. Although individual research studies differed in whether younger or older clients were more satisfied with help provided, a sufficient number of studies reported a moderate or high correlation between age and satisfaction/dissatisfaction (Shapiro, 1997). Only a small number of studies have explored the relationship between gender and satisfaction but the evidence suggests no general tendency for greater satisfaction to be associated with either boys or girls. A more useful approach may be to explore the relationship between client/staff gender combinations (Bernzweig et al, 1997).

There is very little evidence in most studies to demonstrate what impact their findings had on service development or practitioner attitudes and skills. A shift in thinking is required from perceiving children and young people as recipients of health promotion efforts on their behalf or child protection procedures, to accepting children and young people as active participants in the whole process. Another gap in the literature is the limited information on how children and young people felt about being asked their views on the service that they had received. Some children may feel perturbed by this while others are enthusiastic about being given the opportunity to be part of a reflective process.

## Listening to children

Few studies have been undertaken with regard to therapeutic interventions with children and young people experiencing emotional and behavioural difficulties and whether they found the therapy helpful. Abused children are in a bind when it comes to disclosing abuse by parents or other family members during therapy, mindful of the negative consequences. Similar reluctance to disclose abuse or involve the police are found in domestic abuse cases where women fear being further harmed or harassed by a partner/husband. Those undertaken have found generally children speak less than parents when interviewed together; adolescents express themselves in limited ways tending to agree/disagree, while therapists spoke more often to parents than to children when attempting to evaluate the help and support offered (Cederborg, 1997; Walker, 2012). The question is whether this reflects a generalisable aversion to participating in research of this nature or whether the research design militates against inclusion and active participation.

Practitioners have built up a repertoire of therapeutic methods in working with children and young people, and engaging with them in areas of great sensitivity such as bereavement, parental separation or sexual abuse. The same repertoire of research techniques is yet to be developed to ensure that children and young people are being given the best possible chance of contributing to service evaluation.

Strickland-Clark et al (2000) suggest that children's reactions to therapy can be influenced by their attachment style. In families where there are insecure attachments, for example, children can feel constrained to speak more freely because of fears of what the consequences might be and the discomfort in exposing painful or difficult feelings. Ways to engage such children have been developed and could be adapted by researchers. This poses important challenges for practitioners and researchers wanting to research in areas where there are factors likely to inhibit participation. The alternative is to automatically exclude some children and young people and thereby miss the opportunity to gather valuable evidence to improve service provision rather than designing strategies to overcome these difficulties.

Therapy can be usefully evaluated in terms of peoples' experiences of helpful versus unhelpful events. Many studies have simply adapted adult methodologies and applied them to child populations. These are inappropriate. There is nevertheless, an emerging trend to move towards emphasising children's competencies and strengths in being able to describe their own perceptions (Clark and Statham, 2005).

When efforts are made to overcome resistance to incorporating children and young persons' perceptions there is much evidence of creative and sensitive work being undertaken. Hazel (1995) reviewed a number of studies of methods for interviewing children for research evaluation purposes. The conclusion was that there are a number of factors that help a researcher in gaining confidence and the co-operation of young people, together with their perceptions and views. The fieldwork setting needs to achieve a balance between privacy needed for confidential data collection, and openness to public scrutiny for assuring the personal safety of the young person and minimise any risk of allegations of impropriety against the researcher.

Vignettes of relevant social situations presented to a group of children for comment may be a particularly useful tool to use at the beginning of an interview to break the ice and encourage someone other than the researcher to speak. Discussion can then be facilitated around the opinions expressed or particular terms used in the participants' comments. Short stories, presenting well-known catchphrases or sayings, or presenting a problem in the style of a teenage magazine as well as creative work with focus groups and artistic expression can all be used to enable free expression and quality information.

Another area with the potential to provide a rich source of information is in non-verbal communication. The advantage of developing methodologies for interpreting this level of communication is that it can enable access to much younger children's perceptions and those with disabilities, sensory impairments or developmental delays (NSPCC, 2020).

# Human Rights Act 1998

The Human Rights Act (UN, 1998) came into force in 2000 and incorporates into English law most of the provisions of the European Convention on Human Rights. The act applies to all authorities undertaking functions of a public nature, including all care providers in the public sector. The Human Rights Act supports the protection and improvement of the health and welfare of children and young people throughout the United Kingdom. Article 3 concerns freedom from torture and inhuman or degrading treatment. Children and young people who have been subjected to restraint, seclusion or detention as a result of alarming behaviour because of child abuse could use this part of the act to raise complaints.

Article 5 concerns the right to liberty, and together with Article 6 concerning the right to a fair hearing, is important to children and young people detained under a section of the Mental Health Act, the Children Act or within the youth justice system. Social workers involved in such work must ensure that detention is based on sound opinion, in accordance with clearly laid out legal procedures accessible to the individual, and only lasts for as long as the mental health problem persists. If the underlying cause of the problem is child abuse, these measures can be felt by the child as doubly harmful. In the context of youth justice work, particular attention needs to be paid to the quality and tone of pre-sentence reports which can be stigmatising. The formulaic structure of pre-sentence reports might not enable an assessing social worker, working under deadline pressure, to provide an accurate picture of a young person, who could have endured years of neglect (Walker, 2019).

Article 8 guarantees the right to privacy and family life. Refugees and asylum seeking families can become entangled in complex legal procedures relating to citizenship and entitlement. This provision can be invoked when UK authorities are considering whether a person should be deported or remain in this country. Compassionate grounds can be used for children affected by the proposed deportation of a parent or in cases where a parent is not admitted. Social workers attuned to the attachment relationships of often small children can use this knowledge to support Article 8 proceedings. In such circumstances, the maintenance of the family unit is paramount (Walker, 2011).

Social workers involved in care proceedings or adoption work will have to consider very carefully whether such plans are in the best interests of the child but also are consistent with the child's rights under the Convention. For example, the Convention emphasises that care orders should be a temporary measure and that children should be reunited with their family as soon as possible, where appropriate. In the case of a parent with a mental health problem detained in a psychiatric hospital, the Convention could be employed by their children to facilitate regular visits if these have been denied.

Article 10 concerns basic rights to freedom of expression and in the context of child abuse is a crucial safeguard to ensuring that practitioners work actively to enable children and young people to express their opinions about service provision. Professionals have an opportunity within this specific provision to articulate and put into practice their value principles of partnership and children's rights.

Article 14 states that all children have an equal claim to the rights set out in the Convention *'irrespective of the child's or his or her parent's or legal guardian's race, colour, sex, language, religion, political or other opinion, national, ethnic or social origin, property, disability, birth or other status'*. This provision could be used to argue for equality of service provision and non-prejudicial diagnosis or treatment. Social workers and others need to ensure they are employing anti-racist and non-discriminatory practice as well as facilitating children and young people to:

» access information about their rights;

» contact mental health services;

» access advocates and children's rights organisations;

» create children's service user groups.

# Conclusion

Children are not a homogenous group. The age range from childhood to adolescence incorporates several developmental stages which requires attention being paid to the design of developmentally appropriate methods of assessment and intervention in child abuse work. The UK and many of the Western industrialised, advanced nations are evolving as multi-cultural, ethnically diverse and culturally rich places to live. Children and young people from a wide variety of backgrounds and expediences come to live in the UK or are born into families who have settled. The job of all practitioners is to increase awareness and understanding of young people and remember to treat them all as individuals rather than a stereotype applied to a minority group. Indicating some comprehension of their cultural background will help in engaging troubled persons, show respect and form the beginnings of trust, which is crucial. It is important in this context to continue the task of finding out what works best for which children in what circumstances with finely calibrated research methodologies. Children are sometimes thought of as empty vessels waiting to be filled up. They are considered by some to be miniature adults. Services for children and young people have consequently often been based on adult concepts, models and practices. This has led to paternalistic, patronising practices that emasculate children and stifle their creativity and wisdom.

It is still a relatively radical idea to think that children and adolescents are different from adults in fundamental ways that require different ways of conceptualising their problems and providing appropriate services in response. Society is still at the beginning of a process of understanding childhood and adolescence in terms that are relevant to them, rather than to carers/parents or adult-dominated institutions. That understanding can only come from more involvement of children and young people in research, in the design of the research and in the process of the research. The job of adults is to facilitate and support them in gaining more control over their lives.

Social workers and others concerned with child protection are ideally placed to fulfil that role in empowering, participatory practice with children's rights at the heart of everything they do. Social workers are in a highly responsible position but they cannot stop or prevent child abuse without other staff in contact with children and young people being better informed, trained and supported to do their bit. Government also needs to put child protection higher up the political agenda, allocate more resources and integrate child protection into every department or programme of activity. With much more accessible, culturally appropriate parenting support services and outreach programmes, this would be a powerful combination. Teachers have only recently been expected to be more involved with safeguarding children as part of their duties but they require more training and support to be effective. Children in class can be monitored to observe behaviour which can reveal that abuse has been or is happening. They can reveal abuse in drawings or indirect means. Teachers can spot sudden changes in a child indicating something is wrong. They are often the most trusted adult known to the child. The police need to be more proactive in risk assessments where vulnerable parents can be helped to change behaviours before abuse happens. Investigating a report of anti-social behaviour if handled carefully could reveal an underlying problem of child abuse. Domestic violence cases are inherently bound up with child abuse. Communities also need to be less afraid to alert authorities if they are concerned about the safety of a child. After a child dies or is removed from their parents, neighbours or other family members can be found who knew of abuse but weren't able to voice alarm. This relates to the earlier concepts of reluctance to judge, fear of reprisals, the stigma of being perceived as interfering or a feeling that concerns will not be taken seriously. The sanctity of family life and a suspicion about state intrusion also play into a reluctance to 'get involved'. An old African proverb states that '*it takes a village to rear a child*'; the message is as profound as it is simple: safeguarding and protecting children and young people is everyone's responsibility.

# Bibliography

Adam, S and Brewer, M (2004) *The Financial Costs and Benefits of Supporting Children since 1975*. York: Joseph Rowntree Foundation.

Adams, K and Christensen, S (2000) Trust and the Family–School Relationship Examination of Parent–Teacher Differences in Elementary and Secondary Grades. *Journal of School Psychology*, 38(5): 477–497.

Alexandre-Bidon, D and Didier Lett, D (1999) *Children in the Middle Ages: Fifth to Fifteenth Centuries*. Translated by Jody Gladding. Notre Dame, IN: University of Notre Dame Press.

Alexiou, S and Warren, P M (2004) *The Early Minoan Tombs of Lebena, Southern Crete*. Sävedalen: Paul Åströms Förlag.

Anderson, C (2005) An 11th-Century Scandal. *America-The Jesuit Review*, 192(20): 47–49.

Ariès, P (1962) *Centuries of Childhood: A Social History of Family Life*. Translated by Robert Baldick. New York: Knopf.

Australian Institute of Health and Welfare (2016) https://www.aihw.gov.au/reports/australias-health/australias-health-2016/contents/summary (Accessed Oct 2020).

Babbitt, F C (translator) (1928) *Plutarch's Moralia*, Volume II. Cambridge, MA: Harvard University Press.

Bailey, V and Blackburn, S (1979) The Punishment of Incest Act 1908. *Criminal Law Review*, 685–708.

Banister, J (2004) Shortage of Girls in China Today. *Journal of Population Research*, 21(1): 19–45.

Banner, S (2005) When Killing a Juvenile Was Routine. *The New York Times*. Archived from the original on April 12, 2016. (Accessed Jun 2020).

Barlow, J, Kirkpatrick, S, Wood, D, Ball, M and Stewart-Brown, S (2007) *Family and Parenting Support in Sure Start Local Programmes*. London: NESS.

Bass, L (2004) *Child Labour in Sub-Saharan Africa*. Colorado: Lynne Rienner Publications.

BBC (1986) Childwatch. https://genome.ch.bbc.co.uk (Accessed Oct 2020).

BBC (2002) http://news.bbc.co.uk/1/hi/uk/1900155.stm (Accessed Oct 2020).

BBC (2008) http://news.bbc.co.uk/1/hi/uk/7824291.stm (Accessed Oct 2020).

BBC (2009) Ordeal of British Child Migrants. http://news.bbc.co.uk/1/hi/world/asia-pacific/8360150.stm (Accessed Jan 2020).

BBC (2014a) What Medieval Europe Did with Its Teenagers. https://www.bbc.co.uk/news/magazine-26289459

BBC (2014b) Secret History of Children's Homes. https://www.bbc.co.uk/news/magazine (Accessed Jan 2020).

BBC (2015) https://www.secularism.org.uk/news/2015/01/christian-gp-who-performed-exorcism-on-patient-is-struck-off (Accessed Jan 2020).

BBC (2017) https://www.bbc.co.uk/news/world-australia-38877158 (Accessed Jan 2020).

BBC (2018) https://www.bbc.co.uk/sport/football/46453955 (Accessed Jan 2020).

BBC (2018a) https://www.bbc.co.uk/news/world-europe-43697573 (Accessed Jan 2020).

BBC (2019) Children Escape Cult. https://www.bbc.co.uk/news/uk-scotland-49813941 (Accessed Jun 2020).

BBC (2019a) https://www.bbc.co.uk/news/uk-48354692 (Accessed Jun 2020).

Bean, P and Melville, J (1989) *Lost Children of the Empire*. London: The Child Migrants Trust.

Become (2020) https://becomecharity.org.uk/care-the-facts/about-the-care-system/ (Accessed Jun 2020).

Bell, B (2018) https://www.bbc.co.uk/news/uk-england-43400336 (Accessed Jun 2020).

Bernzweig, J, Lewis, C and Pantell, R (1997) Gender Differences in Physician-Patient Communication Evidence from Pediatric Visits. *Archives of Pediatrics and Adolescent Medicine*, 151(6): 586–591.

Betts, C (2008) Cyberbullying: The Legal Implications and Consequences. *Boarding Briefing Paper* 23. http://www.boarding.org.uk/file_uploads/94-BBP23-Cyberbullying.pdf (Accessed Jun 2020).

Biggeri, M and Mehrotra, S (2002) *The Subterranean Child Labour Force: Subcontracted Home Based Manufacturing in Asia*. Innocenti 16. UNICEF.

Bilton, T, Bonnett, K, Jones, P, Lawson, T, Skinner, D, Stanworth, M and Webster, A (2002) *Introductory Sociology*. New York: Palgrave.

Bloch, H (1988) Abandonment, Infanticide, and Filicide. An Overview of Inhumanity to Children. *American Journal of the Disabled Child*, 142(10): 1058–1060.

Boswell, J (1988) *The Kindness of Strangers: The Abandonment of Children in Western Europe from Antiquity to the Renaissance*. New York: Pantheon Books.

Bourke, A (1999) *The Burning of Bridget Cleary: A True Story*. London: Pimlico.

Bowen, D (2002) *Everyday Life in the Muslim Middle East*. Indiana: Indiana University Press.

Brett, K (1991) The Sexual Molestation of Children: Historical Perspectives. *Journal of Psychohistory*, 19(2): 191–214.

Briggs, K (1976) *An Encyclopedia of Fairies, Hobgoblins, Brownies, Boogies, and Other Supernatural Creatures*. London: Pantheon Books.

British Library (2020) https://www.bl.uk/romantics-and-victorians/articles/child-labour# (Accessed Jun 2020).

Brooklyn College (1991) http://www.brooklyn.cuny.edu/web/academics/schools (Accessed Jun 2020).

Bywaters, P, Bunting, L, Davidson, G, Hanratty, J, Mason W, McCartan, C and Steils, N (2016) *The Relationship between Poverty, Child Abuse and Neglect: An Evidence Review*. York: Joseph Rowntree Foundation.

Calder, M (2008) *Contemporary Risk Assessment in Safeguarding Children*. Lyme Regis: Russell House.

Campion-Vincent, V (2008) *CHILDREN AS PREY: A CASE OF THE UTMOST Contemporary Legends of Organ Theft, Children's Disappearances, Kidnappings, and the Sexual Abuse of Children and Adolescents*. Paris: Seuil.

Cannon, R (2014) https://borgenproject.org/10-facts-child-labor/ (Accessed Jun 2020).

Castleden, R (2002) *Minoans: Life in Bronze Age Crete*. London: Routledge.

Catch 22 (2020) *ONLINE HARMS: Supporting Young People Offline and Online to Prevent Harm and Build Resilience*. London: Catch 22.

Cavanagh, K, Dobash, R E and Dobash, R P (2005) Men Who Murder Children Inside and Outside the Family. *BJSW*, 35: 667–688.

Cederborg, A C (1997) Young Children's Participation in Family Therapy Talk. *American Journal of Family Therapy*, 25(1): 28–38.

Channel 4 News (2012) https://www.channel4.com/news/witchcraft-murder-couple-jailed-for-life (Accessed Jun 2020).

Charnovitz, S (1996) Child Labour: What to Do? *Journal of Commerce*, 203–207. Chapel Hill, NC: University of North Carolina Press.

Chase, E. and Walker, R (2015) Constructing Reality? 'The Discursive Truth of Poverty in Britain and How it Frames the Experience of Shame', in Chase, E and Bantebya-Kyomuhendo, G (eds) *Poverty and Shame: Global Experiences*. Oxford: OUP.

Child Labour Index (2020) *Annual Report*. Verisk Maplecroft.

Child Trends (2020) https://www.childtrends.org/publications/state-level-data-for-understanding-child-welfare-in-the-united-states (Accessed Jun 2020).

Children are Unbeatable (2004) https://www.thirdsector.co.uk/newsmaker-children-aposs-champion-peter-newell-co-ordinator-children-unbeatable/article/620855 (Accessed Jun 2020).

Children's Commisioner (2021) https://www.childrenscommissioner.gov.uk/2021/02/17/building-back-better-reaching-englands-left-behind-children/.

Children's Society (2010) *Annual Report*. London: Children's Society.

Children's Society (2020) *Good Childhood Report*. London: Children's Society.

Children's Society (2020a) *Young Refugees and Migrants*. London: Children's Society.

Children's Worlds (2020) https://isciweb.org/wp-content/uploads/2020/07/Summary-Comparative-Report-2020.pdf (Accessed Jun 2020).

Choudhry, V, et al (2018) Child Sexual Abuse in India: A Systematic Review. *PLOS One*. doi: 10.1371/journal.pone.0205086 (Accessed Jun 2020).

Cipolla, C (1980) *Before the Industrial Revolution: European Society and Economy, 1000–1700*.

Clark, A and Moss, P (2005) *Listening to Young Children: The Mosaic Approach*. London: National Children's Bureau.

Clark, A and Stratham, J (2005) Listening to Young Children: Experts in Their Own Lives. *Adoption and Fostering*, 29(1): 45–56.

Clegg, C (2000) *Vladimir Nabokov, Lolita: A Reader's Guide to Essential Criticism*. Icon Books. New York: Norton.

Cohen, M (1995) *Lewis Carroll: A Biography*. London: Macmillan.

Colson, F (1962) *Philo with an English Translation*. Translated by F H Colson. 1–10. Cambridge, MA: Harvard University Press.

Cortes. Letter 105.

Cowan, R (2013) *Roman Legionary AD 69–161*. Oxford: Osprey Publishing.

Crane, J (2018) *Child Protection in England, 1960–2000: Expertise, Experience, and Emotion*. London: Palgrave Macmillan.

Crawford, S (1999) *Childhood in Anglo-Saxon England*. Gloucestershire: Sutton.

Creegan, C and Henderson, G (2006) *Getting it Right for Every Child*. Edinburgh: Scottish Executive.

Cross, T P and Whitcomb, D (2017) The Practice of Prosecuting Child Maltreatment: Results of an Online Survey of Prosecutors. *Child Abuse & Neglect*, 69: 20–28.

CSEW (2019) *Crime Survey for England and Wales*. London: ONS.

Cult Observer (1987) https://www.icsahome.com/memberelibrary/co (Accessed Jun 2020).

Cunningham, H (2005) *Children and Childhood in Western Society since 1500*. 2nd ed. New York: Longman.

Daily Mail (2014) https://www.dailymail.co.uk/news/article-2724386/I-raped-aged-4-aide-Thatcher-Woman-claims-abused-senior-Conservative-MP-visited-notorious-guest-house-paedophile-Cyril-Smith (Accessed Jun 2020).

Daily Record (2020) https://www.dailyrecord.co.uk/news/crime/children-god-rapist-nailed-after-22356632 (Accessed Jun 2020).

Daily Telegraph (2014) https://www.telegraph.co.uk/newsaustralia/10696544/Britains-finest-WWII-general-accused-of-child-sex-abuse (Accessed Jun 2020).

Daily Telegraph (2019) https://www.telegraph.co.uk/news/2019/06/20/uks-senior-catholic-ignored-child-sex-abuse-victims-protect/ (Accessed Mar 2021).

Daily Telegraph (2020) https://www.telegraph.co.uk/gymnastics/2020/07/17/gymnastics-abuse-scandal-continues-widen-revelations-emerge/ (Accessed Mar 2021).

Daly, M and Wilson, M (1996) Violence against Stepchildren. *Current Directions in Psychological Science*, 5(3): 77–81.

Danczuk, S and Baker, M (2014) *Smile for the Camera: The Double Life of Cyril Smith*. London: Biteback Publishing.

Davies, L (2009) *Protecting Children: A Resource Book and Course Reader*. London: Akamas.

Davies, L and Duckett, N (2016) *Proactive Child Protection and Social Work*. London: SAGE.

Dean, S (2018) https://medium.com/more-than-2000-years-and-counting-of-sexual-abuse (Accessed Mar 2021).

De Castellanos (2014) De los timoto-cuicas a la invisibilidad del indigena andino y a su diversidad cultural. http://www.saber.ula.ve/bitstream/123456789/18495/1/articulo3 (Accessed Mar 2021).

DeMause, L (1974) The Evolution of Childhood. *Journal of Psychohistory*, 1(4): 503–575.

DeMause, L (1974) *The History of Childhood*. New York: Psychohistory Press.

DeMause, L (1987) The History of Childhood in Japan. *Journal of Psychohistory*, 15(2): 147–152.

DeMause, L (1990) The History of Child Assault. *Journal of Psychohistory*, 18(1): 1–29.

DeMause, L (1997) The History of Child Abuse. *Journal of Psychohistory*, 25(3): 216–236.

DeMause, L (1998) The History of Child Abuse. *Journal of Psychohistory*, 25(3): 23–37.

Department for Education (2017) *Evaluation of the Safeguarding Children Assessment and Analysis Framework (SAAF)*. London: HMSO.

Department for Education (DfE) (2018) *Working Together to Safeguard Children: A Guide to Inter-Agency Working to Safeguard and Promote the Welfare of Children*. London: Department for Education.

Department of Health (1999) *Lost in Care: Report of the Tribunal of Inquiry into the Abuse of Children in Care in the Former County Council Areas of Gwynedd and Clwyd since 1974*. London: HMSO.

Department of Health (2012) https://www.gov.uk/government/publications/national-action-plan-to-tackle-child-abuse-linked-to-faith-or-belief (Accessed Mar 2021).

Department of Labor (2017) https://www.dol.gov/sites/dolgov/files/ILAB/child_labor (Accessed Mar 2021).

Derevenski, J, ed. (2000) *Children and Material Culture*. London, UK: Routledge.

de Sahagim, B (1956) *Historia General de las Cosas de Nueva Espaha: Yfundada e'n la documentacion en lengua mexicana recogida por los mismos naturales. Angel Maria Garibay K. Edt. Tomo I. Book I*. Mexico City: Editorial Porrua.

De Sahagun, B (1996) *Primeros Memoriales*. Norman, OK: University of Oklahoma Press.

De Vries, J (2000) The Industrial Revolution and the Industrious Revolution. *Journal of Economic History*, 54: 249–270.

Dominelli, L (2002) *Feminist Social Work Theory and Practice*. London: Palgrave.

Driver, E and Droisen, A (1989) *Child Sexual Abuse: A Feminist Reader*. New York: New York University Press.

Drotar, D. and Robinson, J (2000) *Handbook of Developmental Psychopathology*. New York: Springer.

Dube, S R, Felitti, V J, Dong, M, Chapman, D P, Giles, W H and Anda, R F (2003) Childhood Abuse, Neglect, and Household Dysfunction and the Risk of Illicit Drug Use: The Adverse Childhood Experiences Study. *Pediatrics*, 111(3): 564–572.

Dubowitz, H (2017) Child Sexual Abuse and Exploitation—A Global Glimpse. *Child Abuse & Neglect*, 66: 2–8.

Eberly, S (2012) Fairies and the Folklore of Disability: Changelings, Hybrids and the Solitary Fairy. doi: 10.1080/0015587X.1988.9716425 (Accessed Mar 2021).

Eckenrode, J, Smith, E G, McCarthy, M E and Dineen, M (2014) Income Inequality and Child Maltreatment in the United States. *Pediatrics*, 133(3): 454–461.

ECPAT (2008) *End Child Prostitution, Child Pornography and Trafficking of Children for Sexual Purposes*. Thailand: ECPAT International.

EHRC (2019) https://wiseman.co.uk/ehrc-calls-increase-age-criminal-responsibility/ (Accessed Mar 2021).

Eisenstadt, N (2016) *Independent Advisor on Poverty and Inequality: Shifting the Curve - A Report for the First Minister*. Scottish Government.

Elia M (2015) The Cost of Malnutrition in England and Potential Cost Savings from Nutritional Interventions. https://www.bapen.org.uk (Accessed Mar 2021).

Emerson, D (2020) http://dguth.emerson.build/maproject/poems/the-factory-by-letitia-elizabeth-landon/ (Accessed Mar 2021).

Esposito, J (1988) *Islam: The Straight Path*. Oxford: Oxford University Press.

Etienne, R (1976) Ancient Medical Conscience and Children. *Journal of Psychohistory*, 4(2): 131–162.

Eyben, E (1986) What Did Youth Mean to the Romans? *Journal of Psychohistory*, 14(3): 207–232.

Fairchilds, C (1984) *Domestic Enemies: Servants and Their Masters in Old Regime France*. Baltimore, MD: Johns Hopkins University Press.

Fairwear Foundation (2012) https://www.fairwear.org/stories/fwf-new-child-labour-policy (Accessed May 2020).

Featherstone, B, Morris, K, Daniel, B, et al (2017) Poverty, Inequality, Child Abuse and Neglect: Changing the Conversation across the UK in Child Protection? *Children and Youth Services Review*, 97: 127–133.

Ferrara, P, Vitelli, O and Bottaro, G (2013) Factitious Disorders and Münchausen Syndrome: The Tip of the Iceberg. *Children's Health Care*, 17(4): 366–374.

Ferraro, J (2008) *Nefarious Crimes, Contested Justice. Illicit Sex and Infanticide in the Republic of Venice, 1557-1789*. Baltimore, MD: Johns Hopkins University Press.

Fildes, V (1986) *Breasts, Bottles, and Babies. A History of Infant Feeding*. Edinburgh, UK: Edinburgh University Press.

Finkelhor, D (1986) *A Sourcebook on Child Sexual Abuse*. Beverley Hills, CA: SAGE.

Finkelhor, D (1994) The International Epidemiology of Child Sexual Abuse. *Child Abuse & Neglect*, 18(5): 409–417.

Flandrin, J-L (1979) *Families in Former Times: Kinship, Household and Sexuality in Early Modern France*. Translated by Richard Southern. New York: Cambridge University Press.

Flicker, B (1993) Psychohistorical Roots of the War against Children. *Journal of Psychohistory*, 21(1): 69–78.

Food Foundation (2020) https://foodfoundation.org.uk/publications/ (Accessed Jun 2020).

Friedman, S H, Hrouda, D R and Holden, C E (2005) Child Murder Committed by Severely Mentally Ill Mothers: An Examination of Mothers Found not Guilty by Reason of Insanity. *Journal of Forensic Sciences*, 50(6): 1466-71.

Furlong, M and McGilloway, S (2012) The Incredible Years Parenting Program in Ireland: A Qualitative Analysis of the Experience of Parents Living in Disadvantaged Areas. *Clinical Child Psychology and Psychiatry*, 17: 616–630.

Furnari, L (2005) Born or Raised in High-Demand Groups: Developmental Considerations. *ICSA Newsletter*, 4(2).

Gallagher, N (2009) Infanticide and Abandonment of Female Children: Overview. https://referenceworks.brillonline.com (Accessed May 2020).

Gans, B (1970) Battered Babies: How Many Do We Miss? *The Lancet*. doi: 10.1016/S0140-6736(70)91756-3 (Accessed May 2020).

Gardner-Thorpe, C (2010) James Parkinson (1755–1824). *Journal of Neurology*, 257: 492–493.

Gavitt, P (1990) *Charity and Children in Renaissance Florence: Ospedale degli Innocenti, 1410–1536*. Ann Arbor, MI: University of Michigan Press.

Gelis, J (1991) *The History of Childbirth: Fertility, Pregnancy and Birth in Early Modern Europe*. Translated by Rosemary Morris . Boston, MA: Northeastern University.

Gibbs D (1994) Rickets and the Crippled Child: An Historical Perspective. *Journal of the Royal Society of Medicine*, 87(12): 729–732.

Gilbert, N, Parton, B and Skivenes, M (2011) *Child Protection Systems: International Trends and Orientations*. Oxford, UK: Oxford University Press.

Gillard, D (2018) *Education in England: A History*. http://www.educationengland.org.uk/history.

Gladman, A and Heal, A (2017) *Child Sexual Exploitation after Rotherham*. London: Jessica Kingsley.

Goody, J (1983) *The Development of the Family and Marriage in Europe*. New York: Cambridge University Press.

Goody, J (2000) *The European Family: An Historico-Anthropological Essay*. Oxford: Basil Blackwell.

Gove, M (2013) https://www.gov.uk/government/ (Accessed May 2020).

Gray-Fow, M (1987) Child Abuse, Historiography and Ethics: The Historian as Moral Philosopher. *Journal of Psychohistory*, 15(1): 455–466.

Guardian Newspaper (2012) https://www.theguardian.com/uk/2012/mar/01/couple-guilty-boy-murder-witchcraft (Accessed May 2020).

Guardian Newspaper (2015) https://www.theguardian.com/politics/2015/feb/02/thatcher-peter-hayman (Accessed Aug 2020).

Guardian Newspaper (2018) https://www.theguardian.com/uk-news/2018/jun/08/british-army-criticised-for-exam-results-day-recruitment-ads (Accessed May 2020).

Guardian Newspaper (2018a) https://www.theguardian.com/uk-news/2018/mar/30/like-being-raped-three-claims-of-coerced-exorcism-in-the-uk (Accessed Nov 2020).

Guardian Newspaper (2018b) https://www.theguardian.com/uk-news/2018/jul/24/ex-archbishop-george-carey-gave-uncritical-support-to-disgraced-bishop-inquiry-told (Accessed May 2020).

Guardian Newspaper (2019) https://www.theguardian.com/sport/2019/apr/24/15-months-on-from-larry-nassar-usa-gymnastics-struggles-to-find-its-way (Accessed May 2020).

Guardian Newspaper (2019a) https://www.theguardian.com/society/2019/jan/30/scandal-hit-childrens-prison-still-restraining-inmates-unlawfully-report (Accessed April 2021).

Gupta, A (2018) Punishing the Poor: Child Welfare and Protection under Neoliberalism. https://socwork.net/sws/article/view/575/1122 (Accessed May 2020).

Halsey, K and White, R (2008) *Young People, Crime and Public Perceptions: A Review of the Literature (LGA Research Report F/SR264)*. Slough: NFER.

Hanawalt, B (1986) *The Ties that Bound: Peasant Families in Medieval England*. Oxford, UK: Oxford University Press.

Hanawalt, B (1993) *Growing Up in Medieval London: The Experience of Childhood in History*. New York: Oxford University Press.

Hanawalt, B (2002) Medievalists and the Study of Childhood. *Speculum*, 77: 440–458.

Hann, G and Fertleman, C (eds) (2016) *The Child Protection Practice Manual: Training Practitioners How to Safeguard*. Oxford: Oxford University Press.

Hansard (1922) *5 July 1922 [156] 410*. UK: House of Commons.

Hazel, N (1995) *Elicitation Techniques with Young People. Social Research Update, Issue 12*. http://sru.soc.surrey.ac.uk/SRU12.html (Accessed May 2020).

Hearn, D (2015) *Legal Executions in Georgia: A Comprehensive Registry, 1866–1964*. SC: McFarland.

Helenga, K (2002) Social Space, the Final Frontier: Adolescents on the Internet, in Mortimer J and Larson R (eds) *The Changing Adolescent Experience-Societal Trends and the Transition to Adulthood*. Cambridge: Cambridge University Press.

Helfer, M, Kempe, R and Krugman, R (1997) *The Battered Child*. Chicago, IL: University of Chicago Press.

Helman, C G (2005) Cultural Aspects of Time and Ageing. *Science and Society*, 6: 54–58.

Henderson, J and Wall, R (eds) (1994) *Poor Women and Children in the European Past*. New York: Routledge.

Herlihy, D and Klapisch-Zuber, C (1985) *Tuscans and their Families: A Study of the Florentine Catasto of 1427*. New Haven, CT: Yale University Press.

Herrenkohl, T, Leeb, R T and Higghins, D (2016) The Public Health Model of Child Maltreatment Prevention. *Trauma, Violence, and Abuse*, 17(4): 363–365.

Heywood, C (2001) *A History of Childhood: Children and Childhood in the West from Medieval to Modern Times*. Cambridge, UK: Polity.

Higgins, D J (2015) A Public Health Approach to Enhancing Safe and Supportive Family Environments for Children. *Family Matters*, 96: 39–52.

Hindman, H D (ed) (2009) *The World of Child Labor: An Historical and Regional Survey*. Armonk, NY: M.E. Sharpe.

Hobbes, T (1651) *Leviathan*. Oxford, UK: Oxford University Press.

Home Office (2020) https://www.gov.uk/government/statistics/statistics-on-so-called-honour-based-abuse-offences-england-and-wales-2019-to-2020 (Accessed May 2020).

Home Office (2021) *Tackling Child Sexual Abuse Strategy*. London: Home Office.

House of Bishops (2012) https://www.churchofengland.org/sites/default/files/2017-10/guidelines%20on%20deliverance%20ministry.pdf (Accessed May 2020).

House of Commons (1819) *Cotton Mills and Factories Act 1819*. London: HMSO.

House of Commons (2014) https://publications.parliament.uk/pa/cm201415/ (Accessed May 2020).

House of Commons Library (2020) *Youth Custody: Research Briefing*. London: HMSO.

House of Lords (1985) *Gillick 3 All ER*.

Human Rights Watch (2013) *Child Soldiers*. New York: Human Rights Watch.

Human Rights Watch (2010) https://www.hrw.org/news/2010/04/15/corporal-punishment-schools-and-its-effect-academic-success-joint-hrw/aclu (Accessed May 2020).

Humphreys, M (2019) Lost Children of the Empire. https://www.leftlion.co.uk/read/2019/july/margaret-humphreys-home-children-child-migrants-trust/ (Accessed May 2020).

Humphries, J (2016) *Childhood & Child Labour in The British Industrial Revolution*. Cambridge: Cambridge University Press.

IICSA (2019) https://www.iicsa.org.uk/publications/investigation/english-benedictine-congregation-ealing-abbey/part-1-ealing-abbey-and-st-benedicts-school/executive-summary (Accessed May 2020).

# BIBLIOGRAPHY

IICSA (2019a) https://www.iicsa.org.uk/key-documents/9716/view/public-hearing-transcript-8-march-2019.pdf. (Accessed April 2021).

IICSA (2020) https://www.iicsa.org.uk/publications/research/csa-schools (Accessed April 2021).

IKWRO (2020) http://ikwro.org.uk/child-marriage-abuse/ (accessed April 2021).

ILO (2017) *Ending Child Labour by 2025: A Review of Policies and Programmes*. Geneva: Independent Labour Organisation.

Independent Inquiry into Child Sexual Abuse in England and Wales (2018) *Interim Report*. London: IICSA.

Independent Inquiry into Child Sexual Abuse in England and Wales (2020) *Interim Report*. London: IICSA.

Independent Newspaper (2016) https://www.independent.co.uk/news/uk/home-news/christian-fundamentalist-schools-performed-exorcisms-children-and-beat-pupils-religious-rituals-a7312681.html (Accessed May 2020).

India Today (2017) https://www.indiatoday.in/india/story/109-children-sexually-abused (Accessed Oct 2020).

Institut fur Kindheit (2006) *Dialektisch Behaviorale Therapie für Posttraumatische Belastungsstörung nach sexualisierter Gewalt in der Kindheit und Jugend (DBT-PTSD)*.

Internet Watch Foundation (2019) *Annual Report*. Cambridgeshire, UK: IWF.

Juvonen J, Gross EF (2008) Extending the School Grounds?—Bullying Experiences in Cyberspace. *Journal of School Health*, 78: 496–505.

Karma Nirvana (2020) https://karmanirvana.org.uk/factsheet-stats/ (Accessed Oct 2020).

Kay, J (2003) *Protecting Children- A Practical Guide*. London: Continuum.

Kelly, L (1996) Weasel Words: Paedophiles and the Cycle of Abuse. *Trouble and Strife*, 33.

Kempe, H, Silverman, F, Steele, B, Droegemueller, W and Silver, H (1962) The Battered-Child Syndrome. *Journal of the American Medical Association*, 181(1): 17–24.

Khyoon, A Y (2014) The Theme of Child Abuse in Selected Fairy Tales by Brothers Grimm. *al-Mustaqbal al-'Arabī*, 2(210): 33–58.

King, M (1994) *The Death of the Child Valerio Marcello*. Chicago, IL: University of Chicago Press.

King, M (2007) Concepts of Childhood: What We Know and Where We Might Go. *Renaissance Quarterly*, 60: 371–407.

Kissane, A (2017) Child Sexual Abuse? A View from England in the Later Middle Ages, Childhood and Youth. http://www.notchesblog.com (Accessed Oct 2020).

Kissane, A (2017) *Civic Community in Late Medieval Lincoln*. London: Boydel & Brewer.

Klapisch-Zuber, C (1985) Women, Family, and Ritual in Renaissance Italy. Translated by Lydia G. Cochrane. Chicago, IL: University of Chicago Press.

Kremer, W (2014) What Medieval Europe Did with Its Teenagers. https://www.medievalists.net (Accessed Feb 2021).

Kuehn, T (2002) *Illegitimacy in Renaissance Florence*. Ann Arbor, MI: University of Michigan Press.

Laming, H (2003) *The Victoria Climbie Inquiry: Report of an Inquiry by Lord Laming*. London: HMSO.

Lansford, J E, Dodge, K A, Pettit, G S and Bates, J E (2010) Does Physical Abuse in Early Childhood Predict Substance Use in Adolescence and Early Adulthood? *Child Maltreatment*, 15(2): 190–194.

Lenzer, G (2001) Children's Studies: Beginnings and Purposes. *The Lion and the Unicorn*, 25(2): 181–186.

Li, Q (2006) Cyberbullying in Schools. A Research of Gender Differences. *School Psychology International*, 27(2): 157–170.

Liefaard, T and Doek, J (2015) *Litigating the Rights of the Child*. Springer.

Lindsay, G and Totsika, V (2017) The Effectiveness of Universal Parenting Programmes: The CANparent Trial. *BMC Psychology*, 5: 35.

Local Government Association (2020) https://www.local.gov.uk (Accessed Feb 2021).

Lynch, M (1985) Child Abuse before Kempe: An Historical Literature Review. *Child Abuse and Neglect*, 9(1): 7–15.

MacCauley, D (1996) Child Abuse in Sport. *British Journal of Sports Medicine*, 30: 275–276.

Madigan, A, et al (2020) Exploring the Facilitation of Successfully Completing Treatment within a Residential Setting with Veterans Diagnosed with PTSD. *Journal of Veterans Studies*, 6(1): 230–238.

Malet, M, McSherry, D, Larkin, E and Robinson, C (2010) Research with Children: Methodological Issues and Innovative Techniques. *Journal of Early Childhood Research*, 8(2): 175–192.

Marland, H (ed) (1993) *The Art of Midwifery: Early Modern Midwives in Europe*. London, UK: Routledge.

Marten, J (2018) *The History of Childhood: A Very Short Introduction*. Oxford: Oxford University Press.

Marx, K (1868) https://www.marxists.org/archive/marx/iwma/documents/1868/machinery-speech.htm (Accessed Feb 2021).

Mason, P T (1972) Child Abuse and Neglect Part I – Historical Overview, Legal Matrix, and Social Perspectives. *North Carolina Law Review*, 50(2): 1.

Matthews, G and Mullin, A (2018) The Philosophy of Childhood, in Edward N Zalta (ed.) *The Stanford Encyclopedia of Philosophy* (2020 Edition). https://plato.stanford.edu.

McKenna, P (1980) https://www.belfasttelegraph.co.uk/news/northern-ireland/kincora (Accessed Feb 2021).

McLaughlin, M (1974) Survivors and Surrogates: Children and Parents from the Ninth to the Thirteenth Centuries, in Lloyd deMause (ed) *The History of Childhood*, 101–181. New York: Psychohistory Press.

*Micha: Hebrew Bible*. Tanakh. Micha 6: 7.

Middleton, N (1970) The Education Act of 1870 as the Start of the Modern Concept of the Child. *British Journal of Educational Studies*, 18(2): 166–179.

Miller, A (1985) *The Shalt Not Be Aware: Society's Betrayal of the Child*. London: Pluto Press.

Miller, A (1987) *For Your Own Good- The Roots of Violence in Child-Rearing*. London: Virago.

Miller, C (2016) https://wordandsilence.com/2016/09/20/krishna-the-universe-in-his-mouth/ (Accessed Feb 2021).

Mining Accident Database (2021) http://mineaccidents.com.au/mine-accident/202/huskar-colliery-1838 (Accessed Feb 2021).

MOD (2014) *Defence Statistics*. London: MOD.

Money, J (1986) Munchausen's Syndrome by Proxy: Update. *Journal of Pediatric Psychology*, 11(4): 583–584.

Moran, P, Ghate, D and van der Merwe, A (2004) *What Works in Parenting Support?* London: Department for Education and Skills.

Morris, K and Tunnard, J (1996) *Family Group Conferences: Messages from Research*. London: FRG.

Morrow, V and Richards, M (1996) The Ethics of Social Research with Children: An Overview. *Children and Society*, 10: 90–105.

Moulds, J (2020) https://labs.theguardian.com/unicef-child-labour/ (Accessed Feb 2021).

Mounteer, C A (1986) Roman Childhood, 200-B.C. to A.D. 600. *Journal of Psychohistory*, 14(3): 233–256.

Munro, E (2011) *The Munro Review of Child Protection*. London: HMSO.

Musacchio, J (1999) *The Art and Ritual of Childbirth in Renaissance Italy*. New Haven, CT: Yale University Press.

National Center for Victims of Crime (2020) (https://victimsofcrime.org/child-sexual-abuse-statistics (Accessed Jan 2021).

Natov, R (2006) *The Poetics of Childhood*. London: Routledge.

Neimark, E D, De Lisi, R and Newman, J H (1985) *Moderators of Competence*. Hillsdale, NJ: Erlbaum.

Newman, T (2004) *What Works in Building Resilience*. Barkingside: Barnardo's.

NSPCC (2010) http://www.nspcc.org.uk/help-and-advice/worried-about-a-child/talking-to-our-experts/types-of-child-abuse/bullying-definition/bullying_wda75441.html) (Accessed Jun 2020).

NSPCC (2020) https://learning.nspcc.org.uk/research-resources/briefings/research-with-children-ethics-safety-avoiding-harm.

Offside Trust (2018) http://www.offsidetrust.com/resources (Accessed Jun 2020).

ONS (2018) https://www.ons.gov.uk/peoplepopulationandcommunity (Accessed Jun 2020).

ONS (2019) *Child Abuse and the Criminal Justice System, England and Wales: Year Ending March 2019*. London: HMSO.

ONS (2019a) https://www.ons.gov.uk (Accessed Jun 2020).

ONS (2020) https://www.ons.gov.uk/peoplepopulationandcommunity (Accessed Jan 2021).

ONS (2020a) *Infant and Child Mortality 2018*. London: Office for National Statistics.

Orme, N (2001) *Medieval Children*. New Haven, CT: Yale University Press.

Orwell, G (1938) *Homage to Catalonia*. London: Secker and Warburg.

Oxfam (2020) https://www.oxfam.org (Accessed Jun 2020).

Ozment, S (1983) *When Fathers Ruled: Family Life in Reformation Europe*. Cambridge, MA: Harvard University Press.

Petrov, C (2020) Cyberbullying.org.

Picard, C (1935) *Manuel d'archéologie grecque: La sculpture*. Volume I (7-6th centuries BCE).

Pollard, W (1987) Decision Making and the Use of Evaluation Research. *American Behavioral Scientist*, 30(6): 661–676.

Pollock, L (1983) *Forgotten Children: Parent–Child Relations from 1500–1900*. New York: Cambridge University Press.

Polonko, K A, Adams, N, Naeem, N and Adinolfi, A (2011) Child Sexual Abuse in the Middle East and North Africa: A Review, in *Essays on Social Themes*. New York: Akiner Press.

Pope, S (2000) *Dictionary of the Napoleonic Wars*. London: Cassell.

Porter, C (1925) Outbreak of Gonorrhœa in a Children's Home. *The Lancet*. doi: 10.1016/S0140-6736(01)17170-9 (Accessed Jun 2020).

Prügl, E (1999) *The Global Construction of Gender - Home Based Work in Political Economy of 20th Century*. New York, NY: Columbia University Press.

Quinton, D (2004) *Supporting Parents: Messages from Research*. London: DOH.

R v Hopley 2F&F 202, 186.

Radford, L, Allnock, D and Hynes, P (2015) *Preventing and Responding to Child Sexual Abuse and Exploitation: Evidence Review*. Geneva: Unicef.

Raine, S and Kent, S (2019) The Grooming of Children for Sexual Abuse in Religious Settings: Unique Characteristics and Select Case Studies. *Aggression and Violent Behavior*, 48: 180–189.

Reeve, M D (1983) Petronius, in Leighton D Reynolds (ed) *Texts and Transmission: A Survey of the Latin Classics*. Oxford: Clarendon.

Regoli, R M, Hewitt, J D and DeLisi, M (2014) *Delinquency in Society*. 9th ed. Burlington, MA: Jones & Bartlett Learning.

Reinhard, J (2010) *Inca Rituals and Sacred Mountains: A Study of the World's Highest Archaeological Sites (with Constanza Ceruti)*. Los Angeles, CA: University of California.

Robbins, M S, Liddle, H A, Turner, C W, Dakof, G A, Alexander, J F and Kogan, S M (2006) Adolescent and Parent Therapeutic Alliances as Predictors of Dropout in Multidimensional Family Therapy. *Journal of Family Psychology*, 20: 108–116.

Rogers, C (2011) Rogers, Chris 2011. Where Child Sacrifice is a Business. *BBC News Africa*. https://www.bbc.co.uk/news/world-africa-15255357 (Accessed Jan 2021).

Romanou, E and Belton, E (2020) *Isolated and Struggling: Social Isolation and the Risk of Child Maltreatment, in Lockdown and Beyond*. London: NSPCC.

Rousseau, J J (1762) *On the Social Contract; or, Principles of Political Rights*. Napoli, Italy.

Salter, M (2013) *Organised Sexual Abuse*. London: Routledge.

Saradjian, J (1996) *Women Who Sexually Abuse Children*. London: Wiley.

Scherer, A (2012) *Mortuary Landscapes of the Classic Maya*. Austin, TX: University of Texas Press.

Scott, B C (1988) *Parenting and Outcomes for Children*. York: Joseph Rowntree Foundation.

Sex Education Forum (2020) https://www.sexeducationforum.org.uk/resources/evidence.

Shelman and Lazoritz (2005) *The Mary Ellen Wilson Child Abuse Case and the Beginning of Children's Rights in 19th Century America*. New York: McFarland.

Shelter (2019) https://england.shelter.org.uk/media/press.

Silver, C (1999) *Strange and Secret Peoples: Fairies and Victorian Consciousness: Fairies & Victorian Consciousness*. Oxford: Oxford University Press.

Skinner, A E and Castle, R L (1969) *78 Battered Children: A Retrospective Study*. London: NSPCC.

Sky News (2020) https://news.sky.com/story/victims-attack-tokenistic-inquiry-into-organised-child-exploitation-12080433 (Accessed Jan 2021).

Slack, K S and Yoo, J (2004) Food Hardships and Child Behavior Problems among Low-Income Children. *Institute for Research on Poverty* Discussion Paper no. 1290-04.

Smart, C (2000) Reconsidering the Recent History of Child Sexual Abuse, 1910–1960. *Journal of Social Policy*, 29(1): 55–71. Cambridge University Press.

Smith, M (1990) *The Early History of God: Yahweh and the Other Deities in Ancient Israel*. San Francisco, CA: Harper & Row.

Smith, S (1976) The Battered Child Syndrome—Some Research Aspects. *The Bulletin of the American Academy of Psychiatry and the Law*, 4(3): 235.

Smiths Dictionary (1875) *Lacus Curtius: Greek and Roman Sacrifices*.

Soares, C, Ablet, G, Mooney, B and King, S (2019) *Child Sexual Abuse in the Context of Children's Homes and Residential Care*. London: HMSO.

Sommerville, C J (1992) *The Discovery of Childhood in Puritan England*. Athens, GA: University of Georgia Press.

Spock, B (1946) *The Common Sense Book of Baby and Child Care*. New York: Duell, Sloan and Pearce.

Stager, L and Wolff, S (1984) *Child Sacrifice at Carthage: Religious Rite Or Population Control?* London: Biblical Archaeology Society.

Strickland-Clark, L, Campbell, D and Dallos, R (2000) Children's and Adolescent's Views on Family Therapy. *Journal of Family Therapy*, 22(3): 324–341.

Sugg, R (2018) *Fairies: A Dangerous History*. London: Reaktion Books.

Sunday Mirror (2014) https://comresglobal.com/polls/sunday-mirror-independent-political-poll-march-2014/ (Accessed Nov 2020).

Sunderland, M (2001) *Using Story Telling as a Therapeutic Tool with Children (Helping Children with Feelings)*. Milton Keynes: Speechmark.

Swift, L (2014) https://theconversation.com/medea-is-as-relevant-today-as-it-was-in-ancient-greece-29609 (Accessed Jun 2020).

Tag Eldin, M, Tag-Eldin, A, Abdel-Aty, M, Mansour, S G E and Al-Tayeb, M (2008) Prevalence of Female Genital Cutting among Egyptian Girls. *Bulletin of the World Health Organization*, 86: 269–274.

Tanaka, M, Suzuki, Y E, Aoyama, I, Takaoka, K and MacMillan, H L (2017) Child Sexual Abuse in Japan: A Systematic Review and Future Directions. *Child Abuse & Neglect*, 66: 31–40.

Tatar, M (2018) *The Hard Facts of the Grimms' Fairy Tales*. Expanded Edition. New York: Princeton University.

Terpstra, N (2005) *Abandoned Children of the Italian Renaissance. Orphan Care in Florence and Bologna*. Baltimore, MD: Johns Hopkins University Press.

The Children's Center for Psychiatry, Psychology, & Related Services (2017) https://childrenstreatmentcenter.com/sexual-abuse-teachers/ (Accessed Jun 2020).

The Independent (2017) https://www.independent.co.uk/news/uk/home-news/teachers-banned-classroom-sexual-misconduct-record-numbers-statistics-investigation-a7828891.html (Accessed April 2019).

The Independent (2019) https://www.independent.co.uk/news/uk/home-news/withcraft-exorcism-uk-deaths-child-abuse-beating-burning-police-a9201981.html.

The Independent (2020) https://www.independent.co.uk/news/uk/home-news/food-poverty-hunger-child-malnutrition-hospital-layla-moran-coronavirus-a9615161.html. (Accessed April 2021).

The Theos Report (2017) *Christianity and Mental Health: Theology, Activities, Potential*. London: Theos.

The Times (2013) https://www.thetimes.co.uk/article/former-archbishop-of-york-covered-up-sex-abuse-scandal-pm0fgs600f2 (Accessed Nov 2020).

Thomas, N and O'Kane, C (1998) The Ethics of Participatory Research with Children. *Children & Society*, 12(5): 336–348.

Toronto Sun (1986) Beatings, mutilations, in cultish church. *Cult Observer*, October 1986, p. 9. From *The Toronto Sun*, July 11, 1986.

Trevelyan, G M (1977) *English Social History*. London: Longman.

Troy, V, McPherson, K, Emslie, C and Gilchrist, E (2018) The Feasibility, Appropriateness, Meaningfulness, and Effectiveness of Parenting and Family Support Programs Delivered in the Criminal Justice System: A Systematic Review. *Journal of Child and Family Studies*, 27: 1732–1747.

Truth Project (2020) Child Sexual Abuse in Sports. https://www.nelsonslaw.co.uk/truth-project-report/ (Accessed Nov 2020).

Unicef (2007) *The State of the World's Children*. Geneva: Unicef.

Unicef (2011) *The Situation of Palestinian Children in The Occupied Palestinian Territory*. Jordan, Syria and Lebanon, Jordan: Unicef.

Unicef (2017) *Child Labour Data*. Geneva: Unicef.

Unicef (2020) *Refugee and Migrant Children in Europe in 2019 - Accompanied, Unaccompanied and Separated.* UNHCR, UNICEF & IOM.

United Nations (2006) https://documents-dds-ny.un.org.

United Nations (2016) https://www.un.org/preventing-sexual-exploitation-and-abuse/

Unites States Center of Military History (2007) *Medal of Honor Citations.*

UNODC (2014) https://www.unodc.org/documents/southeastasiaandpacific/ (Accessed Nov 2020).

UNODC (2019) *Global Study on Homicide.* Vienna: Unicef.

Večernje novosti (2013) *Momčilo Gavrić - najmlađi vojnik Prvog svetskog rata.*

Visser, M and Moleko, A G (eds) (2012) *Community Psychology in South Africa.* Durban: Van Schaik Publishers.

Walker, S (2001) Consulting with Children and Young People. *The International Journal of Children s Rights* 9(1): 45–56.

Walker, S (2003) *Social Work and Child and Adolescent Mental Health.* Lyme Regis: RHP.

Walker, S (2005) *Culturally Competent Therapy- Working with Children and Young People.* Basingstoke: Palgrave.

Walker, S (2010) Young People's Mental Health: The Spiritual Power of Fairy Stories, Myths and Legends. *Mental Health, Religion & Culture*, 13(1): 81–94.

Walker, S (2011) *The Social Workers Guide to Child and Adolescent Mental Health.* London: Jessica Kingsley.

Walker, S (2011a) *Social Work Assessment and Intervention.* 2nd ed. Lyme Regis: Russell House Publishers.

Walker, S (2012) *Responding to Self Harm in Children and Adolescents- A Professionals Guide to Treatment, Identification and Support.* London, UK: Jessica Kingsley.

Walker, S (2012a) Family Support Services, Chapter in Gray, M, Midgeley, J and Webb, S (eds) *The Sage Handbook of Social Work.* London: SAGE.

Walker, S (2012b) *Effective Social Work with Children and Families- Putting Systems Theory into Practice.* London: SAGE.

Walker, S. (ed) (2013) *Modern Mental Health- Critical Perspectives on Psychiatry.* St. Albans: Critical Publishing.

Walker, S (2017) https://morningstaronline.co.uk/a-fee4-paedophile-inquiry-zero-credibility-1.

Walker, S (2018) https://morningstaronline.co.uk/article/britains-child-soldier-disgrace.

Walker, S (2019) *Supporting Troubled Young People: A Practical Guide to Helping with Mental Health Problems.* St. Albans: Critical Publishing.

Walker S (2019b) https://morningstaronline.co.uk/article/f/vatican-still-covering-up-paedophile-abuse-evidence (Accessed Nov 2020).

Walker, S (2019c) https://morningstaronline.co.uk/article/f/westminster-under-spotlight (Accessed Nov 2020).

Walker, S and Akister, J (2004) *Applying Family Therapy.* Lyme Regis: RHP.

Walker, S and Thurston, C (2006) *Safeguarding Children and Young People: a guide to integrated Practice.* Lyme Regis: Russell House Publishers.

War Child (2018) *Five Myths about Child Soldiers.* London: War Child.

Watkins, S A (1990) The Mary Ellen Myth: Correcting Child Welfare History. *Social Work*, 35(6): 500–503.

Wayback Machine (2013) Momčilo Gavrić – *najmlađi vojnik Prvog svetskog rata.* Archived 26 March 2018. Večernje novosti.

Wells, K (2014) *Childhood in a Global Perspective*. Cambridge, UK: Polity Press.

Wessels, M (1997) Child Soldiers. *Bulletin of the Atomic Scientists*, 53(4): 32.

Wheeler, S, Williams, L, Beauchesne, P and Dupras, L (2013) Shattered Lives and Broken Childhoods: Evidence of Physical Child Abuse in Ancient Egypt. *International Journal of Paleopathology*, 3(2): 71–82.

Wiehe, V (2011) Nothing Pretty in Pageants. https://thetruthaboutamericasyouth.wordpress (Accessed Oct 2020).

Wilkinson, R G and Pickett, K (2009) *The Spirit Level: Why More Equal Societies Almost Always Do Better*. London: Allen Lane.

Williams, L M (1994) Recall of Childhood Trauma: A Prospective Study of Women's Memories of Child Sexual Abuse. *Journal of Consulting and Clinical Psychology*, 62(6): 1167–1176.

Wilsnack, S, Vogeltanz, N, Klassen, A and Harris, T (1997) Childhood Sexual Abuse and Women's Substance Abuse: National Survey Findings. *Journal of Studies on Alcohol*, 58(3): 264–271.

Wolak, J, Mitchell, K J and Finkelhor, D (2007) Does Online Harassment Constitute Bullying? An Exploration of Online Harassment by Known Peers and Online-Only Contacts. *Journal of Adolescent Health*, 41(6) Supplement 1: S51–S58.

Wooley, E (1955) Significance of Skeletal Lesions in Infants Resembling Those of Traumatic Origin. *Journal of the American Medical Association*, 158: 539.

World Bank (2020) https://data.worldbank.org/indicator/SL.TLF.0714.ZS (Accessed Jan 2021).

World Health Assembly (2016) https://www.who.int/mediacentre/events/2016/wha69/en/ (Accessed Oct 2020).

World Health Orgnisation (2006) Preventing Child Maltreatment. https://documents-dds-ny.un.org (Accessed Oct 2020).

World Health Orgnisation (WHO) (2016) https://www.who.int/reproductivehealth/topics/violence/action-plan (Accessed Oct 2020).

World Health Organisation (2020) https://www.who.int/news-room/fact-sheets (Accessed Oct 2020).

World Vision (2020) https://www.worldvision.org.uk/our-work/child-labour/quick-facts/ (Accessed Nov 2020).

Ybarra, M L and Mitchell, K J K (2004) Youth Engaging in Online Harassment: Associations with Caregiver-Child Relationships, Internet Use, and Personal Characteristics. *Journal of Adolescence*, 27: 319–336.

Young-bruhel, E (2013) *Childism: Confronting Prejudice against Children*. New Haven, CT: Yale University Press.

Yuen, K (2004) Theorizing the Chinese: The MUI TSAI Controversy and Construction of Transnational Chineseness in Hong Kong and British Malaya. *New Zealand Journal of Asian Studies*, 6(2): 95–110.

# Index

Adams, E, 32
Afghanistan, 80, 136
Aladdin, 28
Albania, 136
Algeria, 119
*Alice's Adventures in Wonderland* (Carroll), 26
Allitt, B, 43
Alston, P, 152
American Psychiatric Association (APA), 40, 41
American Society for the Prevention of Cruelty to Animals (ASPCA), 59
Anderson, C, 18
Anderson, H A, 25
Angus Reid Public Opinion, 147
anxiety
  colonial economics and, 83
  fairies and, 22
  mental illness and, 89
  physical abuse and, 38, 39
  sexual abuse and, 40, 97
  social, 69
  storytelling and, 26, 27
Arabia, ancient, 15–16
*Arabian Nights, The*, 28
*Arbitrants, The* (Menander), 7
archaeological and cultural evidence, 7–8
Ariès, P, 129
Aristippus, 6
Aristotle, 10
Augustine, 19
Australia, 3, 83
Australian Institute of Health and Welfare (AIHW), 45
Australian Royal Commission, 85–86
awareness, significance of, 36, 64–65
Aztecs, 13

B&Bs, 110
Baiga group, 97
Baker, M, 101
Bakewell, M, 26
Ball, P, 32, 33
Bangladesh, 91
battered child syndrome, 57, 67–70
  child killings and blame culture in, 69–70
  concerns about, 69
  violent parents and, 68–69
BBC, 14, 31, 84, 90, 94
  *ChildWatch* program, 95
Beckford, J, 70
Become, 142

Belize, 81
Belsky, J, 44
Benin, 75
Bennell, B, 105, 106
Berg, D, 31
Bible, 12–13, 65, 86
Bifulco, A, 49, 52
Biggeri, M, 82
Binnicker, B J, 112
Bloch, H, 10
Boeotia, 10
*Boke of Children, The*, 19
Bolles, E, 112
Bourke, A, 23
Bowen, D L, 16
Bradshaw, J, 119
Brandreth, G, 103
Brazil, 80
Brett, K, 7, 10
Briggs, K, 23
British Association for Parenteral and Enteral Nutrition (BAPEN), 111
British Gymnastics, 107
British Library, 76
*British Medical Journal*, 68
British School of Athens, 11
Brittan, L, 101, 103
Bryn Estyn children's home (Wrexham), 93, 103
Bulger, J, 134
*Burning of Bridget Cleary, The* (Bourke), 23
Burundi, 80
*Bury Messenger* (newspaper), 103
Butler-Sloss, E, 33

Caffey, J, 57
Cairney, F, 106
Cambodia, 123
Cameron, D, 101
Canadian Dominion Statutes, 83
cannibalism, 11
Canterbury Cathedral, 16
Carey, G, 32
Carroll, L, 26
Carson, M, 106
Carthage (modern-day Tunisia), 14, 15
Castle, B, 103
Castleden, R, 5
Catholic Church, 9
Catholic University Medical School (Agostino Gemelli Hospital) (Rome), 43
Chad, 75

177

challenge, as protective mechanism, 48
changelings, 22
   benefits of beliefs in, 24
   Oedipus legend and, 24
   significance of, 23–24
changing perceptions, of children, 127
   changing status and, 131–133
   childhood
   philosophical understanding of, 129
   studies of, 128–129
   children in care and, 140–143
   culture, ethnicity, and prejudice and, 130–131
   refugee and asylum seekers and, 135–137
   representations of children and, 133–135
   risk taking behavior and, 137–138
   and young people
   needs, 139–140
   perceptions, 138–139
Chapman, J, 71
child abuse and neglect (CAN)
   significance of, 3, 44, 72, 109, 110, 151, 154
   study of, 146
Child Exploitation and Online Protection (CEOP), NCA, 123
childism, 45, 146
   forms of, 146
Child Labour Deterrence Act, 91
Childline, 3, 96
child marriages, 115–117
Child Migrants Trust, 85
Child Poverty Action Group, 73
child protection plan (CPP), 3, 96
child protection register (CPR), 3, 96
Children (Northern Ireland) Order (1995), 70
Children (Scotland) Act (1995), 70
Children's Act
   1989, 37, 70, 90
   2004, 37, 71, 147
Children's Commissioner for England, 140–141
Children's Hearing System, 71
Children's Services Co-operation Act (Northern Ireland) (2015), 71
Children's Society, The, 119, 135
Children's Worlds Project, 120
Children and Social Work Act (2017), 37, 142
Children are Unbeatable!, 147
Children of God cult, 31
child sacrifice, 10–11, 115
child sex offenders (CSOs), 124
child sex tourism (CST), 122
child sexual abuse (CSA), 39–40
   effects on victims, 40
   forms of, 39–40
Child Sexual Exploitation, 63
Child Soldiers International, 89
Child Trends, 45

China, 5, 80, 112
Choules, C, 87
Christian Brothers, 84, 85
churches and child abuse, 30
   cover-ups and, 32–35
Church of England, 33, 34, 113
Cinderella, 28
cinema cartoon films and fairy tales, 28
Clarke, G, 106
Clegg, C, 134
Climbie, V, 71, 115
Coggan, D, 113
Cohen, M N, 26
Coleman, M, 105–106
Colombia, 120, 122, 136
Colson, F, 9, 11
Colwell, M, 70
Commercial Sexual Exploitation of Children (CSEC), 122
Commission for Social Care Inspection, 51
Committee of Public Accounts, 156
Commons Select Committee, 115
compensation mechanism, 48
Connelly, P, 71
Connolly, J, 109
consulting ethics, 52–54
contemporary scenario, 109–110
   child health and, 110–111
   child marriages and, 115–117
   cyber bullying and, 120–122
   exorcisms of young people and, 113–115
   honour killings and, 117
   housing and homelessness and, 110
   mental well-being and, 119–120
   modern slavery and, 117–118
   online child sexual abuse and exploitation and (CSAE), 124–125
   sex education and, 118–119
   sexual exploitation of children and, 122–124
   youth justice and, 111–113
Cook, B J, 86
Corby, 44, 49
corporal punishment, *see* physical child abuse
corporate parenting principles, 142–143
Council of Vaison (442 AD), 9
cover-up, of child abuse, 32–35
Cowan, R, 86
Crane, J, 57
Crete, 10, 11
Crewe Alexandra, 93, 105
Crime Survey for England and Wales (CSEW), 2, 96
Criminal Law Amendment Act (1922), 61, 62
Criminal Law Revision Committee, of British Parliament, 138
Crompton, M, 27, 35
Crown Prosecution Service, 64, 145

cultural relativism, 50
Cunningham, H, 79
Currie, E, 103
Curtis Committee Report, 70
cyber bullying
   definition of, 121
   research findings on, 121–122
   significance of, 120–121

*Daily Mail* (newspaper), 101
Damian, P, 18
Danczuk, S, 101
Danesford school (1965), 100
Dateo of Milan (Bishop), 9
Dean, S, 65
De Castellanos, 14
DeMause, L, 1, 42, 44, 59
denial of sexual abuse, understanding of, 66
Departmental Committee on Sexual Offences Against Young Persons, 61, 62
deportation, of children, 83-86
depression, 40, 136
   immature mother and, 44
   maternal, 72, 154
   mental illness and, 89
   physical abuse and, 39
   postnatal, 8
   potential, 147
   sexual abuse and, 97
   sin and, 35
   storytelling and, 27
De Sahagun, B, 13
Devamanikkam, T, 34
Dickens, C, 77
Dickens, G, 101–103
Digital Economy Act (2017), 72
Diodorus Siculus, 14
D-notices, 103
Dodgson, C L, *see* Carroll, L
Dolphin Square scandal (2015), 102
Downie, B, 107
Downie, E, 107
DR Congo, 80, 112
Dubowitz, H, 150
Dutch East India Company, 83

Eberly, S, 23
ecological framework, 44
ECPAT, 122
Elementary Education Act (1870), 19
Elm Guest House scandal (2016), 102
England, 116, *see also* Northern Ireland; Scotland; Wales
Epstein, J, 133
Eritrea, 136

Esposito, J, 15
Estonia, 119
Ethical Trading Initiative, 91
Ethiopia, 80, 119
European Committee for the Prevention of Torture, 148
European Committee of Social Rights, 148
European Convention on Human Rights, 159
European Reformation and Enlightenment, 18–20
European Social Charter, 148
Evans, W, 57
*Every Child Matters*, 51
*Exorcism and the Prayer of Liberation* (Vatican course), 114
exorcisms, of young people, 113–115

Factitious Disorder Imposed on Another (FDIA), *see* Munchausen syndrome by proxy
Factory, The" (Landon), 77
Factory Acts (1802, 1819), 78
Fairtrade Label Organisation, 91
Fair Wear Foundation, 91
fairy tales and folklore, 21
   changelings and, 23–24
   cultural meaning in, 25–26
   impact, on children, 22–23
   significance of, 24–25
   storytelling as therapeutic support and, 26–28
family group conferences (FGCs), 155
fantasy, significance of, 66
Favat, AF, 25
Featherstone, B, 41
female genital mutilation, 98
Ferrara, P, 43
Finkelhor, D, 67, 95
Fisher, J, 134
fomite transmission, 60
Food Foundation, 111
football, child abuse in, 105–106
forced marriage, 116–117
Forced Marriage Unit (UK), 116
Forster, W, 19
France, 79, 136
Francis (Pope), 32, 114
Frank, J, 77
Fraser (Judge), 53
Furnari, L, 31

Gallagher, N, 15
Gallipoli campaign, 87
Gans, B, 68–69
Garmezy, N, 48
Gavrić, M, 87
Gaza Strip, 136, 137
Gemmell, B, 102
gendercide, 16

179

Germany, 79, 87, 95, 113, 136
*Getting It Right for Every Child*, 71
Gibbs, D, 111
Gillick principle, 53
*Gin Lane* (Hogarth) (illustration, 59
*Girl from Samos* (Menander), 7
*Giving Victims a Voice* report, 94
global context, 54–55
Global Organic Textile Standard, 91
Global Partnership to End Violence against Children, 149
Golding, W, 133
Gomme, A B, 11
Gove, M, 71
Greece, 136
Greece, ancient, 64–65
  infanticide in, 8–9
  pederasty in, 9–10
  signs and evidence in, 58
Greek mythology, 7–8
Griffin, C, 139
guilt, sense of, 36, 40, 54, 55, 96
Guinea, 81
Guinea-Bissau, 75
gymnastics, child abuse in, 106–107

Hale, D, 103
Halsey, K, 140
Hansel and Gretel, significance of, 27
harm, abuse as, 63, 66
*harpagmos*, 9
Havers, M, 102
Hay, D, 35
Hayes, D D, 106
Hayman, P, 102–103
Hazel, N, 158
Heal, A, 141
healthcare practitioners/professionals, 96–97
Health Select Committee (UK), 85
Heath, E, 105
Helfer, M, 77, 82
Hennessey, E, 155
Higgins, B, 105
Higgins, D J, 46
Hindman, H D, 78
His Rest Christian Fellowship, 114
Hobbes, T, 65
Home Office (UK), 85, 98, 101, 123, 124
Hong Kong, 83
honour killings, 117
Hope, L, 33
Hopkins, E, 57
House of Bishops, The, 114
House of Commons, 62
  Committee of Public Accounts, 156
House of Lords, 53

Human Rights Act (1998), 159–160
  Article 5 of, 159
  Article 8 of, 159–160
  Article 10 of, 160
  Article 14 of, 160
Human Rights Watch, 88, 147
Humphreys, M, 84, 85

ILO, 80, 81
  Convention on the Worst Forms of Child Labor, 88
immunity, as protective factor, 48
Inca culture, 13
income inequality and child maltreatment, relationship between, 3
Indecent images of children (IIOC), 124
  possession, production, and sharing of, 125
*Independent, The* (newspaper), 97
Independent Inquiry into Historic Child Sexual Abuse, 32, 100, 101, 104
Independent Police Complaints Commission (IPCC), 102
India, 5, 80, 82
*Indianapolis Star, The* (newspaper), 106, 107
Indonesia, 80, 82
industrial revolution
  child labour regulation during, 78
  mine disasters during, 77–78
  significance of, 76
  Victorian era and, 76–77
Ineson, M, 34
infanticide, 5
  in ancient times, 6–7, 11
  Arabia, 15–16
  in Knossos, 11
  in Latin America, 13–14
  in Middle East, 12–13
  North Africa, 14–15
  in Rome, 11
  Bible and, 12–13
  maternal, 8
  Philo of Alexandria on, 8–9
infant mortality rate, 110
*Infants of the Emperor, The*, 86
informed consent, 53
INSPIRE, 148–149
*Institut fur Kindheit* (Germany), 95
institutional resistance, 63–64
International Congress on Child Abuse, 67
International Labour Organisation, 79
International Society for the Prevention of Child Abuse and Neglect (ISPCAN), 150
Internet Watch Foundation (IWF), 124, 125
Iran, 112

Iraq, 136
Ireland, allegations in, 33

Jack and the Beanstalk, 28
James, A, 128, 140
Japan, 87, 97–98, 150
Joan of Arc, 22
Johnston, W, 87
Joint Select Committee, 61
Jordan, 136
Joseph Rowntree Foundation, 150–151

*k'ex*, practice of, 13
Kay, J, 48, 55
Kelly, L, 132, 133
Kempe, C H, 67
Kennedy, J F, 75
Kent, S, 30, 31
Kenya, 123
Kincora Boys' Home (Northern Ireland), 93, 102
kindoki practice, 115
King, G, 106
King, S, 37
Kissane, A, 16
Knossos, 11
Kosloski, 9
Kugel, J, 12

labour, children as, 75–76
    deportation and, 83–86
    in early twentieth century, 78–79
    elimination of, 90–91
    impetus behind, 81–83
    industrial revolution and, 76–78
    as soldiers, 86–88
    myths about, 88–90
    in twenty-first century, 79–81
Laguna de Urao (Mérida), 14
Lamb, D, 106
Lambeth Council (1974), 100–101
Laming, H, 71
*Lancet, The* (magazine), 60
Landon, L E, 77
Lanfranc (Archbishop), 16
Lansford, J E, 41
Las Llamas, 14
Latin America, ancient, 13–14
Latvia, 119
Lebanon, 81, 136
legislation, to prosecute cruelty perpetrators, 70–72
Leo IX (Pope), 18
*Lewis Carroll* (Bakewell), 26
*Lewis Carroll* (Cohen), 26
liberation theology, significance of, 29
Liddell, A, 26

listening, to children, 51–52
Lithuania, 119
Little Red Riding Hood tale, significance of, 25
live streaming, 124
Local Government Association, 117, 118
Local Safeguarding Boards, 71
Locke, J, 131
*Lolita* (novel), 134
Longfield, A, 141
*Lord of the Flies, The* (Golding), 133
Loughton, T, 71
Lucy Faithfull Foundation, 123
Luther, M, 23
Luxembourg, 113

MacCauley, D, 105
MacDonald (Lord), 101
Mali, 75
malnourishment, 111, 114
malnutrition, 111
maltreatment
    consequences of, 54
    psychological, 41
    significance of, 3, 38, 45–46, 69, 146
Manchester City, 93, 105
Maplecroft Child Labour Index (CLI), 80, 81
Marten, J, 83, 88
Marx, K, 77
Mason, P T, 6
masturbation, in infancy, 97, 98
maternal infanticide, 8
Matthews, G B, 129
Maurice (Brother), 99
Maya culture, 13
McCafferty, J, 106
McCann, P, 106
Mead, M, 129
Meadow, R, 42
medieval European society, 131–132
medieval evidence, of sexual abuse, 16–18
Mediterranean, ancient, 8
Mehrotra, S, 82
Menander, 7
Mental Capacity Act (2005), 117
mental well-being, 119–120
Methodist Church, 33
Metropolitan Police, 93, 102, 103, 115
Mexico, 5
Middle East, ancient, 12–13
Miller, A, 39, 66, 146
mine disasters, 77–78
*Minipops* (Channel 4), 134
Minoan civilization, 11
misogyny, 8
misopedia, 45
Miss Teen USA, 135

181

INDEX

mistreatment, of children, 1
Moche, 14
MoD, 89, 90
modern slavery, 117–118
Moleko, A G, 137
Monckton, M-A, 107
Money, J, 42
Mongolia, 123
Moor, P J, 99
moral harm, 63
moral purity, aim of, 61–62
Moran, PM, 49, 52
Morocco, 123
Morrison, P, 103
Munchausen syndrome by proxy (MSBP), 42–43
Munro, E, 71
Munro review, of child protection, 128–129
Musonius Rufus, 6, 10
muti murders, 115
Myanmar, 80, 81

Nassar, L, 106–107
National Archives (UK), 98, 102
National Association for People Abused in Childhood (NAPAC), 3, 96
National Audit Office (NAO), 156
National Board for Safeguarding Children in the Catholic Church, 33
National Center for Victims of Crime, 40
National Council for Civil Liberty (NCCL), 138
National Crime Agency (NCA), 123
National Family and Parenting Institute, 47
National Institute for Health Research (NIHR), 111
National Referral Mechanism (NRM), 118
National Society for the Prevention of Cruelty to Children (NSPCC), 1, 68, 94, 121, 123
   Battered Child Research Unit, 68, 69
   78 Battered Children survey, 69
neglect, 1, 21, 33, 59
   child maltreatment and, 38
   effects of, 42
   inequality and child abuse and, 3, 72
   physical, 2
   poverty and, 72
   significance of, 41–42, 45, 146, 151, 154, 157, 160
   in United States, 59–60
The Netherlands, 125
New Zealand, 3, 83
Nicholas I of Russia, 87
Nichols, V, 30
Nigeria, 112, 136
North Africa, ancient, 14–15
Northern Ireland, 70, 71, 93, 102, 105

North Korea, 80
North Wales child abuse scandal, 93

objectification, of children, 134–135
observation bias, 50
*Observer, The* (newspaper), 103, 134–135
Occupied Palestinian Territory (OPT), 136
Ockenden Venture (1965), 99
O'Connor, J, 102
Ocuish, H, 112
Oedipus legend, 24
Office for National Statistics (ONS), 109, 116
Offside Trust, 106
O'Neill, D, 70
online child sexual abuse and exploitation (CSAE), 124–125
online coercion and blackmail, 125
online grooming, 124
Operation Cayacos, 103
Operation Hydrant, 106
Operation Yewtree, 94
Ormond, G, 105
Orosius, 14
Orwell, G, 87
Oxfam, 109

Paedophile Action for Liberation, 138
Paedophile Information Exchange (PIE), 103, 138
Paget, G T, 87
Pakistan, 80, 82, 112, 136
Palestinians, 136
parental consent, 53
parenting, under spotlight, 59–61
Parkinson, J, 132
parliament, 101–103
Pauper Apprenticeship system, 82
Pearce, S, 110
pederasty, in ancient Greece, 9–10
Penney, S, 30
Pentecostal churches, 114
Persons, J, 112
Peru, 5, 14
Philippines, 80, 82, 123
Philo of Alexandria, 8–9
physical child abuse, 31
   significance of, 38–39
physical/health threat, 63
physical neglect, 2
Piaget, 129
Picard, C, 14
Pied Piper of Hamelin, legend of, 22
Pinheiro, P S, 39
Plato, 10, 64–65
Plutarch, 10, 14
political action/inaction, 61–63
Polonko, K A, 98

Porter, C, 60
*Portrait with Background, A* (Thomas), 26
Portugal, 113
post-traumatic stress disorder (PTSD), 89, 90
poverty, 138
    child labour and, 29, 75–76, 81, 82, 88, 91
    definition of, 73
    link with child abuse, 2, 70, 72–73
    malnutrition and malnourishment and, 111
    maltreatment and, 3
    social perspectives and, 44
    in UK, 109, 110, 119, 132, 142, 152
powder monkeys, 86
prevention and early intervention, 45–46
progressive/proportionate universalism, 46
prohibited images, 125
projection, concept of, 58
Prophet Muhammad, 15
*Protection of Children in England, The*, 71
protective factors, 49–50
Protestant Reformation, 18
Prout, A, 128
Prügl, E, 79
psychoanalysis, 66
psychological abuse, 40–41
psychological domain, of abuse, 43–44
psychological harm, 63, 66
public health model, 46
Punishment of Incest Act (1908), 58
Puss in Boots, 28

*qhapaq hucha*' ritual, 13
Qur'an, 15

Raine, S, 30, 31
Ramsey, J B, 135
rape, 88, 100, 102
    medieval evidence and, 16–17
reasons, for abuse, 43–45
reassurance, significance of, 55
registered child marriages, 116
religion and spirituality, significance of, 29
religious cults, 30–31
resilience, 48–52
rickets, 110–111
rights, of children, 145
    child abuse and neglect (CAN) study and, 146, 151
    Human Rights Act 1998 and, 159–160
    legally sanctioned corporal punishment and, 147–148
    listening to children and, 157–159
    parenting support and, 150–152
    progressive practice development and, 155
    protection and, 152–154
    significance of, 155–157
    violence prevention and response and, 148–150
risk factors
    general, 46–47
    specific, 47–48
Robinson, J, 30
Robinson, T, 103
Rochefoucauld, F de la, 93
Rochester Cathedral, 19
Rogers, C, 47
Romania, 119, 120
Rotherham child sexual exploitation scandal, 141
Rousseau, J J, 65, 131
Royal Commission on Venereal Diseases Final Report (1916), 60

Safeguarding Board Act (Northern Ireland) (2011), 71
Saradjian, J, 66
Saudi Arabia, 112
Savile, J, 93–94
Scherer, A, 14
Scotland, 31, 70, 71, 76, 99, 105, 147
Scotland Yard, 115
Secure Children's Homes, 112
Secure Training Centre, 112
Seneca, 6
Senegal, 123
Settle, E, 23
sex and relationship education (SRE), 118
sex education, 32, 118–119
Sex Education Forum, 118
sexual abuse, *see also* child sexual abuse
    in ancient Greece, 10, 58, 64–65
    medieval evidence of, 16–18
    as public
    children's homes and institutions and, 98–101
    in modern times, 94–98
    parliament and, 101–103
    significance of, 93–94
    in sports, 104–107
    voices as not heard and, 107–108
    victims of, 2
    by women, 66–67
sexual exploitation of children, 122–124
sexual exploitation of children in tourism (SECT), *see* child sex tourism
sexual precociousness, 62
Shaftesbury, Lord, 78
Shahar, S, 129
shame, 10, 35, 55, 89, 96, 107
    killing, 117
    poverty and, 73
Shaw, N, 106
Shipperlee, M, 32

Shirley Oaks abuse scandal, 100–101
*Should Every Child That Is Born Be Raised?'* (Musonius Rufus), 6
signs, of abuse, 50–51
signs and evidence, early, 58–59
Silver, C, 23, 24
Silverman, F, 57
sin, significance of, 35
Slater and Gordon, 85
Slim, Lord, 85
Slovakia, 119
Smart, C, 61, 65
*Smile for the Camera* (Danczuk and Baker), 101
Smith, C, 101
Smith, R, 106
Smith, S, 68
social psychological theories, 44
Social Services and Well-being (Wales) Act (2014), 71
social workers
    child abuse scandal and, 93, 108
    child labour and, 84
    family group conferences and, 155
    Human Rights Act (1998) and, 159–160
    Munro review and, 128
    parental violence and, 68–69
    resistance to state interference and, 131
    significance of, 4, 68–71, 93, 145, 161
    storytelling and, 26
sociological perspectives, 44
soldiers, children as, 86–88
    myths about, 88–90
Somalia, 80
South Africa, 115
South Korea, 119
Spain, 136
spirituality, 35–36
    core qualities of, 35
sport, child abuse in
    in football, 105–106
    in gymnastics, 106–107
    significance of, 104–105
stage theory of development, 129
Steel, D, 101
St Gilbert's, Christian Brothers school (1963), 99
stigmatization, 61, 68–70, 88, 89, 159
Stinney Jr., G J, 112
Stockholm World Congress, 122
Stop Educator Sexual Abuse Misconduct & Exploitation (S.E.S.A.M.E.), 95–96
*Stop It Now!* Website, 123
Storey, T, 34
storytelling, as therapeutic support, 26–28
Strickland-Clark, L, 158
St Vincent's school (1948–1949), 99–100
Sudan, 80
Sugg, R, 22

*Sunday Times* (newspaper), 101
Supporting Families', 152
Sure Start programme, 152
*Surrey Comet* (newspaper), 103
Survivors of Organised and Institutional Abuse (SOIA), 103
Sweden, 3, 113, 147
Swift, L, 8
Swiss Gymnastics Federation, 107
Syria, 136
system engagement model, 45–46

Tanaka, M, 98
Tanakh, 12
Tatar, M, 21
Taylor, A, 93
Taylor, R, 89
teachers and child sexual abuse, 97
teenagers, as researchers, 53–54
Ten Hours Bill (1847), 76
Tenochtitlan, 13
Tertullian, 14
Thailand, 82, 123
Thames, M E, 112
Thatcher, M, 94, 102
Theos, 114
Thomas, D, 26
three E's, 154
three P's, 154
*Through the Looking-Glass* (Carroll), 26
Timoto-Cuicas, 14
Tims, H, 103
Tinderbox, The" (Anderson), 25
Tinkler, A, 107
Todd, A, 121
*Toddlers & Tiaras* (TV programme), 135
Together for Girls, 149
Tolkien, J, 30
Toner, W, 105
Torbett, J, 106
Townsend, P, 73
*Traditional Games of England, Scotland and Ireland, The* (Gomme), 11
trauma
    child labour and, 84, 89
    children in care and, 141
    courts and, 145
    emotional, 55
    sexual abuse and, 67
    significance of, 7, 16, 26, 33, 42, 48, 52
    substance use and, 139
Trevithick, P, 55
Truth Project, 97, 104
Turkey, 136
2030 UN Agenda for Sustainable Development, 54

types, of abuse, 38
  Munchausen syndrome by proxy, 42–43
  neglect, 41–42
  physical, 2, 38–39
  psychological, 40–41
  sexual, 39–40

Uganda, 115
UK Cotton Factories Regulation Act (1819), 76
UK Independent Inquiry into Child Sexual Abuse (IICSA), 16, 30, 34, 60, 71, 84–86, 96, 97, 107, 148
UK Parliament, 37
UN Committee Against Torture, 148
UN Committee on the Rights of the Child, 148
UN Declaration of the Rights of the Child (1989), 127
UNICEF, 5, 91, 136, 149
United Nations Convention on the Rights of the Child (UNCRC), 37–38, 90
  impact of, 149–150
United Nations Optional Protocol to the Convention on the Rights of the Child, 88
United States, 79, 111–112
  Articles of Confederation, 111
  1776 Constitution, 111
  state execution of minors in, 111–112
universalist public health model, 46
University of York, 119, 120
UNODC Crime Trends Survey, 5
UN Secretary-General's Study on Violence Against Children, 39
USA Gymnastics (USAG) scandal, 106–107
USA Head Start scheme, 152
US Children's Bureau's National Child Abuse and Neglect Data System, 3

Vatican, 114
Victorian attitudes, significance of, 64
Victorian era, 76
Vietnam, 80, 123
Viljoen, G, 6
Violence Prevention Alliance, 149
Visser, M, 137

Waddington, R, 33
Wales, 3, 19, 23, 70–71, 93, 96, 113, 116, 147, 148
Wales Act (2001), 71
Walker, S, 24–29, 32, 33, 35, 36, 38–41, 44, 51–54, 64, 70, 73, 89, 90, 94, 102, 103, 107, 108, 112, 130, 131, 136, 145, 147, 150–153, 156, 157, 159, 160
War Child, 88
Wells, H, 71
Wells, K, 131
Werlwas, J F, 42
Werner, E, 48, 49
West Bank, 136, 137
Westfield Children's Home (Liverpool) (1965–1966), 99
Whale's Soul and Its Burning Heart, A', 25
Wheeler, S, 7
White, R, 140
Whitsey, V, 34
Why the Sea Moans', 25
Wiehe, V R, 135
Williams, R, 28
Williams, L M, 95
Wilnsnack, S, 139
Wilson, M E, 59–60
witchcraft, 115
women and sexual abuse, on children, 66–67
Woolley, P, 57
*Working Together to Safeguard Children* guidance, 37, 71, 72
World Health Assembly resolution, 149
World Health Organization (WHO), 38
  Global Plan of Action, 149
  on physical abuse, 38–39
  on risk factors, 47
  on violence against children, 54, 148–149
  on young soldiers, 90
World Vision, 75

Yemen, 16, 112
Yeo, S, 29
Young-Bruehl, E, 44, 45, 146
Young Offender Institutions (YOIs), 112
youth justice, 111–113

Zimbabwe, 80